Confessing God

Other Titles in the Cornerstones Series

Confessing God

Essays in Christian Dogmatics II

John Webster

Bloomsbury T&T Clark
An imprint of Bloomsbury Publishing Plc

B L O O M S B U R Y
LONDON · NEW DELHI · NEW YORK · SYDNEY

Bloomsbury T&T Clark
An imprint of Bloomsbury Publishing Plc

Imprint previously known as T&T Clark

50 Bedford Square	1385 Broadway
London	New York
WC1B 3DP	NY 10018
UK	USA

www.bloomsbury.com

BLOOMSBURY, T&T CLARK and the Diana logo are trademarks of Bloomsbury Publishing Plc

First published 2005. This edition published 2016.

© John Webster, 2016

British Library Cataloguing-in-Publication Data
A catalogue record for this book is available from the British Library.

ISBN: PB: 978-0-56765-887-6
ePDF: 978-0-56765-888-3
ePub: 978-0-56765-889-0

Library of Congress Cataloging-in-Publication Data
A catalog record for this book is available from the Library of Congress.

Typeset by Newgen Knowledge Works (P) Ltd., Chennai, India
Printed and bound in India

CONTENTS

ACKNOWLEDGEMENTS

Some of the essays in this volume have been previously published as follows, and the author and publishers gratefully acknowledge permission to republish:

'Theological Theology' as *Theological Theology: An Inaugural Lecture delivered before the University of Oxford on 28 October, 1997* (Oxford: Clarendon Press, 1998).

'On the Clarity of Holy Scripture' as 'Biblical Theology and the Clarity of Scripture', in C. Bartholomew *et al.* (eds), *Out of Egypt: Biblical Theology and Biblical Interpretation* (Carlisle: Paternoster Press, 2004), pp. 349–82.

'Confession and Confessions', in C. Seitz (ed.), *Nicene Christianity: The Future for a New Ecumenism* (Grand Rapids: Brazos Press, 2001), pp. 119–31.

'The Holiness and Love of God', *Scottish Journal of Theology* 57 (2004), pp. 249–68.

'On Evangelical Ecclesiology', *Ecclesiology* 1 (2004), pp. 9–35; also in M. Husbands and D. Treier (eds), *The Community of the Word* (Downers Grove: Inter-Varsity Press, 2005).

'Hope', in G. Meilaender and W. Werpehowski (eds), *The Oxford Handbook to Theological Ethics* (Oxford: Oxford University Press, 2005).

'Evangelical Freedom', in C. Sider-Hamilton (ed.), *The Homosexuality Debate: Faith Seeking Understanding. Fidelity Essays* (Toronto: Anglican Book Centre, 2003), pp. 109–23.

Thanks are also due to Rob Price for his ready help in the preparation of the manuscript.

PREFACE

The essays in this collection were written in the five years which followed its predecessor volume, *Word and Church*. In many respects, they are continuous with earlier work: they treat topics such as the nature of Holy Scripture or the moral life of the believer which had been a preoccupation for some time; they place not a little emphasis on the intrusive character of the Christian gospel, that is, on the impossibility of enfolding it within moral, cultural or religious practice; they often preface consideration of theological teaching by presenting a pathology of modern Christian divinity; they consider theology as church science.

What is new about these papers compared with the previous volume is that in various ways they begin to give voice to a re-ordered conception of the substance of Christian teaching, at the heart of which lay a discovery of the content and consequences of Christian teaching about God's perfection. Earlier writing had edged towards this matter in introducing an emphasis upon the sheer difference between God and the world into the treatment of all manner of theological topics. This accent upon difference was to be found, for example, in what was said about the invasiveness of divine revelation, or about the utterly gratuitous origin of ecclesial and moral existence. Further reading and reflection showed that these instincts could receive more ample expression, and would be a good deal less exposed to distortion, if the fully realized character of God's life in himself is acknowledged as the first truth of Christian teaching and so as an operative principle in any passage of theological thought. Moreover, it became increasingly clear that the governance of all theological topics by the confession of God's aseity and inseity does not entail the separation of God and creatures, because God's perfection is not self-enclosed, but the ground or cause of his creative, communicative, preserving and restoring presence. That presence is both uncaused and utterly benign, the inexhaustibly full animating principle of created life and movement. The essays on the divine attributes, and also those on the church and the Christian life, trace some of the extensions of this conception of God and God's outer works.

Looking back over what was written some time ago, there are, of course, things which ought to have been said or said better. The material on the divine processions is rather rudimentary, and the relation of God's immanent and economic acts is sometimes spoken of as reciprocally determinative in a way which does not cohere with the underlying account of divine perfection. Moreover, the account of the difference between God and the world would be less abstract and more persuasive, as well as more relaxed, if it were articulated through a doctrine of creation: as it stands, it risks a certain abstractness, and is dominated too strongly by the desire to run counter to naturalism. The essays are working papers, on the way to something else. If they retain any value, it is that of gesturing, somewhat inadequately, towards the great and holy matter which forms the object of Christian divinity, reflection upon which is an occasion for intellectual and spiritual joy.

John Webster
St Andrews
January 2015

INTRODUCTION

The matter to which Christian theology is commanded to attend, and by which it is directed in all its operations, is the presence of the perfect God as it is announced in the gospel and confessed in the praises and testimonies of the communion of saints. The essays in this collection, which forms a sequel to *Word and Church*,[1] are a series of attempts to think about the substance of the Christian confession and about the nature, ends and settings of Christian theology, under the tutelage of the perfect God's self-presence in Christ and the Spirit. They are essays, no more: working papers written as initial clarifications of an approach to Christian doctrine of which I hope in the future to offer a more ample and systematic treatment. Most have emerged in the course of work on issues, formal and material, which have come to be major preoccupations in the last few years: the tasks of the study of Christian doctrine and its relation to the ecclesial community and to the modern culture of higher learning; the nature of Holy Scripture and its place in Christian dogmatics; the doctrines of the divine attributes, the church and the Christian life. Though they are occasional pieces, they are integrated by a common understanding of the nature of theology which derives from and is governed by a set of convictions about the Christian gospel, amongst which the concept of God's perfection has come to have great prominence.

The concept of God's perfection is a lovely, spacious and resonant piece of Christian theological teaching, and one which is immensely fruitful, not only in theology proper but also throughout Christian dogmatics. Much of what follows can be read as sketching some of the content and entailments of the doctrine. As I use the term here, God's perfection is to be understood as the

---

1. J. Webster, *Word and Church: Essays in Christian Dogmatics* (Edinburgh: T&T Clark, 2001).

1

sovereign and majestic fullness with which God is himself; it is the
eternal and entirely spontaneous plenitude and completeness of his
life as Father, Son and Holy Spirit. In dogmatic usage, perfection is
not at root a formal concept (maximal instantiation of certain
properties considered characteristic of deity) but a material one: it
indicates that, without restriction or lack, and in fullest measure,
God is *thus*. Its content is therefore to be determined not from
abstract notions of *deitas* but from God's self-demonstration which
is announced in the Christian gospel. The Christian theological
concept of God's perfection is an attempt to give conceptual
expression to the great divine tautology: I am who I am; part of the
force of that tautology is that God both specifies his own perfection
and declares it in the enactment of himself.

God's perfection is the fully realized singularity and unity of the
Holy Trinity. One consequence which is drawn out in a number of
the essays (notably those on ecclesiology and the Christian life) is a
certain understanding of the relation between God and creatures.
The point is sometimes made in the form of a denial: to speak of
the perfection of God's triune life is to prohibit certain ways of
talking of creaturely participation in God. As there can be no
substantial participation of creatures in the being of God, so in no
manner can the moral or liturgical work of the church extend,
complete or realize the divine work. Behind the denial, however,
lies an affirmation that the relation of God and creatures is best
understood through the twin notions of election and fellowship.
The triune God determines that his own blessedness will include life
over, with and for the creatures whom he appoints for fellowship
with himself. Deploying the language of election and fellowship to
describe the relation of God and creatures helps retain a sense of
the imparticipability of the being and work of God. Yet, properly
deployed, this language does not fall into the trap of proposing that
God's perfection can only be safeguarded by denying any relation
between God and creatures, protecting God by segregating him
into remoteness. That way of conceiving God's perfection is
excluded from the beginning in Christian theology, precisely
because the gospel instructs us that God's perfect, self-directed
life includes the willing and execution of a movement of love in
which he glorifies himself by bringing into being a creature for
himself, maintaining that creature, sustaining it against all perils –
above all, against the creature itself – and ensuring that it will
attain its own perfection. God's perfection includes his perfecting
of creatures.

This theology of God's perfection is somewhat muted in contemporary theology. A rather generic concept of divine perfection does a good deal of work in some philosophical theology (hesitations about this use of the concept are set out in chapters four and five). But in systematic theology it awaits a thorough contemporary treatment, and the lack of such a treatment is not often acknowledged. A range of factors could be adduced to explain this unsatisfactory state of affairs: the surprising persistence of the metaphysics of historical process (especially in North American theology) within terms of which the aseity and completeness of God can be articulated only with difficulty; developments in the doctrine of God which have not encouraged sustained reflection on the doctrine of the immanent Trinity; the prestige of the ecclesiology of *communio* and widespread attraction to the language of virtue and practice in talking of the Christian life. Alongside, and often reinforcing, these factors is an aversion to so-called extrinsicist theologies of divine grace which, it is argued, have very badly deformed the theological traditions of the West, both Catholic and Protestant, and which de Lubac and others have exposed and refuted. Whether the refutation is as thorough as is often assumed might be doubted – both on historical grounds (the history has not been presented with anything like sufficient care and thoroughness to warrant large-scale judgements) and on dogmatic grounds (it is not self-evident, for example, that classical Reformed teaching about *solus Christus* and *sola gratia* is as metaphysically ruinous as it is made out to be). But such questions aside, there is clearly a cogent question posed here for the 'exclusive' account of God's perfection implicit and sometimes explicit in the essays which follow: is such an account still enmeshed in a dualistic conception of God's relation to the world? The suggestion explored here (in the essays on the divine attributes, and those on Christology and the doctrine of the church) is that an adequate response to that question must take the form of a well-ordered account of the relation between divine perfection and divine presence.

God's triune perfection includes, though it is not exhausted by, the movement in which he makes himself present to creatures. The works of human reason – including theological reason – take place in the sphere which is brought into being by that divine movement and presence. We might speak of this sphere as the economy of God's revelatory and reconciling grace. God's grace – that is, his free and loving gift of his presence in Christ and the Spirit – summons into being a mode of creaturely existence in which he causes himself to be known, feared and loved above all things. Knowledge, fear and love are inseparable because revelation and reconciliation are inseparable. God's free self-revelation is, precisely, his presence and activity as reconciler, the one who in Christ has already overcome and in the Spirit will perfectly eradicate our opposition to himself which is the root of our wretched and ignorant condition. As revealer and reconciler, God's presence converts creatures to holiness, a holiness which embraces not only the moral and affective life but also the life of reason.

Christian theology is among the works of reason which take place in the presence of the revealer and reconciler. Crucially, this kind of statement is not intended simply as a remote or background account of the work of theology, but as a proximate description of what theologians are appointed to do. Formally stated, the activity might be indicated thus: In Christian theology, the intentionality of rational acts is enclosed, forestalled, chastened and enabled by their object; that object is 'extentional', in that it reaches towards us, bestowing itself upon us with a freedom and originality which reason cannot anticipate or comprehend. 'Revelation' is therefore much more than the subject matter of theology: it is the condition in which it takes place, or – better – the one before whose presence it is ordered to appear. That presence is antecedent. It is not an object of choice, still less is it a reality which we command to appear before us, for it elects us to be the subjects of the knowledge of itself. It is luminous, shedding abroad the knowledge of itself. It is mobile, turning to us in mercy and in so doing both judging and reconciling reason to itself. Theological reason thus shares in the baptismal pattern of all aspects of Christian existence. Caught up by the Holy Spirit into the reconciling work of God in Christ, reason is condemned and redeemed, torn away from its evil attachment to falsehood, vanity and dissipation, and so cleansed and sanctified for service in the knowledge of the truth of the gospel.

The essays which follow are exercises in positive theology. They stem from a sense that God's revelatory and reconciling presence has been given, and that that gift is the law of theological reason. Theology is not a free science; indeed, it is a counter-instance to the (destructive) assumption that science can only be science if it takes its law not from its object but from itself. For may it not be that what inhibits the open exercise of theological reason is not that which gives theology its law but resentment of that law? And, further, may it not be that the difficulties which attend theological work have much to do with our resistance to God's reconciling presence? And may it not therefore be that what is required of the theologian is the formation of judgement through prayer, hearing the Word and deference to the saints?

Theological reason is reason baptized. Baptism, however, concerns not only mortification but vivification; in it, we receive appointment to life and activity in fellowship with God the reconciler. Reason is *renewed*, and thereby restored to a fitting confidence. Such confidence is not a matter of mastery of its object – theology is always *in statu pupillari* – still less of prestige among the other sciences. It is rather what Calvin calls 'the high confidence which befits a servant of God furnished with his sure commands'.[2] Such confidence derives from a sense that theological reason does indeed go about its business in obedience to the commanding presence of the perfect God, a presence which is not an insecure human projection but something 'sure', because given with the authority of the risen Christ in the power of the Holy Spirit. Theological pride is always misplaced; but so also is anxiety about the possibility and legitimacy of positive theological work. Both pride and anxiety sap reason's trust in the fact that revelation and reconciliation have taken place and are now the determining spiritual condition of the work of the mind. Theology thus derives its proper Christian confidence and equanimity from that fact that it takes up its task in the wake of the *deus dixit* of the gospel.

The essays are, accordingly, sketches in evangelical dogmatics: 'evangelical' in the sense of attempting to follow the instruction of the gospel and to stand beneath its judgement and promise (all other senses of 'evangelical' are subordinate to this primary sense). The gospel bears witness to God's revelatory and reconciling presence and act. It is the transcendent, intrusive character of the gospel which preoccupies much of what follows: the gospel is an achieved 'word' which is other than church and theological reason. In a deep sense the gospel is *separate*: it cannot be transformed into an element – even a founding element – of an ecclesial or intellectual culture. It is a reality which is entire in itself, generating and governing its reception by those to whom it addresses itself with sovereign liberty and effectiveness. And it is therefore 'eschatological' in character, in that both its subject matter and the event of its announcement are interceptive divine acts which divide the history

---

2. J. Calvin, *Institutes of the Christian Religion* IV.viii.9 (London: SCM, 1960), p. 1156.

of the hearers and usher in a decisively new stage in God's dealings
with his creatures. This notion of the purity of the gospel has some
far-reaching consequences. In the doctrine of Holy Scripture, for
example, it suggests that the revelatory force, clarity and authority
of Scripture are not co-constituted by God and readers, but precede
all acts of reception. In the doctrine of the church, one of its
entailments is that the practices in which the church most properly
acts out its identity are those which testify to the gospel's free self-
presentation. The widespread commitment in mainstream contemporary theology to talking (in hermeneutics, ecclesiology or moral
theology) of the mediated character of God's presence may give
these essays something of a cross-grained character. But perhaps
that in its turn may raise the question as to whether all is well with
the theologies of mediation.

None of this is to suggest that theology can exist in abstraction
from the life of the church. It is simply to suggest a different
anatomy of the church, one not oriented to the *visibilia* of church
practice but to the *invisibilia* of divine promise, election, Word, and
the Spirit's sanctifying work. Unlike some of the most authoritative
contemporary work in ecclesiology, the theology of the church
which runs through these essays is governed by the twin notions of
divine holiness and divine election, with the consequence that the
church is understood, not so much as a stable tradition of practices
but as the miraculous assembly of the saints. One immediate effect
of this on the way in which theological reason operates is that
theology demonstrates its character as church science most clearly
in its attention to the word of the gospel in its superiority, majesty,
freedom and (Barth's word) 'isolatedness'.[3] But there can be no
question that theology is properly church science, for one of the
ends of God's revelatory and reconciling work is the gathering of
the communion of saints and the renewal of the life of reason in
their midst. This explains something of the 'churchly' rhetoric of
what follows: its modes of argument and appeal, its norms of
persuasion, its fairly frequent use of the genre of thesis exposition
(not intended, it should be noted, to close off arguments but simply
to give the right sort of Christian determinacy to the elaboration of
concepts).

3.   K. Barth, *The Theology of the Reformed Confessions* (Louisville: WJKP, 2002),
p. 48.

Church science can, of course, be undertaken in a variety of institutional settings, and is not necessarily the preserve of church divinity schools. What matters is that the nature, norms and ends of theological reason should be determined by reference to its object (the presence of the perfect God to the saints) and not simply by reference to rules for the operation of reason established for other contexts. Institutions are contingent; positive theology simply needs to cast around for the most habitable and hopeful context in which it can be busy about its calling without deflecting too much energy into self-defence or polemic against the invasive claims of more prestigious sciences.

Over the last couple of centuries, Christian theology has not enjoyed great success in finding such contexts, and has sometimes been persuaded to abandon the search and instead to promote the strange and sad affair of theology apart from the church. At various points, the essays suggest a pathology of modern divinity: over-investment in natural religion and some of its corollaries; a concessive attitude to philosophy or hermeneutical theory; above all, loss of a vivid sense that appeal to Scripture and dogma can both describe and solve theological problems better than appeal to other resources. But though one should not underestimate the extent to which modern theology has allowed itself to become alienated from its subject matter, it is important not to be swept up by general cultural pessimism or by fashionably tragic readings of the modern history of reason. The history of human culture (and therefore of the church and its theology) certainly bears marks of wickedness. But God's presence outbids the world's rational defiance of him. The sign under which the history of reason stands is that of the *regnum Christi* (perception of this is the greatness of Barth's *Protestant Theology in the Nineteenth Century*). Christ justifies and sanctifies reason and calls it to enter his service; his calling overrules its depravity. If there is a critical task to Christian dogmatics, therefore, it can only be ancillary to the much more necessary and joyful enterprise of indicating the gospel in all its scope and vitality. Perhaps the supreme theological virtue which is to mark theology as it goes about this enterprise is that of attention. 'Therefore we must pay the closer attention to what we have heard, lest we drift from it', counsels the writer to the Hebrews (2.1). 'Therefore': Christian theology stands after the conclusion which has already been reached in the fact that God has spoken by a son, one who is the radiance of God's glory, who bears the stamp of God's nature and upholds all things by his mighty word

(Heb. 1.2f.). Theological reason is eschatological reason, reason transfigured by the fact that it does its work 'in these last days' (Heb. 1.2), following the comprehensive reordering of all things in Christ. And so 'we must pay the closer attention to what we have heard': Christian theology does not search out its object, still less create it for itself. Its originating context is the gospel which has already been uttered, in which God expounds his own presence and which is set out in the apostolic word. The task of theological reason is to pay constant and ever-fresh attention to that gospel, with a measure of focus and single-mindedness. 'Lest we drift from it': theological reason is sanctified but not perfected, and so there can be no theological repose, simply because to relax attention is to fall prey to countervailing forces and be tugged away from that which is to absorb us. Such is the summons; the promise to theological reason is that the work of the mind has not been and will not be immune from the preserving work of God.

Theology

1

THEOLOGICAL THEOLOGY[1]

One of the signs of the health of a university discipline is its ability to sustain lively self-critical disagreement about its intellectual processes. It is no doubt true that, in academia as much as in politics or marriage, endless procedural debate usually does nothing more than defer the hour of decision. But universities (like parliaments and marriages) are supposed to be places of contained conflict, conflict which unearths fundamental intellectual and spiritual ideals and holds them up for correction and reformulation. No less than others, theologians ought to be busy about this kind of dispute, both among themselves and in their extra-mural conversations. Among the many gifts which my immediate predecessor brought to the study of theology in Oxford and beyond was a conviction that theology is and ought to be disturbing, for at its heart lie those events in which, according to Christian faith, human life and thought are entirely transfigured. Rowan Williams' intellectual temper – energetic and courteous at the same time, suspicious both of premature resolution and of mere ironic detachment, genuinely hospitable, above all, *prayerful* – sets an extraordinarily high standard for us, above all by its seemingly inexhaustible suggestiveness, its sheerly provocative effect. And so it is fitting that the new occupant of this ancient chair should continue to devote attention to the task of clarifying what the discipline of Christian theology is about, provoking the kind of disturbance of usual business which the recently arrived are permitted to make, if only for a little while.

That being said, it is worth bearing in mind that, in its very first years, the Lady Margaret professorship could hardly have been less provocative. The first of Margaret Beaufort's divinity readers in

1. An inaugural lecture as Lady Margaret Professor of Divinity, delivered before the University of Oxford on 28 October 1997.

11

Oxford was one Dr Wilsford, who gave a set of lectures in the first term on the entirely predictable topic of Duns Scotus' *Quaestiones Quodlibetales*, at the ungodly hour of seven in the morning. We do not know what the good doctor told his audience at that early hour, but from the subject we may surmise that it was in keeping with the faculty conventions of the time, and hardly likely to kindle debate about the basic self-understanding of the discipline.[2] For something really provocative, one would have gone to hear John Colet, back in Oxford from Europe, lecturing on the Pauline epistles with startling originality and turning the discipline inside out.

But if nowadays one were to follow Colet's lead and to try to reconfigure the discipline of Christian theology, the problem would be simply this: hardly anybody would notice. For Christian theology is not taken very seriously in modern Western universities: sometimes encouraged, occasionally attacked, it is most often treated with a benign indifference, so that if one day theology were simply to absent itself, the university's pursuit of its ideals would in no way be imperilled. Above all, Christian theology is not a serious factor to contend with in thinking about the university's intellectual agenda and its modes of enquiry. Why is this? Why is it that Christian theology has for at least two hundred years played so slender a role in establishing the intellectual culture of the modern research university? Two clusters of reasons come to mind. First, the history of the modern research university and its ethos of scholarship has had as one of its major corollaries the marginalization of moral and religious conviction, and thus the discouragement of theological enquiry. Second, most traditions of modern Christian theology in the West have very deeply internalized the models of enquiry which have become normative in modern academic institutions, and so have found themselves increasingly alienated from the subject matters and the cultural and intellectual processes of the Christian religion. This confluence of external and internal factors has had a twofold effect. On the one hand, it has meant that Christian theology has by and large retained its prestige in the university only by taking on the colouring of its environment – by becoming *wissenschaftlich*. On the other hand, it

2. The early history of the chair is recounted in J. McConica (ed.), *The History of the University of Oxford III: The Collegiate University* (Oxford: Clarendon Press, 1986), pp. 347–52, and in M. K. Jones and M. G. Underwood, *The King's Mother: Lady Margaret Beaufort, Countess of Richmond and Derby* (Cambridge: Cambridge University Press, 1992), pp. 206–10.

has meant that the more theology invokes theological doctrine to articulate its nature and procedures, the more precarious has been its tenure in the dominant institutions of intellectual enquiry. What is it about those institutions of intellectual enquiry which has rendered them a generally inhospitable environment for the practice of Christian theological reflection?

Universities work with conventions about what constitutes learning and what are appropriate methods of enquiry. Although we may not necessarily be reflectively aware of these conventions at all times, they are ubiquitous, constituting a shared set of assumptions about what responsible intellectual activity will look like, encouraging certain practices and disapproving of others. The routine invisibility of these conventions ought, of course, to alert us to their ideological potential; conventions which are not regularly subject to inspection and dispute quickly assume an air of necessity and their conventional character is eclipsed. This is not, of course, to suggest that the modern university's conventions of enquiry are *simply* arbitrary, or that their prestige is merely social or political. Modern conventions of intellectual enquiry have acquired their prestige largely because, in a number of culturally dominant fields (notably natural and social science and, to a lesser degree, history), they have consistently displayed extraordinary explanatory power. Nevertheless, we would be unwise to be mesmerized by this state of affairs into thinking that conventions which have proved themselves locally successful can claim universal applicability or normativity. Above all, we need to grasp that '[l]earning is not some eternal essence that happens to enter history at particular times and places, but a long-enduring social practice whose goals, methods, standards of excellence, and legitimating and orienting frameworks of conviction change drastically over time and are often deeply contested'.[3] Taking the point seriously will involve us in coming to terms with the fact that, although the university may often believe itself in pursuit of the permanent essence of scholarship, '[w]hat it is actually doing is lending institutional support and preference to just some versions of that malleable, often-changing, long-enduring social practice

---

3. N. Wolsterstorff, 'The Travail of Theology in the Modern Academy', in M. Volf *et al.* (ed.), *The Future of Theology: Essays in Honour of Jürgen Moltmann* (Grand Rapids: Eerdmans, 1996), p. 37.

that is learning – and excluding others'.[4] What conventions are being referred to here?

The modern research university conducts its business on the basis of a particular 'anthropology of enquiry'. That is to say, underlying its specific practices and preferred modes of research, its norms of acceptability and its structures of evaluation, is an account of the intellectual life, of what intellectual selfhood ought to look like. That anthropology, largely implicit but nevertheless possessed of enormous authority, is bound up with some of the most potent moral and spiritual ideals of modernity. Above all, it is an extension of the ideal of freedom from determination by situation, which is one of the deep foundations of liberal culture.

To give consent to the ideals of the university is to envisage one's intellectual practice as a reiteration of these ideals. Prominent amongst them is the principle that learning is a generic human enterprise. What is of greatest interest in describing the operations of the intellect can be isolated from any contingent, secondary characteristics which happen to be true of particular enquirers in particular fields. No *background* is needed; indeed, if the intellectual life is to proceed properly, then the enquirer has to leave all particular convictions at the portal of the university before stepping inside, since such convictions have to be factored out from the very beginning. For the practice of intellectual enquiry ought to be as unaffected by the specificities of culture, personality, or political and religious conviction as is the functioning of the bodily organs. And so, when theologians routinely admonish first-year students to 'forget everything you have learned so far', they are doing much more than cleaning out the lumber of inherited prejudice; they are as likely as not initiating students into one of the most tenacious conventions of modern intellectual life.

Within that convention lies hidden the notion that what is most basic to responsible selfhood is to be identified, not with the specificities of background, custom or training, nor with the habits of mind and spirit which are acquired from participation in a particular tradition, but with *inwardness*. What is most basic is interiority, and the most characteristic activity of interiority is that of making representations of the world. My most basic act as a reflective self is that act in which I summon the world into my presence, as it were commanding it to appear before me by making

4. Wolterstorff, 'The Travail of Theology in the Modern Academy', p. 38.

a representation of it, interrogating it and making judgements about it. In this model of the practice of reasoned enquiry, the enquiring self is considered to be what the great Canadian philosopher, George Grant, called a 'transcending summonser'.[5] Reason, that is, is instrumental, in two senses. First, its essential task is that of getting hold of the world, objectifying it so that it becomes something of which I can formulate a picture. Second, reason is instrumental in that it is considered a tool, quite unaffected by a particular context in which I might deploy it or any convictions I may have as its user. In short: the anthropology of enquiry of the modern research university is dominated by ideals of procedural rationality, context- and conviction-independence, and representation and judgement. The effect of this anthropology is to isolate and then privilege an ideal of rational competence: 'human rationality is such and the methods and procedures which it has devised and in which it has embodied itself are such that, if freed from external constraints and most notably from the constraints imposed by religious and moral tests, it will produce not only progress in enquiry but also agreement among all rational persons as to what the rationally justified conclusions of such enquiry are'.[6]

This anthropology of enquiry has been formative of the culture of the modern university in at least two interconnected ways. First, it has been a major factor in the decline of *Bildung*, formation, as an ideal of schooling, and its replacement by *Wissenschaft*. When education is understood as *Bildung*, the goal of schooling is the cultivation of a particular kind of person who has acquired certain habits of mind and will, a certain cast or temper of the soul, and so is oriented to what is considered to be the good and the true. Schooling is transformation, and involves the eradication of defects and limitations, as well as the fostering of skills which are learned through engagement in common intellectual practices (of speech and argument) in which the skills are inculcated and refined. Schooling in this mode both depends upon and gives authoritative expression to a particular version of the human good; to be schooled is to be educated into reflective appropriation of the roles and practices of a specific moral and intellectual world.

5. G. Grant, 'Research in the Humanities', in *Technology and Justice* (Notre Dame: University of Notre Dame Press, 1986), p. 99.

6. A. MacIntyre, *Three Rival Versions of Moral Enquiry: Encyclopaedia, Genealogy, and Tradition* (Notre Dame: University of Notre Dame Press, 1990), p. 225.

The ideal of *Wissenschaft* differs from this in a number of ways. Its anthropological ideals exclude any concern with schooling as transformation, precisely because the activities of enquiry are standard to any rational person. Unlike *Bildung*, it does not perceive itself as tradition-specific, for reason is independent of contexts; hence *Wissenschaft* is concerned with intellectual practices which transcend all localities and instead summon those localities for review. And, moreover, *Wissenschaft* is by its very nature anti-authoritarian: given versions of the good and the true, especially when embodied in authoritative traditions, are not there as arrangements to which we must assimilate ourselves, but as matters into which we are obligated to enquire.

This leads to a second way in which the modern university is shaped by its underlying anthropology of enquiry. That anthropology is partly responsible for a shift in the status of texts in university schooling. Though books are omnipresent in the modern university, our relation to them has a distinctly modern cast. The *Bildung* model of education was in large part sustained by agreement about a canon, and flourished within a culture which had as one of its governing instruments a set of interrelated texts, ordered in such a way that at the centre lay Scripture, around which other texts, secular or sacred, were ranged as nearer or more distant commentary, paraphrase or extension. Within this model, learning is by and large a matter of reading: absorbing and reiterating the textual bearers of the culture, and mapping the intellectual terrain with their aid. Argument within this model is very often a matter of citation – not through wooden repetition of proof texts, but through a respectful conversation with the canon, animated by a reverent sense of its richness, depth and catholic applicability. In citation, present argument is concerned to identify and apply the resources of a textual tradition, rather than to find out what happens if we abandon texts and inquire *de novo*. Yet it is just this – the rejection of citation in favour of enquiry – which has become the hallmark of the *wissenschaftlich* university of modernity. There the decline of citation as a mode of argument, and the more general decline of appeal to texts, is related to a repudiation of authority as a vehicle of rational persuasion. In the university, we tell ourselves, we argue not *from* but *towards* authority, and do so only as free enquirers.[7]

---

7. Cf. J. Stout, *The Flight from Authority* (Notre Dame: University of Notre Dame Press, 1981), p. 149.

This anthropology, centred on reason as the power of representation and embodied in intellectual and educational practices, has proved very barren soil for theological enquiry informed by Christian conviction. Substantively, its account of the human self has – despite all manner of attempted syntheses or correlations – proved itself largely incompatible with Christian understandings of the human creature. Procedurally, the method of enquiry has excluded *ab ovo* the modes of reflective activity which have been most commonly deployed in the traditions of Christian theology. And yet, strange as it may seem, Christian theology has – like most other disciplines in the universe of humane letters – experienced considerable difficulty in formulating critical judgements about this barren intellectual context. This in itself is an indication of how successfully the research university has been able to represent itself as definitive of rational practice *tout court*. But more is involved: a certain failure of theological nerve. The nature and extent of that failure of theological nerve can only, I believe, be demonstrated historically, by giving a lengthy account of the fate of Christian self-description since the later Middle Ages (something which, you will be relieved to know, I am not going to attempt on this occasion). In unfolding that history, it is of capital importance that we break free of one of the grandest myths of modernity: the myth that intellectual history is to be read progressively as the gradual reduction of 'obstacles to general enlightenment or the release of self-imposed tutelage'.[8] Freed from that constriction, we may be able to see that the history of modern theology can also be read as its steady alienation from its own subject matter and procedures. If this is true, then the intellectual disarray of modern Christian theology owes as much to its loss of confidence in its own habits of mind as it does to the enmity sometimes shown by its cultural context. Schleiermacher's arguments in favour of theology at the new University of Berlin were, in retrospect, just as damaging for theology's survival as were Fichte's arguments against. If theology finds itself on the margins, responsibility may well lie not only with a desacralized culture but 'within the field of theology itself'.[9]

8. I. Kant, 'What Is Enlightenment?', in L. W. Beck (ed.), *Kant on History* (New York: Macmillan, 1963), p. 9.

9. E. Charry, *By the Renewing of Your Minds: The Pastoral Function of Christian Doctrine* (Oxford: Oxford University Press, 1997), p. 245.

Tracing the history of that alienation of theology from its own habits of thought would mean identifying how it came about that Christian theology began to argue for its own possibility without appeal to any specific Christian content. In his quite wonderful study *At the Origins of Modern Atheism*, Michael Buckley suggests that the alienation of theology begins in the very early modern period, when theology left its own ground in order to debate with natural philosophy over the existence of God. He argues that '[i]n the absence of a rich and comprehensive Christology and a Pneumatology of religious experience Christianity entered into the defence of the existence of the Christian god without appeal to anything Christian'.[10] The result of this concession, Buckley suggests, was the production of 'an emancipated philosophy which eventually negated all religion'.[11] And so, '[a]s theology generated apologetic philosophy and philosophy generated Universal Mathematics and Universal Mechanics, and as these in their turn co-opted theology to become foundations of theistic assertions, theology itself became a *disciplina otiosa* in the justification and establishment of its own subject matter'.[12] A companionable account, this time focused on Descartes and the German idealist tradition, is suggested by Eberhard Jüngel in his slightly earlier study *God as the Mystery of the World*. Here, in a series of sweeps through the history of the relations of modern theology and metaphysics, Jüngel builds up a portrait of the decline of the theological culture within which Christian claims had their home. Like Buckley, Jüngel is concerned above all to delineate the ways in which theology's failure to construe the concept of God in positive Christological and trinitarian terms left it mortally exposed to failure in face of its philosophical critics. Far from ensuring the survival of Christian theology in the face of challenges to its plausibility, the relinquishing of specifically Christian doctrine in favour of generic theism in fact hastened its demise.

If these historical accounts are substantially correct, they demonstrate that the decline of 'theological theology' has a great deal to do with the disorder within Christian dogmatics and the

10. M. J. Buckley, *At the Origins of Modern Atheism* (New Haven: Yale University Press, 1987), p. 67.
11. Buckley, *At the Origins of Modern Atheism*, p. 358.
12. Buckley, *At the Origins of Modern Atheism*, p. 358.

hesitancy of theology to field theological claims. A couple of examples may reinforce the point.

The first is the rise to prominence of the doctrine of revelation in modern Protestant theology. In its full-dress epistemological form, the doctrine of revelation is a fairly modern invention. It is not to be found, for example, in the magisterial Reformers, who generally remain content to handle the question of how it is that we know God, not by the elaboration of a theory of knowledge or consciousness, but by pointing to a feature of Christian teaching about God, namely, God's prevenience. If God is prevenient in all things, then God is prevenient in our acts of knowing, and so our knowledge of God is rooted in God's self-manifestation. If there is such a thing as a doctrine of revelation in the theology of Calvin, for instance (and it is doubtful if his thought can be folded into that shape), it is only as a corollary of a much more basic conviction about divine grace: in the noetic sphere, too, all is to be ordered towards the glorification of the *magnalia dei*. The shift away from this in post-Reformation dogmatics – a shift described by Ronald Thiemann as one 'from assumption to argument'[13] – is not simply a matter of making explicit basic principles of Reformation thought. Quite the opposite: it often takes the form of the replacement of a doctrine of God by an epistemology. Moreover, construed epistemologically, revelation becomes predoctrinal, prolegomenal, the ground of doctrine which is itself explicable in relative isolation from (for example) Christology or pneumatology. Accordingly, revelation migrates to the beginning of dogmatics, taking up its place before the doctrine of God, acquiring greater and greater epistemological sophistication, but at the same time threatening to sever its ties with the loci that follow: Trinity, Incarnation, Spirit, Church.

A second example of the same process is theological talk of the resurrection of Jesus from the dead. In a fashion similar to what took place in the doctrine of revelation, the resurrection shifts from being an *object* of belief to being a *ground* of belief.[14] That is to say, the resurrection comes to perform a function in an apologetic strategy as part of the endeavour of fundamental theology to

---

13. R. Thiemann, *Revelation and Theology: The Gospel as Narrated Promise* (Notre Dame; University of Notre Dame Press, 1985), p. 11.
14. See F. Fiorenza, *Foundational Theology: Jesus and the Church* (New York: Crossroad, 1985), pp. 14f.

defend the possibility of revelation and special divine action. And as its role changes, so also does its content. Extracted from its proper Christological home, it is no longer considered part of the *Credo*. Instead, it is handled evidentially, as furnishing extrinsic grounds for subsequent attachment to the *Credo*. As a result, the more obviously evidential aspects of the resurrection – notably, of course, the empty tomb – come to occupy centre stage, precisely because they can most easily be assigned a job in the search for transcendental foundations for Christian doctrine.

Neither of these moves could have taken place without a certain forgetfulness of the inner structure and dynamic of Christian doctrine, and without the adoption of intellectual procedures which are themselves seriously underdetermined by doctrinal considerations. The effects of this reach deep into theology's self-understanding and practices, and can be seen both in the literary forms of modern theology as well as in the ways in which it has construed itself.

The history of the genres of theological writing is still largely unexplored in any systematic way; yet the importance of such a study for interpreting the situation of theology in modernity can scarcely be over-emphasized. What happens to styles of theological writing when *Wissenschaft* replaces citation as the dominant mode of enquiry and argument? When citation is in the ascendant, the literary forms of theology are generally governed by the fact that the Christian worlds of meaning are shaped by biblical, credal and doxological texts and by the practices which both carry and are themselves carried by those texts. Theology's literary forms and intellectual architecture, its rhetoric and its modes of argument, are controlled by proximity to these sources. Hence its favoured genres: biblical commentary, exposition of texts which have a heavy presence in the tradition (such as the creeds, the Lord's Prayer or the decalogue), or polemic conducted within an agreed frame of reference supplied by a stable canon of biblical materials and of major voices in the tradition. When they function well, these genres are transparent to that into whose presence they seek to introduce the reader. They are not construed as an improvement upon the canon of Christian texts, organizing it more effectively according to scientific principles, or translating its rough, immediate language into a more sophisticated and reflective idiom. Rather, theology maps out the contents of the canon, or applies them in particular circumstances by extended paraphrase of their content.

As enquiry replaces citation, the genres of theology are steadily assimilated to those of standard rational discourse. The canon gradually shifts from being that on the basis of which theology proceeds to that into whose transcendental conditions theology enquires. This shift involves retiring the rhetoric of commentary, paraphrase and reiteration, for those ways of doing theological work cannot serve the goal of enquiry, which is proof underived from the terms of the tradition itself. They are replaced, therefore, by modes of theological discourse which reflect a quite different set of interests, modes of evaluation and standards of justification, whose key feature is undetermination by the self-representations of the traditions of Christian practice. In the writing of Christian doctrine, this can readily be seen by comparing the style of Calvin's *Institutes* – loose, occasional, very close to the biblical ground – with the dogmatics of Reformed scholasticism. Though initially rather inaccessible to the modern reader, the latter texts are rhetorically a good deal closer to modern scholarly writing than those of the sixteenth-century Reformers, above all because they recast their matter by transferring it from the more immediate discourse of faith into an improved, more orderly and better warranted mode of expression. Or compare a modern scholarly biblical commentary with one by Calvin. The difference is not simply the availability to the modern writer of considerably more by way of historical materials, but a changed relation to the text itself and to the act of explication. A modern scholarly commentator has the task of accounting for the text, and a set of tools at her disposal to establish how the text came to be. Calvin's task is at once more modest and more urgent: more modest, because he is simply interested in eliciting the plain sense of the text; more urgent, because his rhetoric positions the reader in such a way as to be accountable to the text, or better, to be called to account by God through the medium of the text. Hence a fundamental criterion for the success of a piece of exegesis is its ability to let the rhetoric of Scripture stand and itself shape the theologian's discourse. If, as often happens, we find this an unilluminating procedure, it is more than likely because modern theology suffers particularly acutely from the effects of the standardization of discourse which has afflicted the humanities in modernity. Reflecting on this standardization in an essay on philosophy and literature, Martha Nussbaum suggests that '[t]here is a mistake made, or at least a carelessness, when one takes a method and style that have proven fruitful for the investigation and description of certain truths – say those of natural science – and applies them without further reflection or argument to a very different sphere of life that may have a different geography and demand a different sort of precision, a different norm of rationality'.[15] And theology, no less than philosophy or literary studies, has not always avoided the mistake.

One consequence of this normalization is that it has made it increasingly difficult for practitioners within the various subdisciplines of theology to state with any clarity what is specifically *theological* about their enquiries. The theological disciplines have, in effect, been 'de-regionalized', that is, they have been pressed to give an account of themselves in terms drawn largely from fields of enquiry other than theology, fields which, according to prevailing criteria of academic propriety more nearly approximate to ideals of rational activity. And so the content and operations of the constituent parts of the theological curriculum are no longer determined by specifically theological considerations, but by neighbouring disciplines – disciplines which can exercise that controlling function because their lack of determination by theological conviction accords them much greater prestige in the academy. This process of assimilation means that, for example, the study of Scripture, or doctrine, or the history of the church draw their modes of enquiry from Semitics, or the history of religions, or social anthropology, from philosophy, or from general historical studies. Individual scholars or schools have no doubt been able to strike various kinds of local bargains with neighbouring disciplines whilst retaining some of the theological ends of their endeavours. But even such bargains, however carefully brokered, nearly always prolong the assumption that, at the level of actual operations, theological doctrine does not need to be invoked, and may at best enter the picture as an ultimate horizon of processes which it does not immediately affect.

So far, then, I have sketched the decline of a theologically informed account of theology as a mode of intellectual enquiry by pointing to two developments: the steady expansion of certain academic practices, rooted in a universalist anthropology of enquiry and largely detached from particular fields of intellectual work, and the decline of the invocation of theological doctrine in

---

15. M. Nussbaum, 'Introduction: Form and Content, Philosophy and Literature', in *Love's Knowledge: Essays on Philosophy and Literature* (Oxford: Oxford University Press, 1990), pp. 19f.

talking about what theology is, as theologians conform their practice to prevalent cultural norms. It is very important, I believe, not to view the problem from one angle only. It is not simply that theology has failed to keep pace with modernity (in one sense, it has kept pace all too well); nor simply that theology was turfed out by rationalism (for theology itself contributed a great deal to its own decline). It is rather a matter of seeing how internal disarray incapacitated theology all the more because it left theologians with such a reduced intellectual capital to draw upon as they sought to make judgements about the ideals, academic and spiritual, which presented themselves for their attention with such institutional force.

Yet those ideals, and the institutions which bear them, are themselves showing signs of strain. Particularly in the world of the humanities, these conventions of enquiry and the understanding of the human situation which undergirds them do not always command immediate assent. A good deal of attention has been devoted in recent years to developing what might be called a critical pragmatics of academic institutions and activities. The work of Foucault, Bourdieu, Guillory and others suggests that what have often been judged to be invariant principles of rational enquiry are in fact customs whose self-evidence has much to do with the plausibility structures which surround them.[16] Oddly enough, then, the very high premium on critical activity in the university may make us insufficiently aware that the university is a customary institution as much as a reflective one: indeed, its critical practices are themselves customary in character. The academy has not always resisted the temptation to idealize itself as a place of total, interest-free reflection, especially in the way it writes the history of its own disciplines. But its reflective practices have sometimes been a good deal less than that. To see this is not just a matter of conceding that the university is sometimes at the mercy of local interests; any member of any university committee knows that. It is more that, in

---

16. See, for example, M. Foucault, *The Order of Things: An Archaeology of the Human Sciences* (London: Tavistock, 1970), and *The Archaeology of Knowledge* (London: Tavistock, 1972); J. Guillory, *Cultural Capital: The Problem of Literary Canon Formation* (Chicago: University of Chicago Press, 1993); P. Bourdieu, *Homo Academicus* (Cambridge: Polity Press, 1988); P. A. Bové, *Intellectuals in Power: A Genealogy of Critical Humanism* (Columbia: Columbia University Press, 1986), and *Mastering Discourse: The Politics of Intellectual Culture* (Durham: Duke University Press, 1992).

representing itself as a sort of disinterested tribunal, the university
may in important respects obscure from itself and others the real
character of its operations: its place as regulator and distributor of
cultural capital, its proposing of ideals of acceptable intellectual
practice, its commitment to determinate moral and political goals.
The most sharp analysis along these lines has emerged in materialist
social science and in some kinds of literary theory. But the uneasy
situation of Christian theology in the academy is another place
where some of these protocols break the surface and become visible.
If this is so – if the fate of theology in the modern university signals
the limitations imposed by compliance with that institution's
account of itself – then theology could in fact have some
considerable critical significance for the university. Far from being
an obstacle to unfettered liberty of enquiry, theology may furnish
one of the chief means through which instrumentalist and
representational ideologies are opened for inspection and critique.
In this way, theology may offer a set of critical tools through which
we may plot a different geography of the academy's intellectual life.
     How might Christian theology make this contribution? The
immediate temptation is to limit theology's role to one of providing
a vaguely moralistic or mysterious tinge to hard-edged intellectual
pursuits, by drawing attention to the realm of so-called 'values', or
articulating the awe which the researcher feels in face of the
unknown. But theology is more than the academy's conscience or
its folk religion. Its contribution to the wider culture of reflective
institutions will rather be this: by holding fast to its own concerns,
pursuing its own goals and fulfilling its own responsibilities by
making full use of its own procedures, theology will raise a question
about the dominant conventions of enquiry. In effect, its
importance for the university will be secured by its being not less
theological but *more* theological, by 'exercising theology's right to
be exclusively theological'.[17] As a significant contemporary practi-
tioner of this kind of theology has put it, 'the discipline lives by its
ability to contribute from Christian sources things that would not
otherwise be said'.[18]

     17.   E. Jüngel, 'Die Freiheit der Theologie', in *Entsprechungen. Gott – Wahrheit –
Mensch. Theologische Erörterungen* (Munich: Kaiser, 1980), p. 15.
     18.   C. Gunton, 'The Indispensability of Theological Understanding: Theology in
the University', in D. F. Ford and D. L. Stamps (eds), *Essentials of Christian
Community: Essays for Daniel W. Hardy* (Edinburgh: T&T Clark, 1996), pp. 276f.

It has sometimes been argued on this basis that the signal contribution of Christian theology to the academy is its talk about God.[19] Certainly, talk about God may function iconoclastically, relativizing false disciplinary absolutisms by setting the whole intellectual enterprise in a transcendent context. But such a task could quite adequately be performed by other disciplines – some styles of philosophy or aesthetics or religious studies, for example – in which we are, as it were, nudged into considering an absolute context for ourselves and our endeavours. The distinctiveness of Christian theology lies elsewhere, however: not simply in its persistence in raising questions of ultimacy, but rather in its invocation of God as agent in the intellectual practice of theology. In order to give account of its own operations, that is, Christian theology will talk of God and God's actions. Talk of God not only describes the matter into which theology enquires but also, crucially, informs its portrayal of its own processes of enquiry. In effect, theology is a contrary – eschatological – mode of intellectual life, taking its rise in God's disruption of the world, and pressing the academy to consider a quite discordant anthropology of enquiry. To try and make some sense of this seemingly perverse point, we may perhaps ponder a proposition which stands near the beginning of an entirely forgotten theological text, Wollebius' *Compendium theologiae christianae*, a brief handbook of Reformed teaching published in 1626, soon after the Synod of Dordt. Wollebius writes: 'The principle of the being of theology is God; the principle by which it is known is the Word of God.'[20] Grasping Wollebius' point involves us in reclaiming two primary convictions which are largely lost to us, one ontological and one noetic. The first is what has been called 'the classical priority of the object of theological study'.[21] Giving priority to the object immediately calls into question any notion that methods of enquiry are set by the subjective conditions of enquirers and not by that to which they direct their loving attention. For theology as Wollebius envisages it, the being of God

---

19. For example, C. Gunton, 'The Indispensability of Theological Understanding', p. 275; D. Ford, 'Christian Theology at the Turn of the Millennium', in D. Ford (ed.), *The Modern Theologians: An Introduction to Christian Theology in the Twentieth Century* (Oxford: Blackwell, 2nd edn, 1997), pp. 724f.

20. J. Wollebius, *Compendium theologiae christianae*, Prolegomena 1.III, in J. W. Beardslee (ed.), *Reformed Dogmatics* (Grand Rapids: Baker, 1977), p. 30.

21. G. Schner, *Education for Ministry: Reform and Renewal in Theological Education* (Kansas City: Sheed and Ward, 1993), p. 33.

is not simply an hypothesis into which theology enquires, but rather is the reality which actively constitutes and delimits the field of theological activity. Talk of God and God's actions will not just describe theology's ultimate horizon, as it were the furthest boundaries of the field, within which theologians go about their business unconstrained. Rather, the field of theology and the activities which theologians perform within that field – its texts, its modes of interpretation, its standards of assessment, its rhetoric and modes of persuasion – will be described by talk of God. What Wollebius calls 'the principle of the being of theology', what we might call its intellectual ontology, has priority over anthropology and epistemology. Theology is simply not a free science.

This leads to the second of Wollebius' points, namely that the noetic principle of theology is the Word of God. His point is not that theology is governed by a doctrine of Scripture or revelation, but something prior to both, namely this: the 'object' to which the theologian's gaze is directed is inalienably *subject*. We would not be far from Wollebius if we were to say that the object of theology is nothing less than the eschatological self-presence of God in Jesus Christ through the power of the Holy Spirit. Theology is oriented to this active presence, and its enquiries are both materially and formally determined, borne along and corrected by that presence. In a very important sense, the notion of the Word of God undertakes here the duty which in later theology will be performed by epistemology and anthropology: it shows how it is that knowledge of God is possible and real. When such language falls away and is replaced by a psychology or metaphysics of the human knower, the object of theological enquiry is itself re-construed as absent, inert or mute. But, as John Macquarrie once remarked, '[t]he subject matter of Christian theology, God in Christ, is not a passive object laid out for our scrutiny ... but the transcendent reality which already encompasses us'.[22] To neglect that point, to forget that the intellect must be 'docile to the given',[23] is to shift into a different intellectual ontology which abrogates the connexion within which alone theology's status as *Wissenschaft* is secure: its reference to the work and Word of God.

---

22.   J. Macquarrie, 'Theology and Spirituality', in *Paths in Spirituality* (London: SCM, 1972), p. 70.
23.   Macquarrie, 'Theology and Spirituality', p. 64.

How on earth does *this* constitute a serious contribution to the life of the academy? In Oxford, at least, the argument since the 1850 University Reform Commission has taken the form that theology's place in the university is to be won by its conformity to an ideal of disengaged reason, an ideal which many theologians have deeply internalized (with the exception of a few crackpots like Pusey, who can safely be dismissed). My suggestion is the opposite: the most fruitful contribution which theology can make to the wider world of learning is by demonstrating a stubborn yet cheerful insistence on what Barth called 'the great epistemological caveat ... [T]he way of thought [of theology] ... is not secure except in the reality of Jesus Christ and the Holy Spirit'.[24]

But the understanding of theology which I am proposing – theology as the articulation of 'Christian difference'[25] – raises a critical question about the university's self-understanding. For it casts doubt on the combination of pluralism and dogmatism in liberal culture – a pluralism which suspends all strong claims and traditions, and a dogmatism which insists that all such claims and traditions present themselves for inspection before the universal bar of reason. By going about its business, by skilful, reflective, self-critical practice within its own world of discourse, theology will suggest a rather different model of academic life and institutions. It will suggest that the university may be conceived as, and its ideal pursued through, a set of orderly, energetic and curious conversations about differing visions of human life and thought, as a contest between strong claims, including strong claims about the nature of enquiry. In such a context, teachers will play a double role: as partisans, speaking as the intellectual voice of a particular culture, and as those concerned to sponsor high-level articulation of difference, in order that the university may be 'an arena of conflict in which the most fundamental type of moral and theological disagreement [is] accorded recognition'.[26] Such conflicts would not be solved by appeal to universal reason; nor, on the other hand, would they be tolerated by making the university into some sort of perspectival free market of inter-disciplinary discussion in which the only thing that matters is that nothing matters. Both rationalism

24. K. Barth, *Ethics* (Grand Rapids: Eerdmans, 1981), p. 98.
25. J. Milbank, *Theology and Social Theory: Beyond Secular Reason* (Oxford: Blackwell, 1990), p. 381.
26. MacIntyre, *Three Rival Versions of Moral Enquiry*, p. 231.

and indefinite pluralism assume that what is most important about the university is what is neutral among the different versions of reality which are brought to the debate. But may it not be that the academy might flourish if it were to foster sets of practices which would maximize the specific logics of different visions and what animates them; maximize opportunities for encounter and exchange; and minimize factors which inhibit fruitful contests (such as the dominance of only one intellectual procedure)?

What is involved here is the 're-regionalization' of intellectual life, taking seriously 'the death of the notion that there is such a thing as *the* logic of *Wissenschaft*'.[27] An institution in which this kind of conflict is a central pursuit will be less concerned to defend abstract, a-contextual norms, and will be more interested in observing reason as a set of practices with a home in particular traditions which over time have come to formulate and refine standards of intellectual excellence. Filling out this picture of the academy would require us to say much more: about teaching as the engendering of the habits of mind of particular traditions (including their habits of self-critique); about the role to be played by awed reading of classical texts; about the need to deregulate the genres of scholarship. But what is most important is to state the claim that what is needed is a renewed 'conflict of the faculties', though not one driven by 'the quest for commensuration',[28] but by a confident sense of the importance of non-conformity. And, crucially, what such conflict requires is not just a better epistemology, but a changed anthropology of enquiry and politics of intellectual exchange, so that differences can be seen not as a curse but as the given condition for the university's life.

All this no doubt sounds like a way of smuggling theology (and perhaps other supposedly disreputable disciplines like Marxist aesthetics or feminist studies) in through the back door. But it is more a matter of trying to see what the university looks like in a different projection. And, moreover, it is worth noting that thinking of the academy and of academic theology in this way by no means leaves theology comfortably intact. Indeed, it requires a quite radical recasting of theology's prevailing self-understanding. Within this recasting, the most important, as well as the most demanding,

---

27. Wolterstorff, 'The Travail of Theology in the Modern Academy', p. 44.
28. R. Rorty, *Philosophy and the Mirror of Nature* (Princeton, NJ: Princeton University Press, 1979), p. 317.

task is that of re-establishing theology's relation to the culture of Christian faith and practice from which it so often finds itself dissociated. All intellectual acts take place in a particular space or region; that is to say, reflective activity is best understood, not by exquisite analysis of modes of consciousness, but by observing the practices of a cultural world. Christian theology's culture is that of Christian faith – its store of memories, its lexical stock, its ideas, its institutions and roles, its habits of prayer and service and witness, the whole conglomeration of activities through which it offers a 'reading' of reality. That culture precedes and encloses reflective theological enquiry, and it is within, not in isolation from, that sphere that Christian language and concepts acquire their intelligibility. This is why the supposed polarity of enquiry and orthodoxy is specious. For it is only a debased form of orthodoxy which is dominated by the compulsive dynamics of repetition, sameness and closure. Practised well, orthodoxy is not about domination but about what my predecessor, in an essay in honour of another great theologian of this university, has called 'shared attention'.[29] Orthodoxy is participation in a tradition which directs itself to a source of convertedness. It involves a setting of the self – including the knowing self – within patterns of common action and contemplation, of speech and hearing. When they function well, those patterns are sufficiently stable to provide focus, and yet sufficiently aware of their own provisionality to enable self-critical adaptability and to offer a check against stasis. 'Orthodoxy' of this kind enables the theologian to articulate a distinctively theological account of the content, methods and goals of the discipline, and offers much by way of resistance to too ready an acquiescence in the protocols of neighbouring intellectual fields. And it also makes theologians worth talking to, because it means they have something distinctive to say. The vigour of theology and its capacity to contribute in a lively way to the conversations of the academy will in large measure depend upon the confidence, vigour and intelligence with which it inhabits its regions of meaning. Not the least requirement for the theologian in the university is competence in the rules of life of the Christian tradition. Such competence, acquired through observation and application, through habits of

---

29. R. Williams, 'Does It Make Sense to Speak of pre-Nicene Orthodoxy?', in R. Williams (ed.), *The Making of Orthodoxy: Essays in Honour of Henry Chadwick* (Cambridge: Cambridge University Press, 1990), p. 18.

prayer and attention and suffering, is a much more serious and fruitful contribution to conversation than the scrupulous bracketing of positive religion which has long been held to be the price of theology's entrance ticket to the world of higher learning.

In the light of considerations such as these, we may see the wisdom of the arrangement whereby this chair straddles the two publics of the academy and the ecclesial community. At first blush, it seems nothing other than a way of making sure that divinity professors know at least the Anglican answer before the evidence is in, once again betraying the interests of free enquiry. After all, was not Kant right that the catchword of the cleric is 'Do not argue, but believe!'?[30] And Kant continued thus in talking of the scholar-priest:

> The use ... which an appointed teacher makes of his reason before his congregation is merely private, because this congregation is only a domestic one ...; with respect to it, as a priest, he is not free, nor can he be free, because he carries out the orders of another. But as a scholar, whose writings speak to his public, the world, the clergyman in the public use of his reason enjoys an unlimited freedom to use his own reason and to speak in his own person.[31]

There is a cluster of assumptions here: about the rational precedence of the world over the congregation; about the inferiority of the merely domestic Christian culture to the free public spaces where reason operates; about the possibility of and necessity for the intellectual to seek out a world without convention and conviction, since freedom and scholarship are antithetical to belonging. But the integration of academy and congregation, of intellect, prayer and attention to Scripture, should serve to highlight the fact that there is no non-local public, no rationality abstract from social practice, no sphere where everything is open for total reflection. The university may not pretend to be such a space, and it may be a particular vocation of theology, when it sticks to its task, to issue that reminder to an institution which has sometimes threatened to convert its customs into axioms.

The university, or, indeed, the faculty of theology where the academic life is envisaged in quite these terms, does not, of course, exist: hence what can be seen as the utopian tone of my remarks. The worldly wise turn away from utopian proposals with a tolerant

---

30. Kant, 'What Is Enlightenment?', p. 5.
31. Kant, 'What Is Enlightenment?', p. 6.

smile. But the function of utopias is to encourage an ironic distance from prevailing conceptions, and to recount the past and envisage the future from a different point of view, thereby provoking serious self-criticism. At its best, the university strives to be a place of non-competitive argument from and about interests, in the hope that things could be other than they are. Theological theology has much to contribute to the fostering of that kind of intellectual polity, and the academy has every reason to expect much from its contribution.

2

ON THE CLARITY OF HOLY SCRIPTURE

I

Theological talk of the clarity of Holy Scripture is a corollary of the church's confession of the radiance of God in the gospel. The gospel attests that, in free majesty and love, the triune God establishes, maintains and completes fellowship with humankind, making himself present and so making himself known as creator, redeemer and giver of life. As the testimony of the prophets and apostles, Holy Scripture is inspired by God to serve his self-communicative presence. The clarity of Scripture is the work which God performs in and through this creaturely servant as, in the power of the Holy Spirit, the Word of God illumines the communion of saints and enables them to see, love and live out the gospel's truth. God lifts up the light of his countenance upon the saints through Holy Scripture, orders their interpretation of the biblical testimony and so builds them up in godliness.

Affirmations such as these are the common stock of classical Christian hermeneutics, though they are more usually familiar to us from sixteenth- and seventeenth-century Protestantism, in which they acquired greater dogmatic precision as well as a certain polemical prominence. They have, however, ceased to have much operative force either in the theology of Scripture or in the theory and practice of biblical hermeneutics, and if they remain present to us, it is most often in coarsened, rationalistic versions. Accounting for their decline would require a full account of the career of modern biblical hermeneutics and its neighbouring disciplines which is well beyond the scope of these remarks. For the present purpose, it may suffice merely to identify an external factor (the changed relation to texts in some general hermeneutical theory) and an internal factor (dogmatic weaknesses in some late expressions of Protestant theology of Scripture) whose conjunction has done much to undermine theological confidence in the viability of this particular tract of Christian theological teaching.

First, decline of confidence in the hermeneutical viability of *claritas scripturae* is related to the prominence of that strand of hermeneutical theory which seeks to secularize and de-absolutize Scripture. In a very suggestive essay, Otto Marquard proposes that one of the commanding forces in the rise of literary hermeneutics and their application to the Bible was the experience of '*a hermeneutical war – a civil war over the absolute text*'.[1] Hermeneutics responds to bloody conflict over the interpretation of Scripture by 'inventing – thus turning itself into pluralizing, which is to say, literary, hermeneutics – the non-absolute text and the non-absolute reader'.[2] Hence '*literary hermeneutics* – by transforming the absolute text into the literary text and the absolute reader into the aesthetic reader – is *given precedence*, as a reply to the hermeneutic civil war over the absolute text'.[3] *Originalitas, non veritas, facit interpretationem.* The effect of this development on the notion of the clarity of Scripture is, of course, highly disruptive, for *claritas*, as conceived by the magisterial Reformers and their heirs, involves two affirmations: (1) that Scripture is indeed 'absolute', not in the sense that it is divine, but in the sense that it is the unsurpassable bearer to us of non-contingent divine revelation; and (2) that the interpretation of such a text cannot be *ad libitum* but must be according to the law which the text sets before us. The hermeneutical directive of the clarity of Scripture is thus an extension of the affirmation *sacra scriptura locuta, res decisa est*; whereas literary hermeneutics (of which hypermodern hermeneutical scepticism is only a late version) can be a near-infinite deferral of decision.

What of the second, internal factor? Post-Reformation theology of Scripture expounded *claritas* as part of a larger dogmatic ontology of the Bible. In doing so it offered an essential check against any strategies of secularizing Scripture, preventing clarity, along with efficacy, inspiration, authority and canonicity, from becoming simply attributes of the subjective *use* of Scripture, and

---

1. O. Marquard, 'The Question, To What Is Hermeneutics the Answer?', *Contemporary German Philosophy* 4 (1981), p. 20. Marquard's sketch might be filled out by J. S. Preus' study *Spinoza and the Irrelevance of Biblical Authority* (Cambridge: Cambridge University Press, 2001).

2. Marquard, 'The Question', pp. 21f.

3. Marquard, 'The Question', p. 24.

insisting instead upon the objective (though not, of course, non-natural) character of Scripture as divine communication. The subsequent history of Protestant bibliology, however, demonstrated a certain limitation in those post-Reformation accounts, namely that, badly handled, the idiom of properties of Scripture could rather easily be separated out from talk of God's reconciling and revelatory activity in the church, and formalized or rendered abstract. If seventeenth-century dogmaticians were usually safeguarded from such formalization by – for example – linking *claritas* to efficacy, later accounts ran the risk of so talking of Scripture's clarity *in se* and *ante usum* that it became extracted from its proper dogmatic location and rendered as a natural property of the Bible *qua* text. This, in turn, made it possible to associate clarity with transparency of authorial intention or original meaning, in such a way that clarity was further distanced from its doctrinal setting and expounded in terms of rational accessibility. Clarity, in other words, becomes confused with historical evidentness; the context of clarity is not the self-communicative presence of God to the community of faith, but the transparency of an historical report to historical reason.

By way of contrast, what is attempted here is a dogmatic account of *claritas scripturae* which expounds the notion through a series of interconnected affirmations: about the self-communicative presence of God; about the ontology and properties of Scripture; about the church as the creature of the Word; and about sanctified interpreters and their acts. Amongst other things, it suggests that a well-rounded theological account of *claritas*, far from undermining the validity of hermeneutical work, recovers the proper vocation of hermeneutics, precisely by reinserting the activity of interpretation into the overall structure of God's communicative fellowship with humankind. And, moreover, the argument here is that attention to dogmatic factors is crucial in explaining the modern history of hermeneutics, and in articulating a Christian understanding of what it means to engage in the interpretation of Scripture. The history of modern theology has been deeply affected by general theory about texts, readers and reading communities, and acts of interpretation, developed in relative isolation from theological considerations, and in such a way as to neutralize, absorb or sometimes even repudiate theological talk of the place of the biblical texts in the revelatory activity of God. In the matter of biblical interpretation, Christian theology has not always managed to keep hold of the rhythm of its own concerns, often looking to general theory to provide it with two things: (1) its *problematic* (that is, an account of the content and structure of hermeneutical reflection, of its primary questions, and of the ways in which they are to be approached); and (2) its *genealogy* (that is, a history of hermeneutics as a comprehensive science of interpretation, in terms of which specifically Christian traditions of biblical interpretation are to be understood). Once this problematic and its attendant genealogy acquire some authority in theology, and demonstrate some success both in explaining how theological hermeneutics has come to be where it is and in recommending how it ought to be conducted, then almost inevitably theological factors tend to be compromised. They come to enjoy only a diminished status, or to be reconceived in the light of dominant hermeneutical conventions. Yet there is no necessity about such developments, and they could have been resisted by more thoughtful drawing upon the resources of Christian teaching about the nature of Holy Scripture, and by a measure of confidence that the church's dogmatic traditions can be of assistance to biblical hermeneutics as it pursues its vocation.

A dogmatic depiction of the topic is an attempt to give an orderly, reasoned portrayal of the church's confession. As a piece of dogmatics, it is, of course, wholly subordinate to the primary work of the church's theology, which is exegesis. Dogmatics, and in particular a theology of Scripture, cannot presume to anticipate or control exegetical work, to which it is an ancillary science. In the case of a doctrine of Scripture, the assistance dogmatics provides is as follows: it offers a description of the origin, nature and ends of Holy Scripture, and of its place in the divine economy. The scope of such an account stretches from consideration of the revelatory purpose and action of God, through an account of the inspiration, sanctification and canonization of the biblical texts, to an account of the faithful reading-acts of Spirit-illumined readers in the fellowship of the saints. A doctrine of Scripture offers a theological ontology of Scripture and an ecclesiology and anthropology of its readers, in terms of which Christian exegetes can understand their place in the divine economy and so more fittingly perform the task to which they are appointed. That is, a doctrine of Scripture does not orient exegetical practice by determining particular results, but by portraying the field of exegetical activity, the divine and human agents in that field, the actions undertaken by these agents, and the ends which they serve. In this way it acts as an auxiliary to exegetical labour.[4]

4. Until recently, there have been few modern precedents from which to take direction in discussing either the doctrine of Scripture in general or the particular issue of *claritas scripturae*. There are now signs that, having languished on the edges of theology for some time, bibliology is returning to theological debate. Among recent English-language works, notice should be taken of K. Vanhoozer, *First Theology: God, Scripture and Hermeneutics* (Leicester: Apollos, 2002), esp. pp. 127– 203; M. Horton, *Covenant and Eschatology: The Divine Drama* (Louisville: WJKP, 2002), pp. 121–276; and T. Ward, *Word and Supplement: Speech Acts, Biblical Texts and the Sufficiency of Scripture* (Oxford: Oxford University Press, 2002). See also J. Webster, *Holy Scripture* (Cambridge: Cambridge University Press, 2003). In German, there is an important study by A. Wenz, *Das Wort Gottes – Gericht und Rettung. Untersuchungen zur Autorität der Heiligen Schrift in Bekenntnis und Lehre der Kirche* (Göttingen: Vandenhoeck und Ruprecht, 1996). The question of *claritas scripturae* still awaits a thorough dogmatic exposition. The recent study of J. Callahan, *The Clarity of Scripture: History, Theology and Contemporary Literary Studies* (Downers Grove: IVP, 2001) makes a beginning, but lacks doctrinal precision. There are treatments of the topic by U. Duchrow, 'Die Klarheit der Schrift und die Vernunft', *Kerygma und Dogma* 15 (1969), pp. 1–17; R. Muller, *Post-Reformation Reformed Dogmatics 2: Holy Scripture: The Cognitive Foundation of Theology* (Grand Rapids: Baker, 1993), pp. 340–57; A. C. Thiselton, *New Horizons in Hermeneutics* (London: HarperCollins, 1992), pp. 179–203; and K. Vanhoozer, *Is There a Meaning in this Text? The Bible, the Reader and the Morality of Literary Knowledge* (Leicester: Apollos, 1998), pp. 314–17. The two-volume study by R. Rothen, *Die Klarheit der Schrift* (Göttingen: Vandenhoeck und Ruprecht, 1990) covers a good deal more than its title suggests, and is best read as a critical account of the theology of Scripture in Luther and Barth. The best overall dogmatic treatment remains G. C. Berkouwer, *Holy Scripture* (Grand Rapids: Eerdmans, 1975), pp. 267– 98. Much of the specialist literature is devoted to interpretation of Luther's debate with Erasmus in *De servo arbitrio*. See in particular: F. Beisser, *Claritas scripturae bei Martin Luther* (Göttingen: Vandenhoeck und Ruprecht, 1966); P. Hayden-Roy, 'Hermeneutica gloriae vs. hermeneutica crucis: Sebastian Franck and Martin Luther on the Clarity of Scripture', *Archiv für Reformationsgeschichte* 81 (1990), pp. 50–68; R. Hermann, 'Von der Klarheit der Heiligen Schrift', in *Studien zur Theologie Luthers und des Luthertums* (Göttingen: Vandenhoeck und Ruprecht, 1981), pp. 170– 255; O. Kuss, 'Über der Klarheit der Schrift', in J. Ernst (ed.), *Schriftauslegung. Beiträge zur Hermeneutik des Neuen Testamentes und im Neuen Testament* (Paderborn: Schöningh, 1972), pp. 89–149; R. Mau, 'Klarheit der Schrift und Evangelium. Zum Ansatz des lutherschen Gedankens der claritas scripturae', *Theologische Versuche* 4 (1972), pp. 129–43; P. Neuner and F. Schröger, 'Luthers These von der Klarheit der Schrift', *Theologie und Glaube* 74 (1984), pp. 39–58; H. Østergaard-Nielsen, *Scriptura sacra et viva vox: eine Lutherstudie* (Munich: Kaiser, 1957); S. D. Paulson, 'From Scripture to Dogmatics', *Lutheran Quarterly* 7 (1993), pp. 159–69; E. Wolf, 'Über "Klarheit der Heiligen Schrift" nach Luthers *De servo arbitrio*', *Theologische Literaturzeitung* 92 (1967), pp. 721–30.

By way of initial orientation, the following proposition may be offered: *To confess the clarity of Holy Scripture is to acknowledge the radiant presence of God who through Holy Scripture sheds abroad the light of the knowledge of his reconciling works and ways in the communion of the saints, assembled by the Word of God and illuminated by the Spirit to hear the gospel with repentance and faith.*

Talk of the clarity of Holy Scripture is a *confession*. To confess is to articulate a truth which is given, presenting itself to the mind, will and affections in its irreducibly spiritual character. To confess is also to commit oneself to act in accordance with and under the tutelage of that which is confessed. Confession is thus a recognition of and a decision for divine teaching. Consequently, confession does not take its rise in natural perception; its origins lie in the conversion of reason through divine instruction. Confession is the articulation of knowledge which comes to us in the course of the great work of reconciliation which is purposed by God the Father, accomplished by God the Son, and brought to full effect by God the Holy Spirit. The clarity of Scripture is a matter for confession because it is not simply a linguistic or semantic property of the biblical text, perceptible *remoto deo*; clarity is that which Scripture acquires by virtue of the presence and action of God, and that which is seen as it makes itself visible to faith. *Claritas scripturae* is 'a "confession" of faith that praise[s] the Word in its clarity'.[5]

Accordingly, in its character as confession, talk of the clarity of Scripture is also an *acknowledgement*. That is, such talk is not in any straightforward way a proposal on the part of the church or the individual reader; still less is it simply a statement of interpretative policy. It is grateful recognition and reception of that which Scripture antecedently is. As with the attributes of God, so here with the properties of Scripture: the logic of theological attribution is not ascription but acknowledgement. The properties of Scripture are not labels attached to Scripture, indicating our attitudes towards, interests in, or intended uses of the biblical text. To talk of *claritas scripturae* is to acknowledge that, by virtue of the action of God, Holy Scripture *is* clear.

Claritas scripturae is, however, not a simple but a complex notion.[6] What it says about the nature and functioning of the

---

5. Berkouwer, *Holy Scripture*, p. 273.

6. My account of the complex character of the notion of *claritas scripturae* has some similarities to that offered by Callahan in *The Clarity of Scripture*, who argues

biblical texts draws upon theological doctrine concerning the nature of God and God's relation to the world, concerning the church in relation to Word and Spirit, and concerning the nature of human interpreters and their acts in relation to Scripture. As with all themes in bibliology, the domain of the clarity of Scripture is the *magnalia dei*, the economy of God's reconciling and revelatory turn to the saints. Its explication therefore requires careful arrangement of materials drawn from across the dogmatic corpus: the doctrine of the Trinity, soteriology, ecclesiology and anthropology. This involves, in particular, reflection upon the fact that the triune God is himself light, and so radiantly present to his creatures, one who wills to be known and loved, and so one whose work of reconciling love can be described as calling his creatures out of darkness into his marvellous light (1 Pet. 2.9). The clarity of Scripture is a refraction of the light which God is and which he sheds abroad. Similarly, talk of the clarity of Scripture involves an account of those who are illuminated by the divine presence, those for whom the Lord is light and salvation (Ps. 27.1). That company – which may be variously described as the fellowship of the saints, the community gathered around the Word, or the *illuminati* of the Holy Spirit – is the setting in which the clarity of Scripture is made a matter of attention and confession, and in which Scripture's clarity guides the work of interpretation. To engage in the interpretation of the clear Word of God requires the Spirit's gifts of repentance and faith as those dispositions of human life in which the gospel may be heard.

All this, then, constitutes the web of affirmations within which the theological logic of the notion of the clarity of Scripture is best displayed. We now turn to their fuller explication.

II

The setting of the clarity of Scripture is the effective illuminating presence of God the revealer who is in himself light and whose mighty

that 'the expression *clarity of Scripture* refers to how Christians account for the union of Scripture that is read, an appropriate reading of Scripture and Scripture's readers. Scripture, when read in a Christian manner, can be said to be clear in itself but not by itself (it has never been isolated from its readings or readers, historically or theologically)' (p. 11). But though Callahan is keen to trace the connections between clarity and the activity of reading, he has little to say about revelation, and runs the risk of detaching clarity as a hermeneutical practice from theology proper.

work of reconciliation overthrows the darkness and ignorance of sin, restoring us to fellowship and establishing the knowledge of himself.

Holy Scripture is clear because God is light and therefore the one in whose light we see light. God is himself light. The splendour and inexhaustible self-sufficiency of God's triune being includes his limitless capacity to enlighten the world by manifesting himself as its true light. As light, God is the one who is glorious in himself and so one who is resplendent. The metaphor of light is particularly fitting to indicate the manner in which, in the depth of his being, God is one whose freedom and sovereignty include a turning to his creatures. For light is not light if it is self-enclosed: light shines, it suffuses or pervades. It does so by virtue of its own inherent potency, yet that potency is precisely the capacity to be self-diffusing, to shed itself abroad. God is light, omnipotent and therefore omnipresent light. The eminence which God is and in which he is the creator and Lord of all things includes the energy or impetus of his self-revelation. God is light, imparting and disclosing his glory, enlightening all things effectively and effortlessly, breaking forth by virtue of his own spontaneous and unfettered power. 'The true and living God is eloquent and radiant.'[7]

It scarcely needs to be said that this divine radiance by which all things are illuminated is no impersonal state of affairs. It is the presence of God the revealer. To speak of the light of God is to speak of a personal action and mode of relation, the free self-disposing of the Lord of all things existing towards and with his creatures. God's radiance is not a simple metaphysical formula but a matter of fellowship between himself and those whom he enlightens by manifesting himself, showing them the light of his presence. As the one who is in himself light, God faces his people, lifting up the light of his countenance and so illuminating them (Pss. 4.6, 13.3, 89.15). In sum: to say that God is light is to confess the effective, illuminating presence of God the revealer.

Yet more must be said. The confession that God is light has to be understood in terms of the divine resolve for fellowship. But this resolve does not run its course unhindered; it faces opposition from the very creature which it seeks to enlighten and bless. Standing in God's light, illuminated by God, shown the light of God's countenance, the creature attempts to wrest itself free of fellowship

---

7. K. Barth, *Church Dogmatics* IV/3 (Edinburgh: T&T Clark, 1962), p. 79.

with God and establish itself in independence from the creator as its own light and giver of life, its own source of truth. But to accomplish this act of rebellion, the creature must resist, even deny, God's light. In defiance of the divine resolve, in an absurd and impotent yet, for all that, utterly destructive act of repudiation, the creature refuses to acknowledge the glory of God, his illuminating presence as creator. And so the creature falls into darkness and ignorance. This darkness and ignorance do not quench the light – for how could the creature extinguish the light of God's glory, or rob the divine being of its splendour, or place an insurmountable obstacle in the path of its radiance? Rather, the creature's act of defiance is a matter of wilful opposition to light, as a result of which the light becomes that which exposes the creature as sinner. The light whose purpose is to illuminate the creature continues to do so; but now what it discloses is the creature's wickedness, laying the creature open to judgement. 'And this is the judgement, that the light has come into the world, and men loved darkness rather than light, because their deeds were evil. For everyone who does evil hates the light, and does not come to the light, lest his deeds should be exposed' (Jn 3.19f.). To 'hate' the light and to refuse to 'come to' the light are the elemental breaches of fellowship which form the essence of sin. From them flow ignorance and blindness, disordered and directionless existence. 'He who walks in the darkness does not know where he goes' (Jn 12.35; cf. 1 Jn 2.11; Prov. 4.19).

With this we reach the soteriological heart of what is to be said about God as light, expressed thus in our proposition: in his *mighty work of reconciliation [God] overthrows the darkness and ignorance of sin, restoring us to fellowship and establishing the knowledge of himself.*

'In him was life, and the life was the light of men. The light shines in the darkness, and the darkness has not overcome it' (Jn 1.4f.). God's Word is life and light. And this Word, in opposition to (and so in mercy upon) the defiant creature and its dark world, becomes flesh. In Jesus Christ the Word incarnate, the world is no longer permitted to hug itself in darkness or refuse to acknowledge that God is light. The sheer perversity of sin, its persistence in refusing the light, is simply overruled by virtue of one single reality: 'The light shines in the darkness, and the darkness has not overcome it'. The 'shining' is entirely undefeated by the darkness which it masters, overwhelms and scatters. And this is because it – or rather *he*, Jesus Christ, God's Word and light as human presence – is the glory of God. He is not simply a refraction of God's glory, still less a witness to the light (Jn 1.8). He is the 'true light' (Jn 1.9) in the world. To receive him is to behold God's self-manifestation, to see in him the glory of God, which is a 'glory as of the only Son of the Father' (Jn 1.14). For he, Jesus Christ, is God of God and therefore light of light. In him and as him there takes place the majestic and merciful disclosure of God. As the embodiment of God's glory, he is at one and the same time the accomplishment of reconciliation and the accomplishment of revelation. He is the definitive act in which fellowship with and knowledge of God are restored. 'The Word became flesh and dwelt among us ... He has made him known' (Jn 1.14, 18). He is the confirmation of the reality: 'God is light'; and he is the one in whom there occurs the fulfilment of the purpose of God, namely 'fellowship with him' (1 Jn 1.6).

This fellowship, to which we are destined and appointed by God the Father and which is secured against human darkness by God the Son, the effulgence of the Father's glory (Heb. 1.3), is made continuously real by the illuminating ministry of the Holy Spirit. And so the apostle prays in Ephesians 'that the God of our Lord Jesus Christ, the Father of glory, may give you a spirit of wisdom and of revelation in the knowledge of him, having the eyes of your hearts enlightened ... ' (Eph. 1.17f.). The God and Father of our Lord Jesus Christ is 'the Father of glory', the resplendent one who gives the Spirit in order to endow those whom the Son has reconciled with wisdom, revelation and knowledge. These benefits which flow from the Spirit's work are summed up as 'the enlightenment of the eyes of the heart'. Knowledge of the scope of God's luminous presence and activity (that is, of 'the riches of his glorious inheritance in the saints') originates not on the creaturely side of fellowship but on the side of the illuminating person of the Spirit. 'That you may know' is strictly subordinate to and dependent upon the giving of the Spirit and his enlightening of the eyes. Seeing God's glory is God's work.

This reconciling and revelatory presence of the triune God gives the frame for theological talk of the clarity of Holy Scripture. The economy of God's communication of himself by scattering the darkness of sin, reconciling lost creatures, overcoming ignorance and establishing the knowledge and love of himself, is the dogmatic location of the notion of *claritas scripturae*. Scripture is clear as the instrument of the reconciling clarity of God whose light is radiantly present in Jesus Christ and the Holy Spirit. Establishing this dogmatic setting is a task of first rank in the doctrine of Scripture, and, once established, it must not simply be assumed or left to one side: it must be operative at every point, and rendered explicit. Unless this is done, and bibliology tied explicitly to reconciliation and revelation, disorder threatens. This disorder, which readily afflicts any theology of Scripture and its properties, results from the extraction of Holy Scripture from the divine economy. Once detached from operative language about the self-disclosure of God in the course of seeking and maintaining fellowship, the theology of Scripture becomes an isolated piece of teaching. It drifts away from a proper understanding of the origin and ends of Scripture (life with God who lifts up the light of his countenance); it runs the risk of attributing to the text perfections which are properly to be attributed to God alone; and it may thereby make the perception of Scripture's properties (including clarity) a matter of rational judgement rather than of faith in God's presence. The only effective safeguard is attentiveness to the architecture of the gospel, a sense of the scope and arrangement of Christian teaching, and a vigilance lest the pressures of confessional polemic or deference to non-theological literary and philosophical theory deform the theological structure and so prevent well-ordered exposition of *claritas* in relation to the being and work of God who is light.

We conclude this section with three instructive examples of the exposition of the doctrine of *claritas scripturae* in terms of its location in the economy of God as reconciler and revealer. First, *Luther*. The discussions of *claritas scripturae* in *De servo arbitrio*[8] are undergirded by a theological presupposition that Holy Scripture and its readers exist in a sphere which is illuminated by the presence of the risen Christ.

> What still sublimer thing can remain hidden in the Scriptures, now that the seals have been broken, the stone rolled from the door of the sepulchre, and the supreme mystery brought to light, namely, that Christ the Son of God has been made man, that God is three in one, that Christ has suffered for us and is to reign eternally? (pp. 25f.)

The clarity of Scripture, that is, is to be understood as a corollary of the fact that the 'supreme mystery' has indeed been 'brought to light'; Scripture is clear because the Bible and its readers stand after the resurrection in the realm of revelation, and because the *res* which Scripture signifies is itself utterly resplendent.

---

8.   M. Luther, *The Bondage of the Will*, in *Luther's Works* vol. 33 (Philadelphia: Fortress Press, 1972), pp. 24–28, 89–99. Page numbers in the following paragraph refer to this edition.

> The subject matter of the Scripture ... is all quite accessible, even though some texts are still obscure owing to our ignorance of their terms. Truly it is stupid and impious, when we know the subject matter of Scripture has all been placed in the clearest light, to call it obscure on account of a few obscure words. (p. 26)

And so Luther continues in a celebrated passage:

> when the thing signified is in the light, it does not matter if this or that sign of it is in darkness, since many other signs of the same thing are meanwhile in this light. Who will say that a public fountain is not in the light because those who are in a narrow side street do not see it, whereas all who are in the marketplace do see it? (p. 26).

What troubles Luther about Erasmus is, more than anything, his scepticism. What Erasmus takes as modesty before the hidden mysteries of God and as a refusal of speculation, Luther views as a perverse refusal to acknowledge that in Christ's resurrection, what was once hidden has now become plain, and that the present time is no longer in half-light but is the domain of full revelation.

> Matters of the highest majesty and the profoundest mysteries are no longer hidden away, but have been brought to light and are openly displayed before the very doors. For Christ has opened our minds so that we may understand the Scriptures, and the gospel is preached to the whole earth (pp. 26f.).

Accordingly, for Luther, establishing clarity involves a great deal more than sorting out obscurities and identifying Scripture's plain (moral) teaching. It entails, rather, grasping the fact that the matter of Scripture is illumined and made plain by the light of the resurrection. What is so striking about Luther's account of *claritas* is his vigorous theological objectivity: Scripture *is* plain because it is illuminated by God's saving work. Failure to perceive this is not to be attributed to some defect in Scripture's clarity, for 'everything there is in the Scriptures has been brought out by the Word into the most definite light' (p. 28), but to 'the blindness or indolence of those who will not take the trouble to look at the very clearest truth' (p. 27). In short: for Luther, *claritas scripturae* is a salvation-historical affirmation, a statement about the light of the gospel in which Scripture stands and which must illumine the reader if Scripture's clarity is to be perceived.

Second, mention may be made of *Zwingli* in his 1522 account 'Of the Clarity and Certainty or Power of the Word of God'.[9] Here much space is

---

9.   H. Zwingli, 'Of the Clarity and Certainty or Power of the Word of God', in G. W. Bromiley (ed.), *Zwingli and Bullinger* (London: SCM, 1953), pp. 59–95. Page numbers in the following paragraph refer to this edition.

given over to the polemical assertion that to be *theodidacti* in interpretation of Scripture necessarily means the exclusion of human teachers: the affirmation 'taught of God' carries with it the negation 'not of men' (p. 89). Behind the polemic, however, is an attempt to set *claritas scripturae* in the wider context of God's fellowship with his creatures. It is for this reason that Zwingli begins his treatise apparently tangentially with discussion of the *imago dei*, expounding the image in terms of the relation between creator and creature: 'we are made in the image of God and ... that image is implanted within us in order that we may enjoy the closest possible relationship with its maker and creator' (p. 65). Hence the 'inward man ... delights in the law of God because it is created in the divine image in order to have fellowship with him' (p. 67). This furnishes Zwingli with the overarching context of the doctrine of the clarity of Scripture, which concerns the way in which the Word (God's communicative presence and action) illumines the 'inner man', so making Scripture clear: 'It is the Word of God, which is God himself, that lighteth every man' so that 'the comprehension and understanding of doctrine comes ... from above' (p. 79). There is, doubtless, the beginning of a problem here, particularly a competitive view of divine and human action: 'not *doctores*, not *patres*, not pope, not *cathedra*, not *concilia*, but the Father of Jesus Christ' teaches the church (p. 79). And this goes hand in hand with the interiorized, a-social anthropology which Zwingli presupposes. Nevertheless, the scope of Zwingli's treatise is such that he sets discussion of *claritas* in a larger frame of the saving relations of God and humankind, and so resists an over-hasty concentration upon textual properties in and of themselves.

It is, however, to Zwingli's successor in Zurich, *Heinrich Bullinger*, specifically in the first three sermons of the first *Decade*, that we should turn for one of the most elegant and shrewd statements of the soteriological and revelatory setting of the theology of the clarity of Scripture.[10] The details of what Bullinger has to say in the third sermon about the relation of Scripture's clarity to the activity of exposition need not detain us at present. What is much more important is the way in which, in the first two sermons, Bullinger prepares for his account of the clarity of Scripture by setting out what is, in effect, a brief history of the revelatory acts of God, in which Bullinger traces 'the history of the proceeding of the Word of God, and by what means it shined ever and anon very clear and brightly in the world' (p. 48). For Bullinger, what is said of Scripture has its place in the fact that 'from the beginning ... of the world, God by his Spirit and the ministry of angels, spake to the holy fathers' (p. 39), so providing that 'no age at any time should be without most excellent lights' (p. 40). Revelation is thus what Bullinger calls 'that lively tradition' of patriarchs and prophets,

---

10.   H. Bullinger, *The Decades* I & II (Cambridge: Cambridge University Press, 1849). Page numbers in the following paragraph refer to this edition.

definitively summed up in the Son of God and then communicated in the
ministry of the apostles. In sum, 'The Word of God is the speech of God,
that is, the revealing of his good will towards mankind, which from the
beginning, one while by his own mouth, and another while by the speech of
angels, he did open to those first, ancient, and most holy fathers; who again
by tradition did faithfully deliver it to their posterity' (p. 56). This theology
of the Word is then related to the end of revelation and the manner of its
reception. As regards its end, Bullinger's emphasis is soteriological: 'the
Word of God is revealed, to the intent that it may fully instruct us in the
ways of God and our salvation' (p. 61); as regards its reception, what is
required is a number of virtues which are themselves gifts of the Spirit –
reverence, attentiveness, prayer, sobriety, faith (see p. 64). What is most
striking in Bullinger's presentation is his firm sense of the proper setting of
doctrinal affirmations about the nature of Scripture, his sense, therefore,
that talk about *claritas scripturae* ought only to be reached after full
depiction of 'the history of the proceeding of the Word of God'. Moreover,
Bullinger offers an especially fine example of the coordination of the
doctrines of revelation and salvation with an untroubled and circumscribed
hermeneutics which is surely the best index of good theological order in this
matter.

III

The radiance of God's presence in the 'proceeding of the Word of
God' avails itself of creaturely instruments. It presents itself in and
through creaturely forms, electing and ordering the course of these
creaturely realities, and acting through their service to accomplish
its end, namely the publication of the *magnalia dei*. Of those forms,
the chief is Holy Scripture, through which the clear word of the
gospel sounds forth. In propositional form: *Holy Scripture is clear
as the sanctified creaturely auxiliary of the communicative presence of
God, through which the promise and instruction of the gospel are
announced by the Holy Spirit.*

Our next task, therefore, is to discuss the place of the biblical text
in the divine economy, and, more specifically, to identify the senses
in which clarity may be understood as a property of Holy Scripture
as text. Discussion of this topic can easily drift into dualist
assumptions which fail to give a properly integrated account of the
relation between divine communicative activity and creaturely
realities. One version of this dualism does not allow that a text, as a
verbum externum, can in and of itself play any role in the divine
economy, for texts are mere natural products, obscure and
indeterminate, and cannot be instrumental in God's self-

clarification. The problem here is what Wenz identifies as a bifurcation of 'concrete and limited creaturely historical means' from 'God's saving action and work'.[11] And it usually results in one of two things: either a rejection of any sense that the text is itself clear, or (more often) a relocation of clarity in readers or reading communities, so that clarity is a property, not of the biblical text, but of the processes of its reception. Another version of the dualism demonstrates the same disintegrated understanding of texts and divine communication, but this time by ascribing to the biblical texts properties or actions which are proper to God, in this way removing the text from the realm of natural, contingent history. On this model, Scripture is without qualification clear *in se*; its perspicuity is such that the divine self-clarification is identified with the text. These two forms of dualism – either naturalization or near-divinization of the text – are two faces of the same coin. Both lack a well-rounded theological treatment of the divine use of creaturely instruments which can coordinate the natural integrity of the text and the incommunicability of divine action. What is required, therefore, is a way of talking of the use of texts in the economy of God's revelatory grace which will compromise neither their naturalness nor their divine use. Such an account can then furnish the basis for a theological understanding of clarity as a textual property.

At the heart of such an account is, I suggest, a notion of Scripture as *sanctified creaturely auxiliary of the communicative presence of God*. Scripture is, first, a sanctified text. By sanctification we refer to the work of the Holy Spirit in electing, shaping and preserving creaturely realities to undertake a role in the divine economy: creaturely realities are sanctified by divine use. This divine 'use', though it is gratuitous, is not simply occasional or punctiliar, arbitrarily employing the creaturely reality and then casting it aside. That is, sanctification has a properly horizontal dimension; it involves the election and overseeing of the entire historical course of the creaturely reality so that that reality becomes in itself a creature made suitable to serve the divine purpose. A sanctified creaturely reality is not extracted from its creatureliness, but ordered in such a way that it can fittingly assist in the work which is proper to God. Sanctified by the Spirit, the creaturely reality is given its own genuine substance as it is moulded to enter into the divine service.

---

11. Wenz, *Das Wort Gottes*, p. 295.

This notion of sanctification can be applied to the nature of the biblical texts and their function in God's revelatory work. As the work of the Spirit, sanctification integrates communicative divine action and the creatureliness of those elements which are appointed to serve God's self-presentation. Thus, to speak of Scripture as *holy* is to articulate two convictions. First, because they are sanctified, the texts are not to be defined and handled exclusively as 'natural' entities: they are fields of the Spirit's action in the publication of the knowledge of God. Second, sanctification does not diminish creatureliness; hence the texts' place in the revelatory economy of God does not withdraw them from human processes. It is *as* – not *despite* – what they are as creaturely that they serve God. The sanctified text is creaturely, not divine, and its place in the divine economy does not need to be secured by ascribing divine properties to the text.

From this, we may draw a fundamental principle for our understanding of the ontology of Scripture: Holy Scripture has its being in the formative economy of the Word and Spirit of God. It is what it is as a sanctified element in the proceeding of the divine Word; the movement of God's self-manifestation determines the text's substance and therefore its properties, including its clarity. At this point, three affirmations intersect. (1) It is proper to speak of the ontology of the text. However much the biblical texts are bound up with their reading and reception, they have a measure of durability and resistance, and can be spoken of *in se*. They are more than a score for performance, much more than an empty space for readerly poetics. (2) The ontology of the biblical texts has to be explicated in theological terms. The confession that the Bible is Holy Scripture stands against the assumption that the being of this text is exhaustively defined by its occupation of a space in a natural field of communicative activity. This assumption is to be controverted because of its underlying claim that a 'natural' understanding of the text is more basic than an understanding of the text as Holy Scripture. The biblical text *is* Holy Scripture; its being is defined, not simply through membership of the class of texts, but by the fact that it is *this* text – sanctified, that is, Spirit-generated and preserved – in *this* field of action – the communicative movement of God. (3) Because the text of Holy Scripture has its being in this divine movement, talk of the properties of the text is a means of indicating that which Holy Scripture is as it fulfils its appointed task and serves God's glorious presence. What does this mean for theological portrayal of clarity as one of the properties of Holy Scripture?

As with the more general notion of sanctification, so here in the question of *claritas scripturae*: effective Christological and pneumatological teaching are central to the success of the enterprise. Scripture's clarity is rooted in the fact that it is appointed to be the instrument of the Spirit's announcement of the gospel of Christ. In the power of the Spirit, Jesus Christ is the prophet of his own reality: he announces himself. Risen from the dead, he is the living Word who declares with divine authority and full effect the reality of and the benefits which flow from his reconciling achievement. Because Scripture is sanctified for the service of this Word, it 'enlightens', bringing the clear Word of God to bear upon the attentive listener. 'When the Word of God shines on the human understanding', writes Zwingli, 'it enlightens it in such a way that it understands and confesses the Word and knows the certainty of it.'[12] Drawing examples from the patriarchs' persuasion of the authenticity of divine commands, Zwingli notes that 'God's Word brought with it its own clarity and enlightenment'.[13] Yet he is careful to add that this clarity is not a quality of the listener's understanding, but the fruit of the Spirit's work in and through the text. Scripture is clear, that is, because of 'the light of the Spirit of God, illuminating and inspiring the words in such a way that the light of the divine content is seen in [God's] light'.[14]

Appeal to Christological and pneumatological doctrine prevents the segregation of the property of clarity from the revelatory work of God. In similar fashion, careful delineation of the connection between the clarity of Scripture and Scripture's efficacy (*efficacia scripturae*) prevents its isolation from its dynamic presence in the communion of saints among whom the gospel is announced by Scripture. Scripture is clear as it performs its task of serving the illuminating presence of Jesus Christ in his church. Clarity is therefore what might be called an historical property of Scripture, an attribute of the text which has its being in the 'proceeding' of revelation. The idiom of the ontology and properties of Scripture is dynamic.

12. Zwingli, 'Of the Clarity and Certainty or Power of the Word of God', p. 75.
13. Zwingli, 'Of the Clarity and Certainty or Power of the Word of God', p. 77.
14. Zwingli, 'Of the Clarity and Certainty or Power of the Word of God', p. 78. On this theme in Luther, see R. Hermann, 'Von der Klarheit der Heiligen Schrift', pp. 210ff.; R. Mau, 'Klarheit der Schrift und Evangelium', pp. 134ff.

This connection of clarity and efficacy is a routine aspect of most modern dogmatic accounts of the topic, and is often associated with Luther. To emphasize in this way that clarity is effectual helps block ideas that *claritas scripturae* is something to hand, 'available' after the manner of an historical report.[15] Scripture is clear as God is clear, namely in the event of his self-bestowal, as gift and not as stored treasure. Moreover, this emphasis ensures that we keep in mind the relation between the clarity of Scripture and the end of Scripture, namely the publication of the promise and instruction of the gospel.

Nevertheless, there is a danger that clarity may be collapsed into or identified with *efficacia*, with the result that clarity is scarcely a property of Scripture as text and much more a property of the divine event of revelation to which Scripture is only somewhat loosely attached. One of the most influential accounts along these lines is Beisser's influential study *Claritas scripturae bei Martin Luther*.[16] Beisser proposes that for Luther the clarity of Scripture is a function of Scripture's effectiveness as a 'living spoken word':

> This word is clear, univocal and accessible to everyone. Its self-evidence is compelling. A spoken word is heard; that is the fundamental form of this self-evidence. But this ought not to be understood as a mechanical process which runs its course automatically. For the word is self-evident not as a static quantity but as a spoken word. The word's self-evidence is not based upon a deposit; rather, it arises insofar as the word's self-evidence is enacted.[17]

The location of clarity is therefore primarily in the event of proclamation:

> The word is external, but although it is external, it is a spiritual quantity. If one takes the letter for itself on its own, it shows itself to be weak, indeed unsuitable. 'Spiritus Sanctus lesset sich nicht, verbis bunden, sed rem profert.' This ought to make clear that for Luther there is no available deposit for that which the Word of God is. The word is real, not insofar as it stands in the book, but because it is preached, because in it God speaks to us.[18]

---

15. See R. Mau, 'Klarheit der Schrift und Evangelium', p. 135; E. Wolf, 'Über "Klarheit der Heiligen Schrift"', p. 726.

16. Beisser is followed, for example, by Duchrow, 'Die Klarheit der Schrift und die Vernunft', and Thiselton, *New Horizons in Hermeneutics*.

17. Beisser, *Claritas scripturae bei Martin Luther*, p. 31.

18. Beisser, *Claritas scripturae bei Martin Luther*, p. 37.

This is undergirded by Beisser's suggestion 'that Luther regards the Bible or the Word of God primarily as oral, preached word':[19] 'when Luther speaks of "Scriptura" or "verbum", he is not thinking primarily of a *text*'.[20]

Beisser is certainly correct to urge that *claritas* ought not to be viewed as a static *depositum* but as a living phenomenon, and therefore as one unavailable for disengaged inspection. 'Notwithstanding the public character of this word, its clarity is not primarily that of universal rational validity, but as it were a clarity which comes from the hand of God. The word is clear, but this clarity is not generally, rationally ascertainable, for the word is clear as *God's* word ... Because of this, one can say for Luther the external word is a spiritual quantity.'[21] And he lays the right kind of emphasis on clarity as a function of the divine radiance: 'the clarity of Scripture is God's clarity'.[22] However, in protecting the notion of clarity from excessively formal or static conceptions, Beisser can hardly avoid an actualistic account of the matter: clarity, in effect, becomes oral clarification to which Scripture as *text* is not sufficiently related.[23] Beisser identifies a distortion which can be introduced into the theology of Scripture when clarity as textual property is discussed. But the safeguard is not to evacuate *claritas* into *viva vox evangelii*, on the grounds that to talk of Scripture as clear *in se* is objectifying. What is required is, rather, a dynamic (but not actualistic) ontology of Scripture which retains the idiom of properties and neither separates nor identifies clarity and efficacy.

Here we may look for instruction to what may at first blush appear to be an unpromising guide, namely Turretin. The received account of his theology of Scripture in the *Institutes of Elenctic Theology* is that it transforms a dynamic theology of Scripture into something static, and so reifies the clarity of Scripture as an objectified textual phenomenon. Callahan, for example, argues that Turretin represents a shift to 'the belief that clarity is a quality of Scripture itself, rather than something brought to the text by the reader (whether ecclesial official or Spirit-illumined believer)',[24] thereby sacrificing the confessional character of clarity. But this is to foreshorten Turretin's account. Clarity is not, for him, mere evidentness; it is rather concerned with the fact that in Scripture the mysteries of faith 'are so wonderfully accommodated by the Lord that the

---

19.   Beisser, *Claritas scripturae bei Martin Luther*, p. 141. Cf. p. 83.
20.   Beisser, *Claritas scripturae bei Martin Luther*, p. 83.
21.   Beisser, *Claritas scripturae bei Martin Luther*, p. 85.
22.   Beisser, *Claritas scripturae bei Martin Luther*, p. 85. Cf. pp. 88, 136.
23.   See Mau's critical comments on Beisser in 'Klarheit der Schrift und Evangelium', p. 130.
24.   Callahan, *The Clarity of Scripture*, p. 144.

believers understand these mysteries sufficiently for salvation'.[25] Clarity as
textual property is inseparable from both divine accommodation and from
readerly activity, which together form the soteriological setting for a
theology of Scripture's attributes. It is true that Turretin's language of
Scripture as *in se* clear occasionally nods, notably at those points where
Scripture itself is spoken of in a rather unqualified way as agent: the
Scriptures, he writes, 'are luminous formally and effectively because like the
sun they emit rays and impress themselves upon the eyes of the beholder'.[26]
But this is a small slip, corrected almost immediately in Q. XVII.xi by talk
of God as the efficient cause of Scripture. Only a slight adjustment to
Turretin would be required to bring out more fully the dynamic element of
what he has to say, and to relate it to the wider economy of salvation.

Clarity is therefore a property bestowed upon Holy Scripture by the
work of the Spirit. Sanctified to do service to the glorious self-
manifestation of God, appointed by Christ as a witness to himself,
Scripture is clear because in and through its texts the Holy Spirit
announces the gospel's promise and instruction. As the older
theology put it, Scripture is clear concerning 'all things necessary
for salvation'. Or in Calvin's phrase (he is commenting on 2 Peter
1.19): the clarity of Scripture is the way in which by divine
appointment it is 'a fit and proper guide to show us clearly the
way'.[27] Clarity does not mean ease or immediacy of access or
absolute semantic transparency. It means that this text is caught up
in God's self-manifestation as the light of the world, and becomes
the means through which the Spirit makes plain the gospel. But
where does the Spirit make the gospel plain, and *to whom*? These are
the concerns of our final sections, on the church and the act of
interpretation.

IV

*The sphere of the clarity of Holy Scripture is the church, the creature
of the Word of God; by the Word the church is generated and
preserved, and by the Spirit the church sets forth the clear Word of
God in traditions of holy attentiveness.*

25. F. Turretin, *Institutes of Elenctic Theology I: First through Tenth Topics*
(Phillipsburg: Presbyterian and Reformed Publishing, 1992), p. 143 (Q. XVII.iii).

26. Turretin, *Institutes of Elenctic Theology I*, pp. 144f. (Q. XVII.viii).

27. J. Calvin, *The Epistle of St Paul to the Hebrews and the First and Second
Epistles of St Peter* (Edinburgh: Oliver and Boyd, 1963), p. 342.

Holy Scripture is an ecclesial reality. This is not because Scripture is the church's invention, whether through production or authorization, and still less is it because the church is Scripture's patron, conferring some dignity on it by adopting it as its symbol system of choice. Rather, Scripture is an ecclesial reality because the place of Scripture is in the economy of salvation, and the economy of salvation concerns the divine work of restoring fellowship through the gathering of the *sanctorum communio*. A soteriology without an account of the church would be incomplete; and a bibliology uncoordinated to ecclesiology indicates a cramped grasp of the scope of the divine economy. By extension, because *claritas* has its sphere in soteriology, it has a necessary ecclesial component: the clear Word of God is the Word of God in, for and over the church. For clarity concerns the luminous character of the gospel of God of which Holy Scripture is the creaturely auxiliary. That luminosity, and the clarity of the text in and through which the gospel bears testimony to itself, is not mere transparency available for inspection by standardly rational persons. It is spiritually perceived; perceived, that is, by those whom Christ and the Spirit gather into the faithful community and who receive the Word with trust and fear of the Lord.

Failure to make sense of the ecclesial aspect of *claritas scripturae* is one of the chief weaknesses of Hodge's account of the matter. Although Hodge cautions that clarity does not spell the end of 'deference to the faith of the church',[28] his argument is driven by an antithesis between private judgement and church authority. 'What Protestants deny on this subject is that Christ has appointed any officer, or class of officers, in his church to whose interpretation of the Scriptures the people are bound to submit as of final authority'.[29] That this is a degenerate version of what can be found in, for example, Zwingli and Turretin, can be seen in the next sentence: God 'has made it obligatory upon every man to search the Scriptures for himself, and to determine on his own discretion what they require him to believe and to do'.[30] Clarity is therefore a necessary condition for the 'right of private judgement' which is 'the great safeguard of civil and religious liberty'.[31] This is surely the wrong idiom for an account of the operations of Scripture. First, it assumes that office or tradition in the church are always

28. C. Hodge, *Systematic Theology*, vol. 1 (New York: Scribner, Armstrong, 1877), p. 184.
29. Hodge, *Systematic Theology*, vol. 1, p. 184.
30. Hodge, *Systematic Theology*, vol. 1, p. 184.
31. Hodge, *Systematic Theology*, vol. 1, p. 186.

instruments of suppression, and never act as guides; second, it thinks of the fellowship of the saints by analogy from the civil realm (as an aggregate of individual bundles of rights and judgements); third, 'judgement' is an odd description of the fear and trembling which the faithful have before the Word. And, most of all, the whole account is curiously deistic in its lack of language about the activity of God.

Similar problems surface in R. T. Sandin's attempt to depict clarity through the philosophy of Wittgenstein (with which he is not well acquainted), to whom Sandin attributes the view that 'all communication by means of language presupposes the self-identity and determinateness of what is spoken/heard (written/read)'.[32] By extension, 'if there is a meaning in Scripture such meaning is clear', and the task of interpretation is simply a matter of removing obstacles in the recipient.[33] There are numerous problems here: the appeal to philosophy rather than theology, the assumption that there is no such thing as special hermeneutics, the absence of language about God, but more than anything, a lack of any reference to the church as the sphere of meaning (all the more surprising in view of Wittgenstein's views on the social character of communication).

Scripture is clear in the gathering of the saints, which is the 'special sphere of influence' of Holy Scripture.[34] If this has, at least until recently, remained a somewhat muted theme in Protestant dogmatics, this is largely because in Reformation and post-Reformation polemic, *claritas* was a key weapon in protest against the authority of interpretative traditions and their agents. At its best, this polemic was not detached either from conviction of the ecclesial sphere in which Scripture functions or from the proper exercise of the office of interpretation. But the demands of polemic against the magisterium could lead to neglect of both. Zwingli's principle that 'enlightenment, instruction and assurance are by divine teaching without any intervention on the part of that which is human'[35] betrays an ecclesiological minimalism which already exposes the Protestant tradition to the threat of the hegemony of private judgement which has been noted in Hodge. Moreover, Zwingli may here (as, perhaps, in his sacramental theology) slip into a dualism in which God's work of illumination is immediate and contextless, making use of no auxiliaries and occurring in empty

---

32. R. T. Sandin, 'The Clarity of Scripture', in M. Inch and R. Youngblood (eds), *The Living and Active Word of God* (Winona Lake: Eisenbrauns, 1983), p. 239.

33. Sandin, 'The Clarity of Scripture', p. 240.

34. K. Barth, *Church Dogmatics* I/2 (Edinburgh: T&T Clark, 1956), p. 685.

35. Zwingli, 'Of the Clarity and Certainty or Power of the Word of God', p. 80.

spaces which are simply the occasions of its imparticipable self-activation.

If we are not to be betrayed into some of these mistakes, what is required is judicious theological specification of both 'clarity' and 'church'. Clarity must be related to churchly acts of interpretation in a way which denies neither that Scripture is clear *in se* and *ante usum* nor that there is a legitimacy to ecclesial interpretation. The churchly component must be articulated in such a way that its role is not one of presiding over or supplementing and so 'clarifying' Scripture, but rather of receiving its inherent clarity in holy attentiveness. The clarity of Scripture, that is, constitutes a determination of the role of the church vis-à-vis Scripture, both in the sense of limiting the church's activity and in the sense of giving it a specific character and direction. The clarity of Scripture forms, check and directs churchly interpretation.

This entails, first, that the church should not be considered to have any constitutive or co-constitutive role in the clarity of Holy Scripture. Scripture is not an initial textual stage in divine revelation which is then completed by churchly activity. Nor is Scripture obscure raw material whose perspicuity derives from ongoing ecclesial clarification. The church does not illuminate Scripture but is illuminated by it and is wholly dependent upon Scripture to dispel its ignorance. For the church, too, Scripture is 'a lamp shining in a dark place' (2 Pet. 1.19), and its clarity is not generated but confessed and received in the church's traditions of reading.

Underlying this are two primary motifs in a theology of the clarity of Scripture. The first is that Scripture's clarity is closely attached to its sufficiency. Supplementation of Scripture is disallowed because as the elected assistant to God's self-manifestation, Scripture is entirely adequate to the task to which it is appointed.

David Brown's recent account of 'tradition as revelation' in *Tradition and Imagination* falters at just this point. 'Revelation is ... a matter of God taking seriously our historical situatedness, our dependence on our own particular environment and setting, rather than attempting to override it. That being so, my contention is that the process of revelation had to continue beyond Scripture, since otherwise the tradition would have become stultified through being trapped within one particular epoch and its assumptions.'[36] Rejecting a 'deposit' view of revelation and contending that

36. D. Brown, *Tradition and Imagination: Revelation and Change* (Oxford: Oxford University Press, 1999), p. 8.

tradition is best understood as 'imaginative reappropriation of the past',[37] Brown presupposes that Scripture is 'part of a living tradition that is constantly subject to change'.[38] If such an account fails, it is partly because within its terms there can be no theologically significant distinction between Scripture and tradition (and therefore, of course, no operable versions of canon and dogma). But it is also because it mischaracterizes tradition itself, whose essential activity it conceives to be 'rewriting'[39] – hardly a fitting term to describe the commentarial traditions which have had such importance in Christian reception of Scripture.[40] To say, on the other hand, that the church finds itself in the light of the clear Word of God, *having been* illuminated, is to suggest that Scripture is possessed of a measure of completeness, a hard edge which marks it off from those acts by which the church receives its radiance.

A second, related motif is that Scripture is the living Word of God, the *viva vox dei* which is not inert and obscure until activated by the church's acts, but *in se* the means of bestowal of life and light. Clarity is not a property which Scripture acquires by virtue of the church's use; as a function of the light and life of the gospel and the gospel's God, its clarity in an important sense precedes the church's reading.

Here we may consider Rowan Williams' proposal that – over against 'closed' accounts of the interpretation of Scripture in which reading is merely a matter of passive reception of already constituted meaning – reading is properly 'dramatic' or 'diachronic'. 'The meanings in our reading', he writes, 'are like the meanings in the rest of our experience, they are to be discovered, unfolded ... So long as our humanity remains unintelligible except as a life of material change, irreversible movement, it is unlikely – to say the least – that we could establish non-diachronic modes of reading as primary.'[41] Or again: 'Christian language takes it for granted ... that meanings are learned and produced, not given in iconic, ahistorical form. It grows out of a particular set of communal and individual histories, and its images and idioms are fundamentally shaped by this fact.'[42] And so:

37.   Brown, *Tradition and Imagination*, p. 65.
38.   Brown, *Tradition and Imagination*, p. 107.
39.   Brown, *Tradition and Imagination*, p. 74.
40.   It is interesting that Brown's examples of tradition in this and the subsequent volume *Discipleship and Imagination: Christian Tradition and Truth* (Oxford: Oxford University Press, 2000) are largely drawn from imaginative literature, the plastic arts and popular piety.
41.   R. Williams, 'The Discipline of Scripture', in *On Christian Theology* (Oxford: Blackwell, 2000), p. 49.
42.   Williams, 'The Discipline of Scripture', p. 49.

Christian interpretation is unavoidably engaged in 'dramatic' modes of reading:

> we are invited to identify ourselves in the story being contemplated, to re-appropriate who we are now, and who we shall or can be, in terms of the story. *Its* movements, transactions, transformation, become *ours* ... [A] dramatic reading means that our appropriation of the story is not a static relation of confrontation with images of virtue or vice, finished pictures of a quality once and for all achieved and so no longer taking time, but an active working through of the story's movement in our own time.[43]

'Dramatic' or 'diachronic' reading thus highlights both the *temporal* and the *active* character of our interpretation of texts; they are a matter of 'a complex of interwoven processes: a production of meaning in the only mode available for material and temporal creatures'.[44] The difficulty here is, once again, not the affirmation that there is an ecclesial component in the reception of Scripture, but that the ecclesial component is of such prominence that the text becomes an occasion for churchly interpretative work, work which is more poetic than receptive.

Clarity is not churchly clarification; the church's traditions of interpretation are authentic insofar as they are a receiving of the clear Word. The ecclesial basis for this is that the church is the creature of the Word. The church is that community which is brought into life and preserved in life by the communicative and reconciling action of the triune God, the one in whose presence and by whose gift the church has its life. That presence and gift are brought to bear upon the church by the action of the Spirit of the risen Christ in and through the prophetic and apostolic witnesses. Holy Scripture, therefore, is the instrument of Christ's rule in the church, and stands over against the church, not as a mere statutory norm but as the sword of the Spirit. Scripture is not something indefinite and opaque, but a divine action of illuminating force and clarity. The office of the church in the matter of interpretation is undertaken, therefore, with deference and submission, wholly subservient and posterior to the divine self-annunciation, whose lively and clear presence it indicates rather than completes or activates. What the church does is, in Bullinger's phrase, a matter of 'giving a setting out to the Word of God'.[45] The church interprets

---

43. Williams, 'The Discipline of Scripture', p. 50.
44. Williams, 'The Discipline of Scripture', p. 55.
45. Bullinger, *The Decades*, p. 72.

the Word by confessing and exhibiting its clarity. There is a parallel here to the churchly act of canonization: the church does not create but confesses the canon and pledges itself to abide under the canon's rule and judgement. So in its acts of interpretation: the church does not create Scripture's clarity but confesses its antecedent character and so pledges itself to continue beneath its consolation and instruction, and thereby to test its interpretative acts against the clear Word, asking whether they are 'genuine audits corresponding to the Word of God or ... no more than speculative constructs out of the Church's creative spirituality'.[46]

There are, doubtless, spiritualized versions of the sort of ecclesiology suggested here which all but eliminate the element of churchly reception, and reduce the interpretation of Holy Scripture to something drastically internal and individualistic. But the issue is not whether the clarity of Scripture eradicates tradition: of course not. The church is visible; it is an historical form of common life and activity. But: what *kind* of tradition? My suggestion is that, in the light of the clarity of Scripture, the church's tradition is best understood as 'holy attentiveness'. Tradition is the church's movement of Spirit-generated and Spirit-governed hearing of the clear word of the gospel which is borne to us by Holy Scripture. It is the *church's* movement, and therefore categorically different from the divine movement of self-manifestation and its creaturely auxiliary; it is not self-moved, and it can claim no perfection. It may, indeed, be corrupt; at certain points it may be a counter-movement to God's revelatory presence, especially when it seeks to preside over that presence as its guardian, or gives itself the task of bestowing on God's revelation a clarity which it lacks. But though it is frail, it stands under the hopeful sign of God's election, and as it is appointed by the Holy Spirit to serve the clear Word of God, so it is made a fitting instrument of hearing. To believe in the Holy Spirit is necessarily to believe in the holy catholic church, the communion of saints; and to believe in the church is to believe in the forgiveness of sins – to believe, that is, that the Spirit can purify a community of the Word of God and make it into a movement in which the Word gains a hearing for itself. Christian interpretation of Scripture exists in that movement, which is not a finished product but an inherited task. Finding ourselves in that movement and the human company

---

46. T. F. Torrance, *Divine Meaning: Studies in Patristic Hermeneutics* (Edinburgh: T&T Clark, 1995), p. 6.

which assembles around it, learning in its school, coming to envisage our own task through those who have also been appointed to attend to the Word, we are quickened to responsible participation in the discernment of the clear Word. Our final task is to offer an initial sketch of that participation.

V

Reconciled to God, drawn into the fellowship of the saints and illuminated by the Holy Spirit, the Christian interpreter of Holy Scripture is summoned and empowered humbly to venture interpretation of the clear Word of God as it is spoken in the words of Holy Scripture.

The clarity of Scripture does not eliminate readerly activity. It is certainly true that there is a correlation between the rise of some strands of general hermeneutical theory in theology and a decline of appeal to *claritas scripturae* in biblical hermeneutics, as attention shifts away from the biblical text as self-interpreting (that is, as the means of the Spirit's clarification of the gospel to the saints of God) towards the text as awaiting interpretative realization. But it would be improper to respond to this development by urging the claims of a naive objectivism, in which Scripture's clarity is such that the interpreter is merely the wax on which the text leaves its clear impression. Clarity does not suspend interpretation; but what is of central importance is to offer a theological rationale for the necessity of interpretation, rather than resting content with, say, the lightly theologized phenomenology of human subjectivity or reader-response theory which often do service at this juncture. In continuation of what has been said about the doctrine of the church, the necessity of interpretation must be grounded in a consideration of the ways and works of God among the saints.

Interpretation is necessary because Holy Scripture is an element in the economy of salvation, the economy whose theme is the renewal of fellowship between God and his human creatures. Interpretation is an aspect of the rebirth of our noetic fellowship with God. The history of reconciliation and revelation is not a unilateral divine history in which there is only a divine agent, with no creaturely coordinate. It is the history of God with us; because its *res* is fellowship, it has a genuine human coefficient. In it, the human creature is restored to *life*, from, with and for God, renewed to inalienable humanness – not to the spurious autonomy of the proud captains of the mind, but to the freedom to confess, to know as we are known. In this sphere of the knowledge of God, therefore, there can be no sense in which revelation is a declaration which achieves its end simply by being uttered. As creative and reconciling speech, revelation calls forth a hearer. It does so *ex nihilo*. The hearer does not precede the divine Word, and is not a creaturely *conditio sine qua non* for revelation's effectiveness. Revelation is effective *in se*, by virtue of its own self-moved and sovereign power. But that movement is a movement which calls into being a partner to this divine self-giving, one who participates, not only passively but also as a real agent, in the movement of the knowledge of God. And as revelation presents itself through the textual form of Holy Scripture, the Word constitutes the creature as reader and interpreter – not just as observer but as one commissioned to act out the right use of Scripture. To say less would be to cut short the reach of the history of salvation.

Revelation is therefore summons and empowerment. It is grace, and therefore wholly creative; it is the self-presentation of the one who brings into being the things that are not. But he really does bring them into being, really does create them and appoint them to stand beneath his summons and to be empowered by him to live, and therefore to hear the clear Word of God and see the light of life.

This sketch of a theological grounding of the necessity of hermeneutics can be contrasted with two other recent Christian accounts of the same territory in which theological factors play a much less prominent role. The first is found in J. K. A. Smith's study *The Fall of Interpretation*. Smith's argument for the necessity of interpretation takes the form of a severe critique of what he claims is a long tradition in Western theology according to which interpretation is a result of the fall, a 'postlapsarian disease'[47] in which immediacy is replaced by hermeneutical mediation. Smith's counter-proposal 'understands interpretation and hermeneutical mediation as constitutive aspects of human being-in-the-world'.[48] In so far as the proposal is doctrinally underwritten, it is by a theology of createdness, for which hermeneutics is 'an aspect of a good, peaceful creation'.[49] The result of this is 'an understanding of the *status* of interpretation as a "creational" task, a task that is constitutive of finitude and thus not a "labor" to be

---

47. J. K. A. Smith, *The Fall of Interpretation: Philosophical Foundations for a Creational Hermeneutic* (Downers Grove: Inter-Varsity Press, 2000), p. 18.
48. Smith, *The Fall of Interpretation*, p. 22.
49. Smith, *The Fall of Interpretation*, p. 22.

escaped or overcome'.[50] An immediate consequence is that Smith can make little positive sense of the notion of the clarity of Scripture, which he sees as expressive of a desire to 'return from mediation to immediacy, from distortion to "perfect clarity" and from interpretation to "pure reading"'.[51] Theological talk of clarity is therefore rejected as 'incipient Platonism (or gnosticism)',[52] resting 'on a dream of full presence',[53] infected with the 'myth of immediacy'.[54] This account is unsatisfactory at a couple of levels. (1) It is historically underdetermined. There have been debased versions of the doctrine of the clarity of Scripture which confuse *claritas* with immediacy and which therefore think of interpretation as a curse from which we have to be redeemed. But neither the Reformers nor the Protestant dogmaticians construe clarity in that way; nor do they fail to emphasize that clarity does not disqualify the activities of interpretation. Smith offers few historical examples of how immediacy excludes interpretation, and his account of the Western theological tradition is remarkably broad-brush in its treatment. (2) In doctrinal terms, the most telling inadequacy of Smith's account is his extraction of the notion of *claritas* from its surrounding dogmatic structure. The classical Protestant construal of perspicuity is a complex arrangement of Christology, soteriology, pneumatology, ecclesiology and sanctification, all undergirded by a doctrine of the ways and works of God in revelation. Only when lifted out of that cluster of affirmations can clarity be reduced to a crude notion of transparency. Smith's inattentiveness to these dogmatic issues, which leads to a seriously stripped-down version of *claritas*, can be traced to the fact that – in the tradition of neo-Reformed philosophers like Dooyeweerd, but in distinction from more classical Reformed thinkers like Bavinck, Barth and Berkouwer – he considers philosophy foundational to the 'special science' of theology.[55] One of the corollaries of this is the development of a notion of creation which has little to do with the economy of reconciliation, but is in fact a metaphysics of human finitude with little real theological freight. In effect, Smith offers a philosophical rationale for the necessity of interpretation, and moreover one which bifurcates *claritas* and interpretation by deploying the wrong doctrinal materials.

Callahan, in *The Clarity of Scripture*, avoids some of these difficulties by providing more extensive theological foundations for his account of the necessity of interpretation. Yet here, too, interpretative acts on the part of readers are not adequately coordinated with divine activity – indeed, the

---

50. Smith, *The Fall of Interpretation*, pp. 22f.
51. Smith, *The Fall of Interpretation*, p. 38.
52. Smith, *The Fall of Interpretation*, p. 134.
53. Smith, *The Fall of Interpretation*, p. 135.
54. Smith, *The Fall of Interpretation*, p. 88.
55. Cf. Smith, *The Fall of Interpretation*, p. 187 n. 22.

doctrines of reconciliation and revelation, though they form the background of the account, rarely come forward to the front of the stage. In
large part, this is because of Callahan's strong concern to ensure that 'the
assertion of Scripture's clarity is immediately related to how readers read'.[56]
In itself this is an uncontroversial, indeed a necessary, concern. But things
go somewhat awry when the description of the reader is undertaken by talk
of 'Christian interpretative frameworks',[57] of 'a pattern of Christian
interpretative interests',[58] or of the reader's 'enactment or embodiment of
the text's display of what was once offered'[59] – all of which give the wrong
sort of scope to the reader. Matters would be more securely stated by a
more modest, soteriological idiom of 'faith', 'hearing', 'attention', and so
forth, in order to avoid the impression that the relation of the reader to
Holy Scripture is simply a particular instance of a general rule about texts
and their reception – an impression reinforced by Callahan's deployment of
reader-reception hermeneutics in the latter part of his study.

The case for the necessity of interpretation is best made, not (as in
Smith's case) through religious philosophy, nor (as in Callahan's case)
through a combination of theology and literary theory, but through a
consideration of the movement of revelation. In this respect, T. Ward's
account in *Word and Supplement* gives much greater space to theological
factors. In distinguishing between sufficiency and self-sufficiency, and
therefore highlighting the text's relations to its readers, he makes careful
use of pneumatology, for it is the Spirit who 'brings the possibility of
appropriate response to the text's illocutionary act'.[60] And Ward's account
is mercifully free of the phenomenology of interpreting subjects which so
clogs many discussions of reading. Yet even here theological arguments are
set alongside philosophical and literary materials, especially speech-act
theory, in a way which does not always leave space for a full deployment of
the dogmatic materials, and which indicates that the book has a firm
apologetic agenda.

In order to describe that to which the Christian is summoned and
for which the Christian is empowered in the matter of the clear
Word of God in its scriptural witness, we need to depict, first, the
context or setting of interpretation, and then, second, the nature
and activity of the interpreter.

---

56. Callahan, *The Clarity of Scripture*, pp. 47f.
57. Callahan, *The Clarity of Scripture*, p. 52.
58. Callahan, *The Clarity of Scripture*, p. 17.
59. Callahan, *The Clarity of Scripture*, p. 42.
60. Ward, *Word and Supplement*, p. 202.

The setting is best described by use of soteriological, ecclesiological and pneumatological teaching: the Christian interpreter is *reconciled to God, drawn into the fellowship of the saints and illuminated by the Holy Spirit.* Of the soteriological and ecclesiological aspects, much has already been said: the Christian interpreter is one who has been extracted from the darkness of sin by the judgement and mercy of God, and set in the sphere of the church, the chosen race, the royal priesthood, the holy nation which is what it is by virtue of the divine call out of darkness into light. Christian interpretation of Holy Scripture is determined by this setting; the 'hermeneutical situation' (that is, the constitutive elements of the business of scriptural interpretation – God, text and readers, and the field of their interactions) is not an instance of something more basic but an episode in the history of salvation. At every point it is defined by the fact that it involves this God (the one who is light and who in Jesus Christ and the Holy Spirit is luminously present), this text (Holy Scripture as the assistant to that presence), and therefore this reader (the faithful hearer of this God in and through this text). Pneumatology has an especially important role in achieving the right kind of theological determinacy in an account of the anthropological, readerly element. As we have noted, theology readily succumbs to the temptation to depict the reader by deploying such bits of philosophical or literary phenomenology as appear companionable to its own interests. Pneumatology forestalls this by demonstrating that the readerly element is ingredient within the compass of God's revelatory presence, and therefore that non-theological supplements are not only unnecessary but may, indeed, deform the content of a theological portrait of interpretation, most commonly by excessive belief in readerly competence. The Holy Spirit is the Lord and life-giver whose work in this sphere is to generate a genuine human correspondent to God's revealing work, that is, genuine acknowledgement and response to the divine summons, and a genuine capacity to hear and see. The 'circuit of the Spirit' thus embraces God's revelatory and inspiring acts and God's illuminating work, so that we do indeed have 'a world of revelation, where God and man are associated again in mutual understanding'.[61]

In this setting, what is to be said of readerly, interpretative activity? The act of interpretation repeats the basic motif of

---

61. J. de Senarclens, *Heirs of the Reformation* (London: SCM, 1963), p. 282.

Christian existence, which is being drawn out of the darkness of sin and turned to the light of the gospel. Holy Scripture is clear; but because its matter is that to which we must be reconciled, readers can only discern its clarity if their darkness is illuminated. 'By what right do we pronounce Scripture to be obscure?' Luther asks. 'With similar temerity a man might veil his own eyes or go out of the light into the darkness and hide himself, and then blame the sun and the day for being obscure. Let miserable men, therefore, stop imputing with blasphemous perversity the darkness and obscurity of their own hearts to the wholly clear Scriptures of God.'[62] Setting aside darkness and turning to the light are not within the competence of readers (theories of readerly virtue usually trip at this point). To discern the light of God is to discern that which itself gives the possibility of its own discernment. We see light in God's light. Interpretation of the clear Word of God is therefore not first of all an act of clarification but the event of being clarified. Reading, therefore, always includes a humbling of the reader, a breaking of the will in which there is acted out the struggle to detach our apprehension of the text from the idolatrous schemas which we inevitably take to it, and by which we seek to command or suppress it or render it convenient to us. 'Behold and see, if thou canst, O soul pressed down by the corruptible body, and weighed down by earthly thoughts, many and various; behold and see, if thou canst, God is truth.'[63] If that is a dynamic of reading, then reading Holy Scripture in its clarity involves subjection to the divine declaration. 'For it is not for us to sit in judgement on Scripture and divine truth, but to let God do his work in and through it ... Of course, we have to give an account of our understanding of Scripture, but not in such a way that it is forced or wrested according to our will, but rather so that we are taught by Scripture.'[64] Reading the clear Word of God involves mortification; as Bullinger notes, true exposition of the clear Word must never be 'after our own fantasies'.[65]

Yet matters cannot remain here. The reader is not simply mortified, stripped of deceit and interpretative hubris, but also vivified: exegetical reason is renewed, and interpretation made

---

62. Luther, *The Bondage of the Will*, p. 27.
63. Augustine, *De trinitate* VIII.iii.
64. Zwingli, 'Of the Clarity and Certainty or Power of the Word of God', p. 92.
65. Bullinger, *The Decades*, p. 75.

possible. Interpretation is not simply a passive letting-be of the text, but a venture of responsibility. The human coordinate to the clarity of Holy Scripture is thus not only negation but also what Barth calls 'freedom under the Word',[66] that is, responsibility for the interpretation of the Word which God has for the church. The church

> cannot allow the revelation attested by Scripture to flow over itself as a waterfall flows over a cliff. Rather, because God's revelation is attested by Scripture and because Scripture furnishes the documentary evidence of this movement of revelation and exists only within it, the church for its part must allow itself to be set in movement through Scripture.[67]

Because *claritas* is inseparable from *efficacia*, then 'the superiority of Scripture over against the church is not the idolatrous calm of icy mountain peaks towering motionlessly above a blossoming valley ... Scripture is itself spirit and life'.[68] In terms of the relation of clarity to interpretation, this means that the churchly readers of Scripture are not simply 'spectators or even objects'[69] of the rule of Scripture in the church, but those responsible for its explanation.

> As the Word of God it requires no explanation ... since as such it is clear in itself. The Holy Ghost knows very well what he has said to the prophets and apostles and what through them he wills also to say to us. This clarity which Scripture has in itself as God's Word, this objective *perspicuitas* which it possesses, is subject to no human responsibility or care.[70]

But this Word assumes the form of a human word, and so incurs the need of explanation. Yet the basic form of this explanation is 'the activity of subordination',[71] which Barth explains thus:

> When the Word of God meets us, we are laden with the images, ideas and certainties which we ourselves have formed about God, the world and ourselves. In the fog of this intellectual life of ours the Word of God, which is clear in itself, always becomes obscure. It can become clear to us only when this fog breaks and dissolves.[72]

---

66. Barth, *Church Dogmatics* I/2, pp. 695–740.
67. Barth, *Church Dogmatics* I/2, pp. 671f.
68. Barth, *Church Dogmatics* I/2, p. 673.
69. Barth, *Church Dogmatics* I/2, p. 711.
70. Barth, *Church Dogmatics* I/2, p. 712.
71. Barth, *Church Dogmatics* I/2, p. 715.
72. Barth, *Church Dogmatics* I/2, p. 716.

Because of this, 'it is true that every interpretation of Scripture consists substantially in the interpretation which the Word gives of itself'.[73] Yet 'it is still the case that this self-illumination does not take place without us, and therefore terminates in that freedom to which as members of the church we are called, and therefore in a human activity in the service of the Word of God.'[74]

Revelation is a movement which moves. Impelled into hearing and responsibility by that movement, the Christian is also authorized and empowered for interpretation. Because they have their place in the formative economy of the clear Word of God, interpretative acts are neither constructive nor creative. But they are work, a straining of our powers to follow, an attempt to discern and articulate the clear Word which does not simply lie before us but which sets itself in relation to us as an address which we do not really hear until we are actively caught up in the movement of which both it and we are part.

Being caught up in this movement means reading according to the law of the text. Scripture's clarity has the character of law. The law of the text is its presentation to us of a definite order and a definite requirement. To read is to trace that order, following its lead, exploring, seeking to say again what it says to us, but all this as discovery of an inherent clarity, a repeating of what is there. We have been schooled by genealogists into acute suspicion of this law of the text, and to regard the associated hermeneutics as 'strict disciplinarian observance'.[75] But surely something more courageous is required of us than compliance with this convention of rebellion? Our almost obsessive scruple about the dangers of pathological versions of the text as law, our fretting at the question of whether texts will deceive, can often be a refusal to have a mature and responsible relation to a text without retreating into agonistics in which we have to master the text or it will surely master us. For the law of the text does not stultify any more than the moral law undermines ethical authenticity. As law the text quickens, summoning us and enabling us actively to discern the structure of its reality and the tasks which it sets before us.

73. Barth, *Church Dogmatics* I/2, p. 718.
74. Barth, *Church Dogmatics* I/2, p. 718.
75. G. Vattimo, *Beyond Interpretation: The Meaning of Hermeneutics for Philosophy* (Cambridge: Polity, 1997), p. 50.

VI

The absence of the notion of *claritas scripturae* in the exegetical and hermeneutical practices of much mainstream Christianity is in part a function of the fact that for a variety of reasons modern Christianity has come to share a widespread cultural assumption, namely, that texts are not and cannot be a mode of *scientia*, and therefore that appeal to the biblical text will not get us very far. Theologians concerned to counter this assumption most often analyse the problem as one of authority: failure to appeal to the text is an exercise in disobedience. This is undoubtedly an aspect of the matter, from which modern Christianity has too readily disencumbered itself. But more is involved: an inability in a non-statutory culture to conceive of how appeal to a text could possibly be a mode of rational inquiry. For are not texts always and only instruments of power, occlusions of real (economic, political, gendered) relations? And cannot texts be resolved without residue into authors or contexts or readers, and so stripped of the determinateness needed to exercise a statutory role?

A recovery of the role of texts requires at least three things. It involves a wider recovery of confidence in substantive rationality. It involves careful theological specification of the nature and properties of Holy Scripture, including clarity, in terms of its place in the wider tapestry of the self-manifesting presence of God among the saints. But it also involves coming to see that the very activity of interpretation is itself an episode in the struggle between faith and repudiation of God. We can cloak our own darkness by calling it the obscurity of the text; we can evade the judgement which Scripture announces by endless hermeneutical deferral; we can treat Scripture not as the clear Word of judgement and hope but as a further opportunity for the imagination to be puzzled, stimulated and set to work. 'Behold and see if thou canst … But thou canst not: thou wilt slide back into those carnal and earthly things.'[76] That is why the promise of *claritas scripturae* is inseparable from the prayer: 'Open my eyes, that I may behold wondrous things out of thy law' (Ps. 119.18). In the answer to that prayer is the recovery of the vocation of biblical theology and biblical interpretation.

---

76. Augustine, *De trinitate* VIII.3.

3

CONFESSION AND CONFESSIONS

I

What follows is an attempt to address some fundamental theological questions about the nature and function of creeds and confessions in the life of the church. Its basic positive claim is that creeds and confessional formulae properly emerge out of one of the primary and defining activities of the church, the *act of confession*. In that act, which is constantly to characterize the life of the church, the church binds itself to the gospel. Confession is the act of astonished, fearful and grateful acknowledgement that the gospel is the one word by which to live and die; in making its confession, the church lifts up its voice to do what it *must* do – speak with amazement of the goodness and truth of the gospel and the gospel's God. Creeds and confessional formulae exist to promote that act of confession: to goad the church towards it, to shape it, to tie it to the truth, and so to perpetuate the confessional life and activity of the Christian community. In this way, creeds and confessional formulae are the servants of the gospel in the church.

Alongside this positive claim run two polemical points. One – largely implicit – is that when the church tries to do without the offices of these servants of the gospel it endangers its relation to the gospel. In the same way that the church's life can be threatened by misrule, arbitrariness or pollution if it neglects canon, sacraments or order, so also it will be exposed to peril if it attempts to exist without the act of confession and its formalization in credal texts. The second polemical claim is that the creed is a good servant but a bad master: it assists, but cannot replace, the act of confession. The church, that is, cannot have the creed but somehow bypass the act of confession, for to do so is to convert the event of confession into an achieved formula, graspable without immediate reference to the coming of the Holy Spirit. Whatever else we may say by way of commending the place of the creed in the life of the church, we must

69

not promote the notion that the creed's significance is merely statutory. Creeds serve, but cannot of themselves comprise the totality of, what it means to be a confessing community.

Both the positive claim and its polemical corollaries rest on a conviction that we need a *theological* description of creeds and confessional formulae, that is, an account which talks about creeds by talking about God. The creeds must not be naturalized; that is, they must not be depicted merely immanently, as functions of the Christian religious community or tradition, naturally considered. Modern critical historical theology has offered a natural history of the creeds, presenting their development as a history of the church's absorption of cultural and philosophical convention, and as social tradition. In the case of giants like Baur or Harnack, such natural histories of the creeds had a fundamentally critical intent, demoting the creeds by offering an immanent explanation of their genesis, so that – like canon and order – they no longer encounter the church as it were from outside with a transcendent claim, but are simply an item in its domestic life. More recent attempts to depict the creeds as instruments of community self-description, identity-avowal, social differentiation or formation in virtue, while they are more alert to the religious functions of creeds, still run the risk of immanence. My suggestion, by contrast, is that what is required is not a more elaborate natural history, sociology or cultural geography of the creeds, but a dogmatic depiction. What is required, in other words, is an account of creeds which sees them as features in the landscape of the church, *theologically considered* as that reality of human history transfigured by the Spirit, visible to faith and therefore to be described spiritually. What is said about the nature and functions of creeds and confessions must be rooted in talk about the triune God in the economy of salvation, tracing these human texts back to their source in the church's participation in the drama of God's saving self-communication in Christ through the Spirit's power. This is not, of course, to cancel out the natural history of the creeds, any more than to talk of a canon of Holy Scripture is to cancel out the natural history of canonization. It is simply to say that the history of the creeds is part of the history of the church – part, that is, of that sphere of human life invaded and annexed by God, and characterized by astonished and chastened hearing of the Word, and by grateful and afflicted witness.

Before pressing the claim of the creed as the basis of a renewed ecumenical convergence around some sort of generous orthodoxy, therefore, it is crucial that we put in place a theological account of the act of confession and its credal instruments. If we fail to do so, what we say will be in the wrong register, and we will fall victim to the shrill juridical and factional hostilities which so often afflict calls for renewed confessionalism. Confession is an act of the church, a spiritual act; and it is a matter, therefore, for theological description and judgement.

II

To try to grasp what lies at the heart of the act of confession, we may ponder Paul's statement in 2 Corinthians 9.13 concerning 'the obedience of your confession of the gospel of Christ'. What Paul has to say there forms part of the great flow of his celebration of the abundance of God. To God's abundance, God's open-handedness, there correspond two fundamental acts of the church: material generosity and confession of the gospel. Both acts are echoes of what Paul calls (v. 14) 'the surpassing grace of God in you'; both, that is, are brought into being by the limitless lavishness of God which Paul celebrates in the climactic words of the chapter: 'Thanks be to God for his inexpressible gift' (v. 15). It is in this context – the celebration of God's overwhelming generosity – that I suggest we root our understanding of the church's act of confession. Before it is proposition or oath of allegiance, the confession of the church is a cry of acknowledgement of the unstoppable miracle of God's mercy. Confession, we might say by way of definition, is that event in which the speech of the church is arrested, grasped and transfigured by the self-giving presence of God. To confess is to cry out in acknowledgement of the sheer gratuity of what the gospel declares, that in and as the man Jesus, in the power of the Holy Spirit, God's glory is the glory of his self-giving, his radiant generosity. Very simply, to confess is to indicate 'the glory of Christ' (2 Cor. 8.23). This can be expanded in three directions.

First, *the act of confession originates in revelation*. This human act takes its rise in the divine act which is generative of the life of the church in its entirety: God's communicative self-presence, the gracious and saving self-communication of God the Lord. Revelation is enacted and declared salvation, the open and visible hand of God's mercy. And what revelation generates is the church, the assembly of those called to new life in forgiveness, freedom from sin, and fellowship with God. Confession flows from this electing and life-giving self-manifestation. Confession is not primarily an act of *definition*; it is, rather, a 'thankful, praising, self-committing *acceptance* of God's self-revelation in Christ'.[1] Moreover, this impulse lying behind the act of confession is, as Paul puts it in 2 Corinthians 9, 'surpassing' and 'inexpressible'. It lies wholly beyond our intellectual or spiritual or moral reach; it is not one of the things which we can appropriate and assign a place in our world; in this matter, we are not competent. And because God's self-communication is thus permanently disorienting – because it is a movement of God, a gift which cannot be converted into a possession – confession is more a matter of *astonishment* than an attempt at closure.

Second, therefore, *the act of confession is a responsive, not a spontaneous act*. In Paul's terms, it is an act of *obedience*, a term which connects confession both to submission and to attentive listening. Obedient confession of the gospel of Christ is not first and foremost a proposal on the part of the church; it is an act *of* the church which follows upon an act done *to* the church. As Barth puts it, in making its confession in the *credo*, 'the church bows before that God Whom we did not seek and find – Who rather has sought and found us'.[2] Once again, therefore, a thorough description of the church's act of confession must be rooted in a trinitarian account of God's self-manifestation. As Father, Son and Spirit, God wills, effects and completes saving fellowship with himself: God alone is its origin, its accomplishment and its realization. And in a real sense, therefore, God alone is the origin, accomplishment and realization of the act of confession. 'Confessions cannot be made; they can only be received as a gift.'[3]

Third, accordingly, *the act of confession is an episode in the conflict between God and sin which is at the centre of the drama of salvation*. Confession is a counter-movement to human wickedness, a counter-movement brought about and sustained by the overflow of God's abundance. Sin is in part the refusal to confess – the sullen and hard-hearted refusal to acknowledge God's self-gift, failure to respond to God's lavishness by voicing God's praise. Confession refuses these refusals. It is a repentant act, a turning, and therefore a decisive 'No' to silence about God or to that murmuring against

1. O. Weber, *Foundations of Dogmatics*, vol. 1 (Grand Rapids: Eerdmans, 1981), p. 29.

2. K. Barth, *Credo* (London: Hodder & Stoughton, 1936), p. 7.

3. E. Schlink, *Theology of the Lutheran Confessions* (Philadelphia: Fortress Press, 1961), p. 16.

God which is the response of the wicked to God's generosity. Confession, therefore, is an aspect of the church's holiness. To be holy is to be elect, caught up in God's drastic negation of disorder and unrighteousness; and confession is the first work of the elect as they are separated by God for acknowledgement and praise of God.

In short: 'the Community confesses, and it "exists" in its confessing'.[4] The point of stressing this is to highlight how confession is *act* or *event* before it is *document*. Textual formulae are instruments of confession, but they do not in any way render the act of confession superfluous. This point is of considerable importance, not least because we are sometimes tempted to think that confessional formulae represent fixity, that they are a means of settling doctrinal disputes. In one sense, of course, confessional formulae do just that: they articulate dogmatic decisions, and so move the life of the church to a new stage which the church cannot repudiate or neglect without redrawing its identity. But the dogmatic decisions which the church articulates in confessional formulae cannot simply be thought of as capital in the bank. Confession is a permanently occurring event; the church never reaches a point where the act of obedient confession can be put behind it as something which *has been* made, and which can be replaced by a text which will become the icon of the church as a confessing community. Properly understood, a confessional formula does not put an end to the act of confession but attempts to ensure its persistence. A creed does not ensure the church's safety from interruption – quite the opposite: it exposes the church to the need for an unceasing renewal of confession of the gospel, of hearing, obedience and acknowledgement of that which the formula indicates.

III

With this in mind, we turn to look more closely at the nature of the creeds and confessional formulae which emerge from the act of confession – at confession as *text*. In propositional form, my suggestion is this: *a creed or confessional formula is a public and binding indication of the gospel set before us in the scriptural witness, through which the church affirms its allegiance to God, repudiates the*

---

4. Weber, *Foundations of Dogmatics*, vol. 1, p. 29.

falsehood by which the church is threatened, and assembles around the judgement and consolation of the gospel.

1. A creed or confessional formula is a *public and binding indication of the gospel*. A little more will be said about the 'binding' character of creeds later; for the present, I want to draw attention to their necessarily *public* character. 'A confession', says Barth, 'cannot be spoken *mezzo forte*.'[5] That is, a confession or creed is a proclamation, a publication or making known of that which is confessed. To confess is not to reflect, even to reflect theologically; it is to herald the gospel. A confessional formula, therefore, shares the vividness and directness of the act of confession by which it is generated. To confess is to testify and to testify with a bit of noise.

It is crucial, however, that we realize that this necessarily public character of a creed does not derive from the busy, authoritarian or loud personalities of the confessors. When that sort of brashness happens – as it often does when calls for a renewed confessionalism are issued – the creed becomes hopelessly distorted, because it is no longer the articulation of an act of confession but merely of pressure-group dynamics, of the desire not just to confess the gospel but to win. Unless that temptation is resisted, confession – however vigorous – will not be obedient confession of the gospel but simply brandishing a weapon in the church's face. The counter to the temptation is to build into the dynamics of the confession a deep sense of the transcendence of that which we confess. A creed is not a programme, a platform, a manifesto to mobilize our forces. It is an amazed cry of witness: 'Behold, the Lamb of God who takes away the sin of the world' (Jn 1.29). Confession is attestation, not self-assertion.

Because confession is public attestation, it is inseparable from conflict and affliction. To recite the creed is to enter into revolt against the world and against the church in so far as it has not yet left the world behind. Public confession challenges by setting the whole of the life of the church and the world beneath the judgement of the gospel. It therefore involves a denial of untruth, and a glad and courageous affirmation of truth. A confession which fails to do this – which is not *dangerous*, which does not venture to contradict – is not a confession worth making, but simply a domestic inventory of Christian attitudes. Real confession is closely linked to

---

5.   K. Barth, *Church Dogmatics* I/2 (Edinburgh: T & T Clark, 1956), p. 639.

martyrdom: both are testimony; both are attestations of the truth which evoke conflict and suppression. The suppression takes various forms: violence, counter-argument, indifference, liturgical routinization. But a church which confesses will demonstrate in its practical attitude a dogged resistance to such pressures. It will simply not conform, because it *cannot* conform. The church which confesses knows that it has been overwhelmed by the gospel and that part of being overwhelmed is publishing the name of Jesus. If once the church allows itself to be stifled in making that confession, it has put itself beyond martyrdom and therefore turned away from the lavishness of God. But if – with fear and trembling, with human uncertainty, with anxiety yet with courage – the church refuses to be arrested in making its confession, then it says in public the one word which slays the devil.

2. Second, a creed or confessional formula is *an indication of the gospel set before us in the scriptural witness*. A written confession is a testimony, pointing to that which is other than itself. What the confession attests is not, first and foremost, the teaching of the church, nor the commitments and self-understandings of those who make use of the confession to profess their faith. A confession is most properly an indication of the gospel. The gospel is normatively set forth in Holy Scripture, for Holy Scripture is that collection of writings generated by and appointed to serve the self-communication of God. Because it is in this way a 'means of grace', an instrument through which God acts to lay bare the gospel, Holy Scripture is prior and superior to all acts of confession, and all acts of confession are subordinate to Holy Scripture. A confession always thinks 'from below'[6]; only by virtue of this subordination does it have any claim on the life of the church. Creeds and confessions have no freestanding existence; they are not a replacement for, supplementation of, or improvement upon, Holy Scripture; they are not even a non-negotiable, normative 'reading' of Scripture. Creeds and confessions are wholly a function of the Word of God which is given in Scripture as through the power of the Spirit the risen Jesus testifies to himself. The rule, therefore, is this: 'Scripture remains Scripture, unique, incommensurable, outside the series'.[7] Hence the authority of the creed is inseparable from

6. Barth, *Church Dogmatics* I/2, p. 39.
7. K. Barth, *The Theology of the Reformed Confessions* (Louisville: WJKP, 2002), p. 20.

its 'expository dependence on Holy Writ'.[8] Its claim is the claim of an anatomy of divinity, a brief outline of the biblical gospel. Its task is to enable the church's reading of Holy Scripture. We may think of the creed as an aspect of the church's exegetical fellowship, of learning alongside the saints and doctors and martyrs how to give ear to the gospel. But such fellowship is fellowship in a *task* which is also ours now. The creed is not a substitute for the church's reading of Scripture, a sort of achieved exegetical steady state. It is, rather, the exemplary instance of the church's submission of all aspects of its life to the prophetic and apostolic witness. It may guide and chasten and correct our reading, but it cannot absolve us of responsibility in the present. The creed does not mean the *end* of one of the church's chief occupations, which is hearing the gospel through attention to Holy Scripture. Hearing the Word is not an inheritance but an event: creeds and confessions structure and guide that hearing, but they do not make it dispensable. Nor, in one sense, do they make hearing *easier*. Truly attending to the creed means not finding safe water but entering into the disruption which is the inevitable accompaniment of encountering the gospel of God.

3. Third, a creed or confessional formula is *one of the means through which the church affirms its allegiance to God*. Confession – like praise, proclamation, holiness and service – is a human echo of the electing mercy of God. To confess is to take sides, to pledge involvement with a particular cause, by binding oneself to a particular reading of reality. To confess in the words of a credal formula is to acknowledge that there are times in the life of the church when indifference, irony, hesitation or scruple are false spiritual stances, and that the church's relation to the truth requires the adoption of a position and the publication of that position in an act of loyalty. Not every moment in the life of the church demands such acts; but some do. Some occasions – not necessarily those which affect our own immediate interests – require an affirmation of allegiance, which ties those who make it to certain options, which excludes others, and which governs the thought and speech of the church's members.

To confess in this way is a counter-cultural move, and we should not underestimate the extent to which, in acting in this way and affirming its allegiance, the church goes against the grain of some

8.   Schlink, *Theology of the Lutheran Confessions*, p. 12.

deep-seated modern instincts. Those instincts are exquisitely described by Kant in the remarkable treatment of conscience in *Religion within the Boundaries of Mere Reason*.[9] Kant fears that public assent to a confessional statement always undermines real integrity and loyalty, because profession is mere external conformity, simulated conviction and not the disposition of a free conscience. Kant is quite right, of course, to protest against the deceit which accompanies the enforcement of a confession. But the mistake here is an assumption which Kant shares with modern liberal Christianity: the assumption that confession is always bad faith. And – again like modern liberal Christianity – Kant's remedy for bad faith is *conscience* – but conscience transformed so that it is a function of will and judgement, not of given truth. If Kant and his modern Christian heirs can make little sense of a confessional formula as an act of allegiance, it is because of a deep commitment to a picture of the human self as free only when undetermined, and as fruitful only when engaged in critical inquiry.

But an act of allegiance expressed through a confessional formula is not an act of self-determination but of acknowledgement. It is an act whose origins lie not in the will but in the self-presenting, lovingly coercive reality of the gospel. It is an act which involves *trust* – trust in our mothers and fathers in the faith then, and in our sisters and brothers in the faith now. And it is an act of obedient acquiescence rather than of critical appraisal – an act, we might even say, of judgement broken by the truth rather than of enthroned reason. Confessing the creed means leaving behind the omnicompetence of conscience and rationality.

All of that is by way of stressing that the creed is an act of allegiance. Once again, it is very important not to overinvest in the human dynamics of profession. The centre of gravity must not become the personal authenticity of the act of allegiance made in assenting to a formula. This is partly to make sure that we do not create a nastily suspicious culture in the church, because if we do so we will oppose the gospel. But it is also because the *fides quae* – those things which are believed – have priority over the *fides qua* – the act of belief by which they are believed. We would be very unwise indeed to defend orthodoxy by attacking the sincerity of

9. I. Kant, *Religion within the Boundaries of Mere Reason*, in A. W. Wood and G. di Giovanni (eds), *Religion and Rational Theology* (Cambridge: Cambridge University Press, 1996), pp. 202–6.

those in the church who appear to deny or compromise their profession. What is wrong with false professors is not just that they have broken their oath but that they have denied the truth.

4. Fourth, through a publicly affirmed creed or confessional formula *the church repudiates the falsehood by which it is threatened.* In a creed the church says 'Yes' to truth, and in saying 'Yes' it thereby also says 'No' to falsehood. It says 'No' only because it first says 'Yes', and it says 'No' with fear and trembling, only because it *must* do so. Nevertheless, in affirming the church also denies, turning from its own complicity in falsehood and striding repentantly and hopefully towards the truth.

This means, first, that – as Bonhoeffer put it – 'the concept of heresy belongs necessarily and irrevocably with the concept of a credal confession'.[10] What is so grievous about the loss of an operative notion of heresy is that it is symptomatic of the loss of an operative notion of truth. Once voluntarism and nominalism grasp hold of the church – once, that is, the Christian faith is no longer considered an onslaught on idolatry but a fertile opportunity for its exercise – then the notion of heresy atrophies and eventually falls away. Very simply, this must not happen, and one of the ways of ensuring that it does not happen is by serious attention to the confessional life of the church.

A confession is a move against falsehood, whether in the form of error or of indifference. A confession worthy of the name will – implicitly or explicitly – include an anathema, an assertion that a teaching or practice is outside the church. We should therefore not be too ready to concede to critics of the confessional attitude that the notion of heresy and the practice of anathematizing are intrinsically flawed, inseparable from the dynamics of scapegoating, exclusion and diminishment of that which is other than the norm. Certainly it is irrefutable that 'orthodoxy' is a political practice as well as a theological concept; certainly an orthodox doctrine is often a successful doctrine; certainly the orthodox have always shown an unwholesome appetite for depicting their opponents in the worst possible light. But to use the notion of heresy in such ways is to abuse it – to deploy it as a means of creating an unpolluted church with a watertight skin. For truth is not a culture or a political practice or a structure for discipline, however much those

---

10.   D. Bonhoeffer, *Christology* (London: Collins, 1978), p. 75.

things may serve the truth. Truth is a miracle; truth is the creation of the Holy Spirit. The notion of heresy and the practice of anathematizing are ways of following or being caught up in the miracle of truth. They are spiritual practices, aspects of the transformation of human knowledge and government by the coming of the Word of God.

5. So far, then, it has been suggested that a creed is a public and binding indication of the gospel as set out in Holy Scripture, through which the church affirms its allegiance to God and repudiates falsehood. In doing these things, a creed is, finally, *a means through which the church assembles around the judgement and consolation of the gospel.* We may ask: What happens when the Christian community professes its faith by reciting the creed? If it is to be of any spiritual worth, such an act must be more than a cheerful or even solemn repetition of a safe formula. A creed places the church under judgement. In the paragraph from *Religion within the Boundaries of Mere Reason* to which reference has already been made, Kant says this:

> Let the author of a creed or the teacher of a church, indeed, let every human being, so far as he inwardly stands by the conviction that certain propositions are divinely revealed, ask himself: Do you really dare to avow the truth of these propositions in the sight of him who scrutinizes the heart, and at the risk of relinquishing all that is valuable and holy to you?

And he adds, 'I would have to have a very unfavourable conception of human nature ... not to suppose that even the boldest teacher of the faith must quake at the question'.[11] And Kant is right – if the creed does not make us quake, if it is not recited with fear and trembling and penitence, then it is not recited with an eye to the one who scrutinizes the heart.

In fear and trembling we place ourselves beneath the truth which we confess. And in so doing we come to know that truth as endless consolation. The consolation which the gospel brings is its announcement that the world really is a place where God in Christ reigns with the unleashed power of the Holy Spirit; where faith, hope and love are *truthful* because they are in accordance with the way the world is. The church's task is to live out the new order which has been made at the resurrection of Jesus from the dead, and

11. Kant, *Religion within the Boundaries of Mere Reason*, pp. 205f.

so to turn its back on the old order of sin and death. That kind of energetic counter-practice requires that the church be committed to a fierce realism; it needs a deep conviction that the church can refuse the conventions of sin because they are a sham. And not the least of the functions of credal formulae is to lodge that kind of realism in the church's heart. The world is the place in which it is a truthful and joyful thing to confess that God is the Father Almighty, maker of heaven and earth; that there is one Lord, Jesus Christ, who is one in being with the Father; that for us and for our salvation he came down from heaven; that the Holy Spirit is Lord and life-giver. To confess these things is to confess the gospel's consolation and so to sponsor cheerful and confident practice on the basis of the gospel's announcement that God has once and for all put an end to the pretence of wickedness.

IV

We return to the question of the *binding* character of creeds and confessional formulae. What authority do these texts have in the church? In what way do they stand as a norm of teaching and practice?

Very simply: they have the authority of a norm which is itself normed; they have real yet conditional, limited and subordinate authority to bind the church; they are a penultimate but not an ultimate word. Creeds and confessional formulae have authority, but only in a twofold subordination. They are subordinate, first and foremost, to the fact that the God of the gospel is free transcendent presence and not merely the immanent soul of the church. God is present as Jesus Christ is present – the one risen from the dead, the one who has been lifted from our sight at the ascension; God is present as the Holy Spirit is present – the one who *comes* to us but is not a principle of immanence. The creed cannot replace God's presence; it can only reach after it, and identify where that presence gives itself to us. Second, creeds and confessional formulae are subordinate, as we have seen, to Holy Scripture, for it is Scripture, not creed, which is appointed by God as the instrument of his self-communication. Whatever else we may say of the creed, therefore, we have to say that it is a *normed* norm. This emphatically does not give us any excuse to fall into soft relativism. To say that the creed is conditional or penultimate is worlds apart from the idea that the creed is merely one not very good attempt at pinning down a God whom we cannot really know. The creed is *confident* of its object; it *knows* this God. To talk of the provisionality of the creed is not an expression of scepticism; it is not the antithesis of earnestness; it is not an attempt to undermine genuine confession. It is simply a sober consequence of the fact that sinners – even redeemed sinners – cannot comprehend God's revelation. It simply acknowledges the constantly self-reforming character of the church's thought and speech. Reformation is needed, not in order to keep step with the world – why on earth would we want to do that? – but in order to make sure that we are properly out of step with the world and therefore trying to keep pace with God. Once again, this is not a matter of promoting instability, having everything open to revision all the time: such an attitude risks denying the reality of the gift of the Spirit to the church. All we are saying is that the creed is not God's Word, but ours; made, not begotten.

On this basis, we can approach the question of the juridical structures which surround the creed: in what way is it *legally* binding on its subscribers? Church law is an aspect of the church's visibility; that is, its life as a human historical society. Law is one of the instruments through which the Holy Spirit ensures the orderly shape and regularity of the church's existence in space and time. It is scarcely possible to conceive of any kind of enduring ecclesial reality without legal instruments for the maintenance of its common life, and confessional formulae are clearly part of the statutory life of the community. Creeds need a legal framework of subscription and assent. Creeds without subscription are hardly likely to serve the church's life in the gospel, and run the risk of becoming what Anglicans sometimes call 'historic formularies' – by which they often mean charming curios which can be safely tucked away at the back of the prayer book.

Creeds need a legal framework. But there is an 'important qualification here: the juridical and statutory have only instrumental significance. We are sometimes impatient with the transcendence of the object of our confession, and tempted to manage it through law. But church law is not domestication; it safeguards, but it does not codify, the free self-presence of the church's Lord and his testimony to himself in Scripture. In short – the authority of the creed, its power to bind, is not primarily positive and juridical but spiritual.

This means that a confession binds in so far as it is in agreement with Holy Scripture: it binds by saying 'Scripture says'. As with all instruments of the church's order, the authority of the creed is inseparable from its submission to the Word of God; it has the authority of the herald, not the magistrate.

On the one hand, this means that we should not use the confessions of the church to press the church to take on the wrong sort of visibility – a purely 'natural' visibility in which the church is identified too closely with its visible forms. When this happens, and a credal formula becomes the article by which the church stands or falls, then the transcendent, eschatological reference of the visible church is compromised, and confessions come to embody, not testify to, the gospel. But when the church becomes properly visible through its confessions, it does not leave behind Spirit, faith, the hiddenness and freedom of God; it does not convert the drama of redemption into a set of propositions to be policed. *Confessional* visibility is *spiritual* visibility. On the other hand, there is the wrong sort of *in*visibility. We can, for example, so emphasize the incomprehensibility of the object of confession that formulae are simply ruled out from the beginning. Or we can, as many moderns do, treat confessional formulae as merely the external dress of inner conviction and experience – and we prefer our church naked. Both rob the church of its proper visibility; both make oversight of the church's public life acutely difficult; both risk undermining the church's relation to the truth of the gospel.

In sum: creeds bind because and only because the gospel binds. And hence we have to say (1) that the gospel does bind, and that confessions are a place where we encounter the obligatory force of the truth; and (2) that the statutory claim of the creed binds only as it presents the gospel's claim. Figuring out a practice to express these principles is no easy matter. The common options – either libertinism or authoritarianism – are not open to a church with any sense for the gospel. What is required more than anything else is the discernment and prudence which are the gifts of the Spirit, and so matters not of policy but of prayer.

V

We sum up these reflections by noting how the credal life of the church expresses each of the four marks of the church: its unity, holiness, catholicity and apostolicity. The creed points to the unity of the church, not in mere fellow-feeling but in the given realities of one Lord, one Spirit, one God and Father of all. It points to the holiness of the church because it is a confession of election – of the drastic separation between the church and sin which the mercy of God opens up and which the mind of the church must honour. It points to the catholicity of the church because to profess the creed is not to set up a party banner but to read the gospel in the fellowship of the saints. It points to the apostolicity of the church because it is only in confession of the truth that the church can live out the faith and mission of the apostles.

We should be under no illusion that renewed emphasis upon the creed will in and of itself renew the life of the church: it will not. The church is created and renewed through Word and Spirit. Everything else – love of the brethren, holiness, proclamation, confession – is dependent upon them. Yet it is scarcely possible to envisage substantial renewal of the life of the church without renewal of its confessional life. There are many conditions for such renewal. One is real governance of the church's practice and decision-making not by ill-digested cultural analysis but by reference to the credal rendering of the biblical gospel. Another is recovery of the kind of theology which sees itself as an apostolic task, and does not believe itself entitled or competent to reinvent or subvert the Christian tradition. A third, rarely noticed, condition is the need for a recovery of symbolics (the study of creeds and confessions) as part of the theological curriculum – so much more edifying than most of what fills the seminary day. But alongside these are required habits of mind and heart: love of the gospel, docility in face of our forebears, readiness for responsibility and venture, a freedom from concern for reputation, a proper self-distrust. None of these things can be cultivated; they are the Spirit's gifts, and the Spirit alone must do his work. What we may do – and must do – is cry to God, who alone works great marvels.

Dogmatics

Dogmatics

4

THE IMMENSITY AND UBIQUITY OF GOD

I

Christian dogmatic language about the divine attributes explicates the nature of the triune God by offering an analytical depiction of God's identity. For the Christian confession, God's identity is singular and antecedent; it is possessed of its own incomparable uniqueness and of a majesty which can only be characterized as it sets itself before us in the free acts of God's aliveness. Because it is responsible rational articulation of the church's confession of that aliveness, Christian dogmatics is a positive science, and so from the beginning it is prohibited from according any orienting or controlling function to abstract considerations of *deitas* in its account of the attributes of God: in dogmatics, questions of the divine nature are wholly resolved into questions of the divine identity, from which alone dogmatics receives its direction. The divine identity is disclosed in the acts of God's being. That is, the singularity of God is learned, not by the adoption, refinement and qualification of a religious, philosophical or ethical conception of deity, but by attention to God's self-enactment in his inner and outer works. God is himself in the plenitude, unity and differentiation of the inner divine life of love and fellowship, in the relations and processions of Father, Son and Spirit. And God is further himself in the unhindered, effortless and wholly loving missions of the triune persons, in willing, reconciling and perfecting creatures as the counterpart to the love and fellowship which God is in himself. In the inseparability of God's inner and outer works, in their strictly irreversible sequence and no less strict reciprocity, Christian dogmatics has to discern the one who is the object of the church's praise. God's identity becomes a matter for dogmatic explication because it expounds itself in and through the history of God's engagement with humanity, God's creature, sinner and child caught up in the judgement and renewal of all things. That history is the drama of God's self-exposition; in it and through it, the *essentia dei* sets itself forth with majestic force and mercy. The divine *essentia* may not be constructed in advance of or in isolation from that history, nor may that history be considered in advance of or in isolation from the antecedent perfection of God. To offer a dogmatic presentation of the attributes of God is, therefore, to indicate *this one* in the supreme radiance and completeness of his triune being and act in which he freely turns to his creatures, claiming them and directing them to himself.

In formal terms, this means that if a dogmatics of the divine attributes is to serve the articulation of God's identity, it must achieve a fitting coordination of 'immanent' and 'operative', 'absolute' and 'relative'. In the matter of the divine immensity and ubiquity, this requirement must be obeyed with particular strictness. This is because, like all the so-called 'metaphysical' attributes, immensity and ubiquity have in some measure been bent out of shape by being harnessed to an abstract conception of God as 'perfect being' and to abstract exposition through the 'logic of perfection' or 'supremacy'. Examples are ready to hand in some recent Anglo-American philosophy of religion which explores divine omnipresence by mapping the logic of the concept of a perfect being.[1] Such a being, the argument runs, must of necessity be characterized by freedom from limitation, that is, by infinity, and must therefore be present at once to all things in a manner which is incorporeal, spiritual and lacking in determinate spatial location. In and of themselves, of course, such statements are hardly unexceptionable; what makes them problematic is their attachment to a distinctly formal conception of deity largely uncorrected by the event of God's free self-enactment as Father, Son and Spirit.

Proponents of these styles of philosophical engagement with the attributes of God consider that 'perfect being theology' is continuous in a quite straightforward way with the theology of Augustine, Anselm and Aquinas, and, indeed, often develop their ideas in conversation with classical texts.[2] The similarities are,

1. E.g., J. Hoffman and G. S. Rosenkrantz, *The Divine Attributes* (Oxford: Blackwell, 2002); K. Rogers, *Perfect Being Theology* (Edinburgh: Edinburgh University Press, 2000); R. Swinburne, *The Coherence of Theism* (Oxford: Oxford University Press, 1993); E. Wierenga, *The Nature of God: An Inquiry into the Divine Attributes* (Ithaca: Cornell University Press, 1989).

2. E.g., S. MacDonald, 'The Divine Nature', in E. Stump and N. Kretzmann (eds), *The Cambridge Companion to Augustine* (Cambridge: Cambridge University

however, more formal than substantial: there is all the difference in the world between spelling out the logic of *a god* and indicating the particular perfection of the God manifest in Jesus Christ and in the Spirit's presence. The *aliquid quo nihil maius cogitari possit* of pre-modern Christian theology is not so much a proposal about deity as an indicator of a name to be confessed. It refers back to the divine enactment, and it is concerned with the conceivability of *deitas* only as a consequence of being overtaken by the 'supreme and inaccessible light' before which the eye of the mind is 'dazzled by its splendour, overcome by its fullness, overwhelmed by its immensity, confounded by its capacity'.[3] The antecedent of 'perfect being theology' is thus not the pre-modern theology of the church, but rather the development from the seventeenth century onwards of a systematic natural theology, in which the divine attributes are deduced from a conception of God which is itself established as part of the project of giving a theistic explanation of the world.[4] For the historical forebears of 'perfect being theology', therefore, we should look not so much to the work of Augustine, Anselm or Aquinas, but – for example – to the Newtonian natural theology of Samuel Clarke, whose *Demonstration of the Being and Attributes of God* (1705) endeavours 'to show to such considering persons as I have already described that the being and attributes of God are not only possible or barely probable in themselves, but also strictly demonstrable to any unprejudiced mind from the most uncontestable principles of right reason'.[5] The setting of such an account of God's perfections is not the prayer of faith – Anselm's 'Your countenance, O Lord, do I seek'[6] – but rather the project of 'demonstration', a project whose norm is only 'the bare force of reasoning', and whose procedure is coherence 'to the rules of strict and demonstrative argumentation'.[7] Thus, like his analytical heirs,

Press, 2001), pp. 71–90; E. Wierenga, 'Anselm on Omnipresence', *New Scholasticism* 52 (1998), pp. 30–41; B. Davies, *The Thought of Thomas Aquinas* (Oxford: Oxford University Press, 1992), pp. 98–117.

3. Anselm, *Proslogion* 16, in J. Hopkins and H. Richardson (eds), *Anselm of Canterbury* (London: SCM, 1974), p. 104.

4. See here C. Schwöbel, *God, Action and Revelation* (Kampen: Kok Pharos, 1992), pp. 46–62.

5. S. Clarke, *A Demonstration of the Being and Attributes of God*, ed. E. Vailati (Cambridge: Cambridge University Press, 1998), p. 7.

6. Anselm, *Proslogion* 1, in Hopkins and Richardson, (eds), *Anselm of Canterbury*, p. 91.

7. Clarke, *A Demonstration of the Being and Attributes of God*, p. 7.

Clarke argues from the demonstration of a self-existent being to the proposal that 'the self-existent being must of necessity be infinite and omnipresent', for '[t]o be self-existent ... is to exist by an absolute necessity in the nature of the thing itself. Now this necessity being absolute in itself and not depending on any outward cause, it is evident that it must be *everywhere* as well as *always* unalterably the same.' And hence 'the infinity of the self-existent being' must be 'an infinity ... of immensity'; this being must exist 'absolutely in every place and be equally present everywhere, and consequently must have a true and absolute infinity both of immensity and wholeness'.[8]

This is surely problematical, not simply because Clarke reaches his affirmation of divine omnipresence by the wrong route, but much more because tucked within the method is substantive teaching about God. Following the method commits him in advance to a theology of omnipresence in which neither the immanent triune life of God nor his loving relations to his creatures play any perceptible role, so reducing omnipresence to a kind of continuous substrate of the coherence of the universe. As a consequence, ubiquity is drastically narrowed by being subsumed under God's (naturally discerned) providential work, thereby eliding its soteriological and pneumatological character. And in this, 'perfect being theology' fares little better, for the same disposition of doctrines (a maximal investment in providence and the cosmological aspects of ubiquity, a correspondingly minimal investment in trinitarian distinctives) is largely retained in exploring the logic of a supreme being. If, by contrast, good dogmatic order is to prevail, what is required is a thoroughgoing theological correction of concepts like 'perfection', 'supremacy' or 'self-existence'. As they have been deployed in natural and philosophical theology, they have been characteristically too abstract, and therefore too susceptible to being laden with the wrong content, in effect answering the question 'What is God?' before the question 'Who is God?' Something a good deal more descriptively dense and rich is required, something more transparent to the particularity of God's self-enactment. Dogmatics has no concern with that than which nothing greater can be conceived *in abstracto*; its responsibility is to God's particular perfection. Or, as Barth put it, what matters in an account of God's perfections is '*Gott selber, sein eines,*

---

8.   Clarke, *A Demonstration of the Being and Attributes of God*, pp. 32–34.

einfaches, eigenes Wesen, God himself, his one, simple, distinctive being'.[9]

Christian dogmatics attempts to indicate God's enacted singularity. Yet in pursuing this task, in not allowing itself to be governed by prior conceptions of *deitas* in general, a dogmatics of the divine attributes soon faces another danger, namely, that of countering abstract conceptions of divinity by simply abandoning consideration of the 'metaphysical' or 'absolute' attributes of God and orienting itself exclusively to the economy of God's works *extra se*. But no less than the abstractions of generic notions of deity, this hypertrophy of the *attributa operativa* fails to grasp the perfectly mutual correspondence between God's inner being and his outer works. In the matter of divine omnipresence, as in all the divine attributes, it is of capital importance that, under the tutelage of God's self-enactment, theology does not fall into a bifurcation of the *essentia dei* and God's revealed will and activity. That bifurcation can happen (as in 'perfect being theology') by determining the doctrine of God in advance of God's works. But it can also happen from the other end: by giving a wholly 'economic' account of the attributes of God without roots in God's being *in se*. Dogmatics can protect itself against this division only by developing an integrated answer to what Chemnitz believed to be the two fundamental questions for a comprehensive dogmatic article *de deo*: 'What is the essence both in the divine unity as well as in the three persons of the Deity?', and 'What is the will of God, revealed in His activity, both in the creation of the universe and the sustaining of all created things, as well as in the creation of special benefits for the sake of His church?'[10]

Consequently, a theology of divine omnipresence needs to offer a fully integrated account of *immensitas dei* and *ubiquitas dei*. There is no *immensitas* which is not known in God's *omnipraesentia operativa*; there is no ubiquity which is not grounded in God's wholly free, transcendent majesty as the measureless one. And if dogmatics affirms this inseparable and equiprimordial character of immensity and ubiquity, it is, once again, not because of some prior conception of what Pannenberg calls the 'true Infinite'[11] – an

---

9. K. Barth, *Die kirchliche Dogmatik* II/1 (Zurich: TVZ, 1946), p. 362; *Church Dogmatics* II/1 (Edinburgh: T&T Clark, 1957), p. 322.

10. M. Chemnitz, *Loci theologici*, vol. 1 (St Louis: Concordia, 1989), p. 55.

11. W. Pannenberg, *Systematic Theology*, vol. 1 (Edinburgh: T&T Clark, 1991), p. 412.

unhappily detached notion whose persistence throughout his account of the divine attributes is unsettling. Rather, it is because only in this way can dogmatics hope to indicate the one who as free Lord of all things is without limit and everywhere present in power and mercy.

II

God's immensity is the triune God himself in the boundless plenitude of his being, in which he is unhindered by any spatial constraint, and so is sovereignly free for creative and saving presence to all limited creaturely reality.

God's immensity is commonly identified as a mode of his infinity. Thus Charles Hodge: 'His immensity is the infinitude of his being, viewed as belonging to his nature from eternity.'[12] Accordingly, it is expounded by describing a set of contrasts with limited, spatial reality: possessed of *immensitas*, God is one to whom *ubietas* may not be attributed, for space is a mode of existence pertaining only to creatures, and God is *illocalis*, his being is *sine mensura*. Such a procedure offers formal assistance to dogmatics by some primary conceptual clarifications; but it is an inherently risky enterprise if it is allowed to overwhelm substantive dogmatic considerations. In particular, two weighty qualifications have to be kept in mind. First, the concept of infinity must not be deployed in such a way that it becomes an inverted image of the finite; an *immensitas dei* which is simply the antithesis of the local, which is reached merely by stripping away the attribute of spatiality, will by no means necessarily be adequate to indicate the boundless plenitude of the triune God. Second, therefore, whatever is said by way of negation is only an interim concept, something said on the way to a positive statement of God's immensity, and its function is therefore not so much to deliver a substantive doctrine of what God is not, as to articulate some contrasts which will bring into relief the particular perfection which God is. Infinity is not indefiniteness or indistinctness of being. As the immense one, unconditioned by space and unrestricted by relations of adjacency, God is not unspecific: he is *this one*. Infinity is not lack of identity, but rather the absolute *Istigkeit* of God's being; it is intensive perfection. Immensity, therefore, means that God is – in Bavinck's phrase – 'limitless in the

---

12. C. Hodge, *Systematic Theology*, vol. 1 (New York: Scribner, 1877), p. 383.

intensive, qualitative, positive sense'.[13] Lack of finitude, transcendence of all circumscriptive measure and limitation, are the backcloth to the particular freedom in and as which God is God; to speak of God's absence of limitation is to indicate the boundless liberty of God to be and act as he determines in relation to space. Immensity concerns the plenitude, richness, sufficiency and effectiveness of God and so of God's disposition of himself in relation to creaturely space.

Immensity is commonly identified as an 'absolute' attribute of God, referring to God *in se*, apart from his relation to creation, and thereby distinguished from the 'relative' attribute of omnipresence, which is his spatial infinity with respect to the creature. The success of any such distinction depends on retaining the integrity and inseparability of 'absolute' and 'relative': only in that way can an account of the divine attributes fittingly refer to the unique and simple identity of the one who in himself and in his acts towards the creation is Father, Son and Spirit. Certainly, the conceptual mapping of God's identity in terms of the distinction between absolute and relative may have a certain formal or heuristic justification (parallel to the distinction between God *in se* and God *pro nobis*, of which it is a corollary). And, more importantly, it may (like, again, a doctrine of the immanent Trinity[14]) preserve the sovereign and gratuitous character of the ways and works of God in the economy. But these distinctions must not be pressed in such a way that the 'absolute' acquires greater weight than the 'economic' in determining the *essentia dei*. In the case of God's immensity, therefore, this means, first, that immensity cannot be expounded without immediate reference to omnipresence, to which it stands in an inseparable and mutually conditioning relation. And it means, second, that, as with all the divine perfections, talk of divine immensity is wholly referred to the enacted identity of God in his sovereign self-presence as Father, Son and Spirit. Accordingly, dogmatics must give precedence to *definition by description* over *definition by analysis*; its account of the being of God and of God's perfections is to be determined at every point by attention to God's given self-identification – and thus by biblical-historical description

13. H. Bavinck, *The Doctrine of God* (Edinburgh: Banner of Truth Trust, 1977), p. 154.

14. See the important recent articulation of the tasks of this doctrine in P. Molnar, *Divine Freedom and the Doctrine of the Immanent Trinity* (London: T&T Clark, 2002).

of the particular freedom which God exercises in his lordly acts –
rather than by construction of what is fittingly ascribed to a god.
Certainly we cannot climb out of our concepts, for they are all we
have. But neither can we leave them undisturbed, or assume that
they are inherently adequate to render God to us. They must be
converted, made serviceable by correction, above all through being
filled out by descriptive reference to the event and name of the God
whom they attempt to indicate.

God's immensity is his transcendence of space. But in theological
usage, transcendence, like infinity, is non-comparative: its content
cannot be reached either by the magnification of creaturely
properties (so that immensity is mere vastness) or by their negation
(so that immensity is simply lack of spatial limitation). God's
immensity is his qualitative distinction from creaturely reality, and
can only be grasped on the basis of its enactment in the ways and
works of God. *Immensus*, as MacKenzie notes in a reflection upon
the Athanasian Creed, is an aspect of *increatus*, and the latter term
'points to the being of God as utterly qualitatively distinct from the
existence of creatures, their attributes and limitations'; immensity is
thus not quantitative disparity but a 'differential of quality'.[15] 'In
terms of space, size and place are not applicable to him. Neither is
he their mere negation. He is qualitatively and utterly other than
these, both positively and negatively.'[16] One task, therefore, of the
language of immensity is to press theology into a quite different
conceptual register, one in which we do not talk about the divine
perfections by maximizing a creaturely conception of immeasur-
ability or infinite extension, but rather by emptying our thinking
about God of the connotations of spatiality, positive and negative.
But again, this 'emptying' is not an end in itself: if it were, the word
'God' might simply indicate some kind of void. Rather, it is both a
preparation for and a consequence of attentiveness to God's wholly
unique being and act. Subject defines predicate; predicate can be
resolved in its entirety into subject.

God's immensity is the free, gratuitous, non-necessary character
of God's relation to space. As *immensus*, God's being has in itself its
own particular depth, its own plenitude and perfection in the
relations of Father, Son and Spirit. God stands under no external

---

15. I. MacKenzie, *The Dynamism of Space: A Theological Study into the Nature
of Space* (Norwich: Canterbury Press, 1995), p. 78.
16. MacKenzie, *The Dynamism of Space*, p. 81.

constraints by virtue of the spatiality of created reality, and his relation to creation does nothing to complete his being. Possessed of immensity, God is self-moved, replete, *ipse sibi et mundus et locus et omnia*.[17] This, once again, differentiates a Christian theology of divine immensity from pantheism or panentheism, which fail because they cannot coherently affirm the difference between God and the world. Not only do they impugn the aseity of God, rendering God and the world mutually constitutive, but they also cannot give a coherent account either of God's action upon the world or of the world's relative independence. Moreover, both assume an abstract conception of divine immensity as pure remoteness, a conception which, if it is to have any cosmological significance, must be secularized by identifying God's immensity with infinite space. It is precisely this abstract conception of immensity which dogmatics must replace with a more richly formed notion of immensity as the surpassing excellence of God which includes within itself the boundless capacity for nearness: immensity is the transcendent fullness of God which is also the energy of his fellowship with his spatial creatures in the works of creation and incarnation.

God is the lordly creator and keeper of the spaces of heaven and earth. His act of creation is a work of effortless supremacy, authority and effectiveness in which he determines that, alongside the utter perfection of his triune life, he will have his being in relation to another reality. This act is *ex nihilo*; that is, it is wholly original, requiring for its fulfilment nothing other than the mighty enactment of God's will. As creator, God brings into being the things that are not, and orders those things by structuring their existence through spatial and temporal relations. Space is not pre-existent but a created mode of relation between contingent realities which emerged out of nothing. 'God does not stand in a spatial or temporal relation to the universe but ... spatial and temporal relations are produced through his creation of the universe and maintained through his interaction with what He has made.'[18] God's immensity thus includes his majestic priority over the space which he brings into being; he does not contain space (surrounding it as a vast vessel), nor is he dispersed through it or spatially

---

17. Tertullian, *Adv. Prax.* 5.
18. T. F. Torrance, *Space, Time and Incarnation* (Oxford: Oxford University Press, 1969), p. 23.

immanent in it as its life-force, nor is he circumscribed by any of its places. 'Heaven and the highest heaven cannot contain thee' (1 Kgs 8.27). Yet none of this denotes the creator's absence, but rather the free, unconditioned character of his sustaining presence to spatial reality and of his employment of it as one of the media in which he makes himself known. The immensity of the triune creator of heaven and earth is his unqualified transcendence of spatial relation even as the one from whose creative act all spatial relations originate and by whose providential work they are held in being. Immensity is at one and the same time the 'otherness' of God over against created space and the divine capacity to stand in relation to space and to act in space without compromise to the divine freedom.

Something of the same may be suggested of God's interaction with creaturely space in the incarnation. The Word becomes flesh and dwells among creatures; thereby he appropriates to himself creaturely conditions, including spatiality. Yet no less than in the act of creation, the act of incarnation is an act of divine self-movement, a *becoming* or condescension which does not entail the abandonment or restriction of God's immensity. For the Word's entry into space is not to be thought of as local removal; his taking to himself a body does not indicate confinement and thus spell the end of his transcendence over space. The Word becomes flesh, certainly, taking to himself a body of matter and its relations to other bodies. In the passion he enters into the agony of bodily conflict in the constriction and elimination of his space. But he does all this in fulfilment of the divine resolve and in the plenitude of the divine being. He does not need to hide or divest himself of the immensity of deity in order to become flesh. In the form of a slave, obediently taking upon himself the contingencies of space, he is no less in the form of God. Even as one who is embodied, one to whom *ubietas* may be attributed, he fills all things. In his spatiality, he is – to use the Reformed parlance – 'outside' (*extra*), unhindered in his immensity. And again, to speak thus of God's immensity even in the act of incarnation is not to detract from the fullness of his humanity; it is simply to spell out that *vere deus* and *vere homo*, immensity and embodiment, are not competing and mutually contradictory accounts of the identity of the Son of God. Incarnation is not confinement, but the free relation of the Word to his creation – the Word who as creator and incarnate reconciler is *deus immensus*.

In sum: a dogmatic account of God's immensity must follow the rule of all well-ordered thought about the divine perfections, namely, that the integrity and reciprocally determinative character of God's aseity and God's works *ad extra* must not be compromised either by their separation or by the exposition of one at the expense of the other. On the one hand, an account of God's presence to and in all created things detached from consideration of God's immensity will be incapable of adequate articulation of the sheer liberty and originality of God's omnipresence.[19] On the other hand, an account of God's immensity developed in relative abstraction from consideration of God's creative, saving and perfecting presence will be incapable of adequate articulation of the direction of God's self-movement as *immensus*.[20] Good order will only prevail

19. From this point of view, the account offered by H. Berkhof, *Christian Faith* (Grand Rapids: Eerdmans, 1986) is unsatisfactory. Berkhof takes 'God's condescendence' as his starting point (p. 121), and so reinterprets those attributes which appear to suggest God's supernatural exaltation, seeking to relate them more effectively to revelational encounter with God. Accordingly, the conception of divine omnipresence 'rests on the belief that God, who often seems far away, has the unlimited ability to be present with his judgement and grace, his help and guidance, even when man does not in the least expect it. One who begins to see that dares to believe that such a God will never and nowhere lose sight of his creation, and may *therefore* be said to be present everywhere' (p. 122, my italics). 'Therefore' gives it away: omnipresence is experientially deduced, and the result is that, precisely because it lacks roots in God's *immensitas in se*, the 'unlimited ability' of God is not allowed any depth of its own, but is of only ancillary significance, as the 'whence' of a human 'belief'. In effect, the divine *perfections* become little more than divine *benefits*. Inattention to *immensitas dei* is often motivated by an (entirely justifiable) resistance to the incursion of metaphysics into the doctrine of God; the resistance emerges as a desire to give priority to (salvific or existential) 'presence' over ubiquity (see, for example, O. Weber, *Foundations of Dogmatics*, vol. 1 (Grand Rapids: Eerdmans, 1981), pp. 449f.). At other times it is motivated by a concentration on biblical-historical-economic concerns without due consideration of God *in se* (for a good example, see Y. Congar, *Le Mystère du temple ou l'Economie de la présence de Dieu à sa créature de la Genèse à l'Apocalypse* (Paris: Editions du Cerf, 1958)). More effective integration of aseity and economic presence can be found in, for example, H. Thielicke, *The Evangelical Faith*, vol. 2 (Edinburgh: T&T Clark, 1978), pp. 122f., or C. Schwöbel, *God, Action and Revelation*, pp. 57–61.
20. Immensity is thus not simply (to use Kathryn Rogers' term) 'aspatiality' (*Perfect Being Theology*, p. 59): the term lacks a proper sense that God's immensity is the energy of his personal movement in the economy. Much the same can be said of Schleiermacher's scruples about talk of the presence of God as 'repletive', which he believes takes us too close to 'the analogy with expansive forms' (F. D. E. Schleiermacher, *The Christian Faith* (Edinburgh: T&T Clark, 1928), p. 209), and his resistance even to the notion of immensity which he again reads as a material idea of

when the doctrine of the Trinity is allowed to play a determinative role in a theology of the divine attributes.[21] This is not to 'use' the doctrine of the Trinity as a device to achieve a certain result; it is, rather, simply to follow the direction indicated by the church's confession of the coeternity and coequality of Father, Son and Spirit, and to affirm the singular and richly differentiated life and activity of God in which there is enacted the oneness of freedom and fellowship in God's life before, over and with his creatures.

III

The God who is in himself limitlessly majestic is present without restriction in and to his creation. The necessity of this presence is only that of his self-determination to be who he is. But if in this matter theology submits to the instruction of the gospel, it must also say that God's limitless self-determination really includes his determination to be present to the creation, and that this determination is not accidental to his holy being but of its essence. In – not despite – his immensity, God is everywhere present to the whole creation, and is present to order, sustain and perfect it and to direct human creatures to fellowship with himself. To the *immensitas dei* there corresponds in the closest possible way his *omnipraesentia*. This is so because God's immensity is a perfection of his triune life: the full, unhindered majesty of God as Father, Son and Spirit includes his glorious self-presentation as the creator and reconciler who gives to all things their end and brings all things to their fulfilment. His immensity, because it is *his* immensity, is not bare absence of relation, not simply an unchecked will in a void. God is immense as the Father who speaks the limitlessly effective word of creative love, as the Son who is the redeemer and head of the entire creation, and as the Spirit who is over all as Lord and giver of life. In this triune act of self-presentation and relation,

'infinity regarded as substance' (p. 210). On the basis of these scruples, Schleiermacher prefers the stripped-down notions that 'God is in Himself' (p. 209), or 'the absolutely spaceless causality of God' (p. 206). Although Schleiermacher concedes that 'the effects of [God's] causal being-in-Himself are everywhere' (p. 209), his account as a whole is vitiated by a division of immanent and economic, and therefore of immensity and presence.

21. On this, see C. Gunton, *Act and Being: Towards a Theology of the Divine Attributes* (London: SCM, 2002).

God's immensity makes itself operative and known as his omnipresence in the creation.

By way of rough orientation: God's omnipresence is his entire and constant presence in and to all things, the ceaseless and sovereign lordship in which the Most High, who is without measure or limit, inclines to be present to his creation and so holds and renews it in life. But how is the omnipresence of the God confessed in Christian faith to be characterized more closely? Once again: the question 'How is the triune God present?' is not the same question as 'How is a god present?' God's triune presence is thus to be characterized, not by thinking of God as 'exemplifying necessarily a maximally perfect set of compossible great-making properties',[22] but rather descriptively, attending to God's particular greatness which is present in the events of his self-naming, to which the prophetic and apostolic witness bears testimony.

In Scripture, God's presence is characteristically to be understood in relation to his exaltation. God is 'God Most High, maker of heaven and earth' (Gen. 14.19, 22; cf. Mt. 11.25), and therefore the one who as transcendent creator possesses and rules the entirety of that which he has brought into being, for he is one to whom 'heaven and the heaven of heavens, the earth and all that is in it' belong (Deut. 10.14; cf. Exod. 19.5). Exalted in this way, he is 'uncontainable' – most particularly in relation to the temple, which cannot in any way 'house' God. 'Will God indeed dwell on the earth? Behold, heaven and the highest heaven cannot contain thee; how much less this house which I have built!' (1 Kgs 8.27; cf. 2 Chron. 2.6, 6.18; the theme is picked up again in Acts 7.44–50). In the prophetic tradition, this thought acquires greater polemical force as a protest against locative religion in which God and place can be identified, and sacred space used to guarantee (and so effectively tame or resist) the divine presence. 'Do not trust in these deceptive words: "This is the temple of the Lord, the temple of the Lord, the temple of the Lord"' (Jer. 7.4; cf. 7.14; Isa. 66.1). Yet the correction to this idolatrous conception of local divine presence is to emphasize, not God's remoteness, but rather the entirely gratuitous character of his universal presence as the Most High. There thus takes place, as de Margerie puts it, a simultaneous process of 'délocalisation' and 'omnilocalisation' in order to state

---

22. T. V. Morris, 'Jesus and the Attributes of Deity', in *The Logic of God Incarnate* (Ithaca: Cornell University Press, 1986), p. 76.

that '*sans cesser d'être transcendent, Il est proche*'.[23] Precisely as the one who is uncontainable in a particular locale, God is present without restriction; his transcendence as maker and possessor of all space is the unhindered capacity with which he is in all places. His presence is omnipotent and unrestricted, and no creature can block or escape the judgement which it brings. 'Am I a God at hand, says the Lord, and not a God afar off? Can a man hide himself in secret places so that I cannot see him? Do I not fill heaven and earth? says the Lord' (Jer. 23.23f.; cf. 16.16f.; Prov. 15.11; Amos 9.2–4; Obad. 4; Acts 17.27f.; Heb. 4.13). Above all in Psalm 139.7–12, ubiquity concerns God's majestically unconstrained and therefore inescapable presence as the truth which discloses: 'Whither shall I go from thy Spirit? Or whither shall I flee from thy presence?' (Ps. 139.7).

In conceptual terms: God's omnipresence is a free mode of relation. It is free, willed presence, *ubivolpraesentia*, a term used in Lutheran eucharistic theology as a contrast to *omnipraesentia generalis*, but which may fittingly serve to indicate that God's omnipresence is *his* presence, self-moved and wholly original. As *ubivolpraesentia*, omnipresence is not a retraction, setting aside or suspension of divine immensity. It is a movement of the one who is replete in himself. But this does not, however, imply that God's omnipresence is arbitrary, punctiliar or unstable, or that there are occasions or places from which it might be withdrawn. Occasional presence is not omnipresence, for omnipresence is without exception, universal, all places being comprehended in the *ubi* to which God wills to be present. The will of God is simple, and therefore undeviating and dependable. Omnipresence has the unshakeable reality of the divine promise: its certainty and constancy is that of the unqualified divine declaration: 'I am with you always'. But the reliability of a promise is not that of a material or natural condition, and cannot be converted into a state of affairs graspable apart from the will of the giver without falling into idolatry: 'They did not trust that [God] was near them unless they could discern with their eyes a physical symbol of his countenance', Calvin comments on the children of Israel in the wilderness.[24] In its character as *ubivolpraesentia*, therefore, omnipresence repeats the

23.   B. de Margerie, *Les perfections du Dieu de Jésus-Christ* (Paris: Editions du Cerf, 1981), pp. 196f.

24.   J. Calvin, *Institutes of the Christian Religion* I.xi.8 (London: SCM, 1960), p. 108.

general nature of God's relation to the creation, namely that it is a relation rooted in God's aseity, springing from but in no way completing the limitless sufficiency of God's self-relation as Father, Son and Spirit.[25]

The affirmation of God's omnipresence as willed presence is wholly incompatible with any sort of account of continuity of being between God and the world, whether in Stoicism or in process philosophy. Where the world is, there is also God? Only in the sense that where the world is, there also God wills to be and act. Otherwise, the fundamental distinction between God and creation is eroded, and no mutuality or fellowship between them is possible, for they are the same substance in the same space. In the relation between God and the world of which omnipresence is part, it is always a matter of the 'sheer inequality' in which God wholly precedes and transcends the creaturely element.[26] Only in precedence and transcendence (but really in them) is God present to all things as Lord. Otherwise, theology simply ends up in the flat contradiction of divine freedom in which 'God is omnipresent of necessity'.[27]

Omnipresence is free *relation*, *ubivolpraesentia*. The direction taken by the freedom of the triune God includes a direction towards relation to the creation in its totality and in each particular. This relation is personal relation. It is not simply a state or condition, which could readily be converted into a natural property of the creation without reference to God. God's omnipresence is not simply the presence of an infinite supersensible reality without physical limitations, but the presence of the Lord God. It is purposive; and it is known not as simple cosmological fact, but in the course of the drama of God's dealings with his creation as its maker and as the agent of its reconciliation and perfection. God's presence is 'the power of his creative nearness':[28] it is 'that which is

---

25. This point is sometimes stated by a dialectical pairing of concepts (such as remoteness/proximity or presence/absence). These expressions are a little unhappy, in that they may suggest that immensity and omnipresence are in some way in tension with one another. The language of *ubivolpraesentia* offers a way of talking of omnipresence as the self-movement of the limitless God which is both more concrete and more effective in integrating transcendence and presence.

26. Barth, *Church Dogmatics* II/1, p. 312.

27. H. Martensen, *Christian Dogmatics* (Edinburgh: T&T Clark, 1898), p. 94.

28. I. U. Dalferth, *Gott. Philosophisch-theologische Denkversuche* (Tübingen: Mohr, 1992), p. 9.

absolutely productive and in no sense produced, ceaselessly effective and not effected, utterly self-presenting and never simply there, the absolute event of nearness and never simply a reality which is to hand.'[29] Or in Aquinas' terms, God's omnipresence is the omnipresence of his agency: *Deus est in omnibus rebus, non quidem sicut pars essentiae, vel sicut accidens, sed sicut agens adest ei, in quod agit.*[30] And as the presence of this limitlessly free agent, God's omnipresence is repletive, a presence without bodily or spatial hindrance, filling and acting on all things which have their being in him: God *replet omnia loca, quod dat esse omnibus locatis, quae replent omnia loca.*[31]

Some negations follow: God's presence is not definite, local or circumscriptive, for he is not present in the world after the manner of a finite physical body encompassed by space. The heavy emphasis upon of these negative characterizations in the Western theological tradition owes a good deal to Augustine (most of all in Letter 148 and Letter 187, the so-called *de praesentia dei liber*).[32] God is 'a spiritual substance not susceptible of division according to local distance or dimension, or even confined within the limits of bodily members',[33] and so 'is not diffused through space or confined within limits, having one part in one place, another in another, a smaller in less space, a greater in a larger'.[34] This is because the spatial relations of created bodies are definitive, whereas God is defined by no such relations. 'Take away the spatial relations of bodies, they will be nowhere, and because they are nowhere they will not be at all. Take away bodies from the qualities of bodies, there will be no place for them to be, and, as a necessary consequence, they will not exist.'[35] Yet it would be rash to conclude that Augustine is simply repeating neo-Platonic commonplaces. The negations are corollaries of affirmations; Augustine does not

29. Dalferth, *Gott*, p. 8.

30. Aquinas, *Summa Theologiae* I.8.i.

31. Aquinas, *Summa Theologiae* I.8.ii.

32. The best account remains S. J. Grabowski, *The All-Present God: A Study in St Augustine* (St Louis: Herder, 1954).

33. Augustine, *Ep. cxlviii*, I.ii (Corpus scriptorum ecclesiasticorum latinorum 44, p. 333).

34. Augustine, *Ep. cxlviii*, I.iii (p. 333); see also *Ep. clxxxvii*, XI (Corpus scriptorum ecclesiasticorum latinorum 57, p. 90) and XIV (p. 92): God 'is not distributed through space by size so that half of him should be in half of the world and half of him in the other half of it'.

35. Augustine, *Ep. clxxxvii*, XVIII (p. 96).

stop short at emphasizing the disembodied, non-spatial and non-dimensive character of God's presence, and such denials serve to draw attention to two positive avowals. First, God is simple and therefore, in Augustine's refrain throughout both letters, God is *in se ubique*, or *ubique incorporaliter tota*. Second, this simple, self-moving and wholly present God is present not just as an invisible spiritual substance but *creatively*, sustaining and ruling the world: God is not a *qualitas mundi* but the *substantia creatrix mundi sine labore regens et sine onere continens mundum*.[36] In sum: the triune God is present in all places, in free majesty, undividedly, neither localized nor extended but spiritually, graciously and creatively present to undergird and glorify all things.

God's omnipresence is a confession of faith. Knowledge of it does not derive from inspection of the nature of created reality but from God's self-presentation as the one who is Lord. No less than knowledge of God's mercy, faithfulness or patience, knowledge of his immensity and ubiquity is a matter of a divinely given perception. Yet to emphasize the confessional character of our knowledge of omnipresence is not to restrict the scope of this piece of Christian teaching simply to the soteriological, at cost to its cosmological implications. That kind of restriction has been common enough in modern Christian dogmatics, especially those of an anthropological cast, in which omnipresence quickly becomes a coordinate or perhaps a contrastive background to experiences of being sought and found by God. Thus Macquarrie suggests that the term immensity indicates 'the deeply felt contrast between man's limited, fragile existence and what has in the revelatory moment touched his life – overwhelming Being'.[37] Or Aulén: a Christian theology of omnipresence affirms that 'there is no place closed to the sovereign power of divine love. God can reach us wherever we are, and it is useless for a man to attempt to flee from his power.'[38] In and of themselves, such statements are relatively unexceptionable. But they risk defining omnipresence simply in terms of saving proximity, with the result that, first, the background of ubiquity in God's *in se* immensity is accorded little significance, and, second, its implications for the spatial character of the created order are left unexplored. Some remarks on this last question may be in order.

36. Augustine, *Ep. clxxxvii*, XVIII (p. 96).
37. J. Macquarrie, *Principles of Christian Theology* (London: SCM, 1966), p. 188.
38. G. Aulén, *The Faith of the Christian Church* (London: SCM, 1961), pp. 150f.

In brief: for Christian dogmatics, God's relation to the creation as the immense and omnipresent creator and redeemer is fundamental for the determination of the nature of space. Space is not to be considered as a 'fact of nature' whose meaning is self-evident without reference to the divine presence and claim upon creatures. Nor is space simply a field of spatial politics or poetics, ungrounded spatial practices not rooted in the deep structure of being. Space is an objective, given form of created existence and relation, one of the media through which the human creature has its existence in relation to the natural order, to other creatures and to God. Above all, space is defined by God's limitless presence, by the simple confession that God is *in se ubique*. Because creatures have their existence in this form, then space is not a mere *brutum factum*, nor a commodity, nor raw material for manipulation. It is a law of creation in which we are to discern the structure of created being and in which, therefore, we encounter a summons to act fittingly, as the spatial creatures we *are*.

In more detail: the doctrine of *creatio ex nihilo* is to be the 'head and pattern' of theological thinking about space, above all because that doctrine articulates the utter gratuity and contingency of created being: 'It is the doctrine of God so creating all things *ex nihilo* and sustaining them and fulfilling them by that selfsame Word, which is the theological principle guiding and controlling all theology's thoughts about the nature of space and time.'[39] Space is therefore not absolute or unoriginate, some sort of pre-existent medium; nor is it simply a register of acts and attitudes on the part of creatures who make space for themselves by disposing of themselves in the world. In both cases (roughly, that of Newtonian conceptions of space as the *sensorium dei*[40] and that of late modern poetics of space[41]) space has become detached from God's acts of creating and maintaining the creaturely realm and reconciling it to

---

39. MacKenzie, *The Dynamism of Space*, p. 21.

40. The classic account is A. Koyré, *From the Closed World to the Infinite Universe* (Baltimore: Johns Hopkins University Press, 1996). For the longer perspective, see E. Grant, *Much Ado about Nothing: Theories of Space and Vacuum from the Middle Ages to the Scientific Revolution* (Cambridge: Cambridge University Press, 1981), and A. A. Davenport, *Measure of a Different Greatness: The Intensive Infinite, 1250–1650* (Leiden: Brill, 1999).

41. See G. Bachelard, *The Poetics of Space* (Boston: Beacon Press, 1969); H. Lefebvre, *The Production of Space* (Oxford: Blackwell, 1991); D. Harvey, *The Condition of Postmodernity* (Oxford: Blackwell, 1990).

himself. In effect, space is secularized: the measure of space is not God's presence to and action upon creatures but either the immanent bodily relations of things or the project of world-construction. Christian theology resists this secularization by a cluster of trinitarian affirmations: by its doctrine of creation, according to which created reality is not self-originating but contingent on the unoriginate will and activity of God the Father; by what it has to say of the relations borne to the creation by the Son or Word of God who orders all things as the one 'in whom all things hold together' (Col. 1.17) and who 'upholds all things by his word of power' (Heb. 1.3); and by the confession of the Holy Spirit as the perfecting cause of creation. From the work of the triune God are derived the origin, order and fulfilment of creaturely space. As creator, God is *immensus*, transcending any contingent spatial relations to that which he calls into being; as Lord of creation he is omnipresent, making space into a medium of relations between the creation and its God.

The centre of theological concern, we might say, is less the physics of space or the poetics of space than the 'economics' of space, its significance in God's ordered administration of created reality.[42] This order is, of course, to be conceived dynamically and historically: the economy of creation is not a set of immobile co-presences but an unfolding dramatic process of interrelation. Space is brought into being and held in existence by the activity of the omnipresent creator who grants to what he has made its own space in distinction from himself. This spatial distance is precisely the condition for mutuality and togetherness. In thus differentiating the creation from himself, God does not leave the creature in isolation, but stands with and acts upon every creature as the omnipresent Lord from whom nothing is absolutely remote. To this active divine presence there corresponds the creature's active occupancy of the space bestowed by God. In actively occupying its given space, the creature exists with and alongside other creatures, in the mutually determinative relation of distance and proximity.

Space is closely connected with interpersonal communion. Space acquires and maintains a surer reality when it has reference not only

---

42. Cf. MacKenzie, *The Dynamism of Space*, p. 136: 'Through his Word [God] orders all things. He administers οἰκονομία, the ordering of the household of creation ... He is Place, for he is the bestower of place for every constituent part of what he has brought into being, and on his Place all things depend.'

to myself but to other persons as well, of whom I can and must say: from me to such a one the distance is this. Space, like time, is interpersonal relation. It distinguishes and unites us, and indicates the perspective of a still greater nearness.[43]

This mutuality of spatial relation involves the creature's 'making room' for itself in relation to and distinction from other creatures. Space as the 'law' of existence is not simply a static location, some kind of pre-existent slot into which the particular creature is placed. It is, rather, a summons to the creature to fulfil its divine calling by actively entering into its particular nature, for 'God makes room for all creation. He allows everything in the freedom which it has as that which is created to express itself in making its place.'[44]

In this lies the potential for the sinful perversion of spatial relatedness. The relative independence which is the necessary condition for spatial relation can become spatial autonomy; mutual determination of creatures can become agonistics; the gift of space can become possessed territory. At this point, the cosmological and the soteriological converge. The good order of creaturely existence under God's omnipresence (*Allgegenwart*) is restored by God's saving presence (*Heilsgegenwart*) in the Word incarnate and in the Spirit. In Jesus Christ the Word of God takes upon himself the full reality of creatureliness, including its spatiality. The Word does so without abandonment or retraction of his immensity as the Word who upholds all things. But as this one, in free self-disposition, he takes flesh and occupies created space. In his passion he bears the full weight of the creature's hatred of the presence of other creatures and of God. He is 'taken away', 'cut off out of the land of the living'; his presence is destroyed, and his place becomes the no-place of the grave (Isa. 53.8f.). But that is not all: he is risen from the dead, and is seated at the right hand of the Father in the heavenly places, from where he rules all things as their head and fills all places with his presence (Eph. 1.20–23). He has set an end to the wicked project of spatial autonomy. In him all creaturely places are reordered, by being claimed with the full authority of the one who is Lord of heaven and earth, as the spaces in which we are to discover the presence of God. And being so claimed, they are also made into places of adjacency to other creatures. In sum: in Jesus Christ, now

43. D. Staniloae, *The Experience of God: Orthodox Dogmatic Theology*, vol. 1 (Brookline: Holy Cross Orthodox Press, 1994), p. 173.
44. MacKenzie, *The Dynamism of Space*, p. 138.

present to all places through the Spirit's power, space is made a medium of fellowship. And 'one cannot obtain such a presence of him without, at the same time, possessing life'.[45]

IV

All this is no more than an initial dogmatic sketch, clumsily executed. The most proper language with which to speak of God's omnipresence and ubiquity is that of praise, of which Traherne may offer a fitting example:

> His omnipresence is an ample territory or field of joys, a transparent temple of infinite lustre, a strong tower of defence, a castle of repose, a bulwark of security, a place of delights ... a broad and vast extent of fame and glory, a theatre of infinite excellency ... Our Bridegroom and our King being everywhere, our Lover and defender watchfully governing all worlds, no danger or enemy can arise to hurt us, but is immediately prevented and suppressed, in all spaces beyond the utmost borders of those unknown habitations which He possesseth. Delights of inestimable value are there preparing, for everything is present by its own existence. The essence of God being therefore all light and knowledge, love and goodness, care and providence, felicity and glory, a pure and simple Act, it is present in its operations, and by those Acts which it eternally exerteth is wholly busied in all parts and places of His dominion, perfecting and completing our bliss and happiness.[46]

45.   Calvin, *Institutes* II.x.8 (p. 435).
46.   T. Traherne, 'The Fifth Century', 9f. in *Centuries* (London: Faith Press, 1960), pp. 227f.

5

THE HOLINESS AND LOVE OF GOD[1]

Among the many significant contributions which Wolf Krötke has made to the renewal of Christian theology, his work on the doctrine of the divine attributes is first in rank. *Gottes Klarheiten*[2] is a very fine book, notable above all for its theological and spiritual concentration, the mature fruit of a lifetime devoted to the utterly demanding and joyful calling of thought and speech about God. After Barth, it has not proved easy for evangelical theologians to write about the perfections of God, simply because Barth's treatment in *Church Dogmatics* II/1 is such a compelling and creative re-inhabitation of the tradition that it is difficult to know how else to set about the task. That Krötke has indeed achieved 'a new interpretation' of such cogency and penetration is a testimony to his remarkable theological gifts. One of the most distinctive features of *Gottes Klarheiten* is the way in which it offers a thoroughly trinitarian account of the attributes – a feature which Krötke's work has in common with at least one other important contemporary study of the topic, that of the late Colin Gunton in his last major publication *Act and Being*.[3] Much may be learned from reading the two books in tandem, most of all about the way in which, in the light of the Christian confession of God as Father, Son and Spirit, the doctrine of God's attributes takes on a very different appearance. In what follows, I attempt to reflect upon the same themes (1) in some preliminary considerations concerning the task of a dogmatic theology of the perfections of God, and (2) in

---

1. This paper was given at a colloquium in Berlin, February 2004, in honour of the 65th birthday of Professor Wolf Krötke.
2. W. Krötke, *Gottes Klarheiten. Eine Neuinterpretation der Lehre von Gottes 'Eigenschaften'* (Tübingen: Mohr, 2001).
3. C. Gunton, *Act and Being: Towards a Theology of the Divine Attributes* (London: SCM, 2002).

some proposals concerning the inseparability of the triune God's holiness and his love.

I

A Christian dogmatics of the divine perfections is a positive science in the church of Jesus Christ whose task is the rational articulation of the singular identity of God the Holy Trinity, freely presented in the works of God's triune being.

A Christian dogmatics of the divine perfections is a *positive* science; its *positum* is God in the infinitely rich and full singularity of his perfect being. Dogmatics is positive, first, by virtue of the *object* by which it is brought into being, through which it is to be guided in all its operations, and in which it has its end. This object is *given* to dogmatic science. It is given, initially, in the confession of the church, but only *in* the confession of the church because it is first of all given *to* the confession of the church by a majestic act of mercy on the part of the church's Lord, as he expounds himself in his works. The divine self-exposition – revelation – sets dogmatics on its way. The *positum* of a dogmatics of the divine perfections is thus not some inherited 'topic' or a set of questions which emerge from the analysis of the concept of deity: Christian dogmatics is not concerned with deity but with God. But precisely because *this* is its given matter, the object of dogmatics is never something simply to hand, a reality which can in some way be schematized by theological reason; however much it may give itself as a reality for knowledge, the *positum* of dogmatics cannot become an object of exhaustive theological projection. This is because dogmatics has to do with a reality which, even in its presence to the mind, remains utterly replete, immeasurable in its fullness. For what is given to dogmatics is the event of God's personal presence, his engagement with humankind as creator, saviour and perfecter in which he unfolds his being and will for us. That presence is irreducibly itself; it cannot be converted or broken down or in any way rendered amenable to reason's comprehension. It is, quite simply, the presence of the glory of God. It is God's spiritual presence, free, majestic, giving itself to be known in its own terms and by its own original act, claiming reason but not in any way circumscribed by reason's measure. Of that claim upon reason, the positive science of dogmatics is one of the fruits.

Further, dogmatics is positive by virtue of its *sphere*: it is a positive science *in the church of Jesus Christ*. God's lordly presence creates a creaturely domain for itself, bringing into being a sphere of human life and fellowship in which God is known, loved and praised. That domain is the church, which is the 'spiritual culture' within which theology fulfils its office. In the church, common life, thought and speech are being transfigured by the reconciling and sanctifying work of God, delivered from the ignorance, vanity and constriction of sin and set free for true knowledge of God in the gospel. The realm of the church is the realm of dogmatics; like all theology, dogmatics is ecclesiastical science. Dogmatic science is not a transcendent moment, an act of the mind which rises above the merely domestic life of the Christian community and submits that life to critical evaluation. It is, rather, an activity of the *sanctorum communio*, and so can fittingly be described as a work of 'holy' reason, reason set apart for service of the gospel in the assembly of the saints.

The task of this positive ecclesiastical science is the *rational articulation* of the reality of God which is given to the church in the gospel. Rational articulation of God's reality is a matter of thought and speech which follow the 'law of the object' by whose commanding presence they are governed. The 'law' of the object is the inherent order in which that object presents itself and which constitutes a claim upon reason. The object is what it is, and not something other; it presents itself in its own unique and particular act; that uniqueness and particularity command the works of reason, summoning them in a particular direction. The intentionality of theological reason – its movement towards the object – is anticipated or graciously overtaken by the extentional presence and action of the object itself. The extentionality of God's presence and action has imperative force. It claims reason, requiring of reason that, if it is to be set free from falsehood and to discover truth, it must exercise itself to follow the object's instruction. This is 'following' the law of its given reality. Yet such a following is by no means merely passive or receptive, because the law of the object quickens reason so that reason may exercise its capacities as it is reconciled to God and made fitting for the service of the knowledge of him.

Dogmatics is a *critical* science only because it is a positive science which does its work under the tutelage of this given reality and its law. It is a critical science because it inquires into the adequacy of the church's thought and speech about God in relation to the *positum* by which the church is claimed. An uncritical dogmatics would not be Christian dogmatics, precisely because it would

assume the identity between its own representations and the reality
of God – or at least the adequacy of those representations – and
would thereby absolve itself from undertaking any fresh acts of
seeking and following the command of God's presence. Were that
to happen, the law of the object would become a mere statute, not a
quickening imperative. The task of critical theology is to work
against such paralysis. But critical theology is not authorized to go
beyond this: it has no mandate to inquire into the conditions of
possibility of there being a given reality which controls the
dogmatic thinking of the church, or to seek to establish such a
possibility on grounds other than the object's self-presence, or to
treat the law of the object with ironic distance. Whatever
judgements critical theology makes must emerge from reason's
having been judged, absolved and summoned into activity by the
gift of God's truth.

Why is all this a necessary preliminary to a dogmatics of the
divine perfections? Because thinking about God's perfections
involves reason's conversion by and reordering towards its object,
which is the singular identity of God the Holy Trinity, freely
presented in the works of God's triune being. How is that identity
to be described?

The Christian doctrine of God is concerned with God's *identity*.
It is charged with the task of giving an account of the particular
character (*Eigenart*) of the God who is confessed in the church, the
one who is himself as he executes his own being in his acts as
Father, Son and Holy Spirit. To inquire into the attributes of God
is thus not to ask about supposed attributes of deity in general,
about what a god must be. It is to ask about the particular
perfection in which God is himself, inquiring into the characteristic
and wholly unique depth of the divine being in which God confirms
himself in all his abundance and grace. It is to ask, not *what* God is
but *who* God is. And it is to ask with a measure of confidence that
such a question can only (but really!) be answered out of attention
to the movement which is God's triune being and act. It is this
'special divine character', this 'special essence of the divine being',
which is the *positum* of a Christian doctrine of the divine attributes.[4]
Two consequences follow.

First, dogmatics will not invest in the attempt to establish the
perfections of God by first determining the necessary attributes of a

---

4.   K. Barth, *Church Dogmatics* II/1 (Edinburgh: T&T Clark, 1957), p. 298.

maximally perfect being. Approaches to the doctrine along these lines enjoy some prestige among Anglo-American philosophers of religion, who have attempted to articulate the attributes of God, first, by establishing a set of great-making properties and then, second, by following the logic of supremacy, envisaging God as (to repeat Morris' phrase) 'exemplifying necessarily a maximally perfect set of compossible great-making properties'.[5] Such arguments (supposed by their proponents to be Anselmian in character, but in fact only doubtfully so) are of little dogmatic utility. Most of all this is because they are pervaded by an abstract conception of *deitas*; in effect, they generate a notion of divinity not governed by the specific contours of God's being and action, which then serves as the frame for positive theological teaching. But it proves to be a very constricting frame. Dominated by the apologetic interests of natural religion and natural theology as they developed from the mid-seventeenth century, this approach deploys the doctrine of God's attributes as part of a larger project of offering a rationally demonstrable theistic construal of reality. As a result, it tends to give high profile to the 'metaphysical' divine attributes, since those attributes are conceptually necessary if God is to be presented as the author and governor of contingent reality. Not only does this mean that the immanent life of the Trinity plays almost no perceptible role in determining the attributes of God (since it is supposed that triunity adds nothing to the conception of God as maximal causal power). It also means that attributes which indicate God's personal, historical relations with his creatures (including, of course, holiness and love) are pushed to the margins. The *identity* of God is determined by the *function* of God as perfect world-cause and world-sustainer.

Second, dogmatics will not attempt to ground what it has to say about the divine attributes in a phenomenology of, for example, love or holiness. Whether they derive from philosophical anthropology, the study of religions or cultural theory, these phenomenologies share a weakness with 'perfect being theology': they determine the *essentia dei* by first determining the content of a predicate such as holy or loving, and then applying the result to God. Even when the predicate is stretched by its application *in divinis*, the problem remains that the predicate is not fully shaped

---

5. T. V. Morris, 'Jesus and the Attributes of Deity', in *The Logic of God Incarnate* (Ithaca: Cornell University Press, 1986), p. 76.

by the acting subject, and the acting subject is therefore rather readily reduced to being an exemplification of a concept derived in advance from elsewhere. As this happens, the singularity of God is compromised, for it is not allowed to emerge in its own free clarity and distinctive form. For dogmatics, on the other hand, the point of language about the attributes of God is simply to indicate God's name. God's name is his enacted identity, his sheer, irreducible particularity as *this one* who is and acts *thus*. More simply: God's name is his uniqueness. As the bearer of this name, God is not indeterminate deity, but the self-determining one who is beyond the reach of any comparison or class. 'I am the Lord, that is my name' (Isa. 42.8). As the incomparable one who is in every respect *a se*, God names himself: God speaks the name which he bears. And so when human speech takes it upon itself to repeat this name, it does not *ascribe* but *confess*. God receives his name from no one but himself, for his identity is altogether self-originating. Dogmatic talk of the divine attributes is thus not a proposal, the projection of a category on to God. It is a repetition of the name of God, or, perhaps better, a conceptual expansion of that name which does not add to it or go beyond it but simply utters it as it has already been uttered, returning to that name as something which cannot be enhanced, mastered or resolved into anything other than itself. In Christian talk of God, the nominal precedes the predicative. All dogmatic talk of God's perfections traces God's own pronouncement of his name; it simply says, in effect, 'the Lord, he is God; the Lord, he is God' (1 Kgs 18.39).

The identity of God of which Christian dogmatics is the rational articulation is the identity of *God the Holy Trinity, freely presented in the works of God's triune being*. God becomes a matter for human thought and speech because he makes himself present to his creatures. God is present to himself in the fullness and inexhaustible sufficiency of his triune being, and in this fullness he has need of no other and owes nothing to any other being. But the fullness which is proper to him includes (though it is not exhausted by) the willing, executing and completing of a repetition of his presence to a reality which is not himself. The circle of God's repleteness, the whole and integrated fellowship which he is as Father, Son and Spirit, is not a closed circle. In its very completeness, it is a life-giving movement, bestowing, guarding, healing, restoring and perfecting the life of what is not God, as its lordly creator and preserver. Thus: 'God is who He is in His works.'[6] But to say this is not in any way to empty the doctrine of God of reference to everything apart from the economy of the *opera dei ad extra*, because these *opera* are the *opera dei*, the works of God's utterly sufficient being. Thus: 'In His works He is revealed as the One He is.'[7]

The formal consequence of this is that, because God the Holy Trinity is the agent of his own presence, he does not become a matter for human consideration because the creature makes God present by a speculative or religious or poetic act. The presence of God is never a function of the self-presence of the creature, but is always pre-eminent, self-moved, commanding, absolutely original. Consequently, the attributes of God are not labels attached to a deity called into the creature's presence, but are indicators of the name of the one who summons the creature to account for itself and its thinking in his presence.

The material consequence is that the doctrine of the Trinity is fundamental for any account of the perfections of God. God's being presents itself in his works; in his works God presents his own most proper being. But God's being is his being as Father, Son and Holy Spirit. There is all the difference in the world between the attributes of deity and the perfections of the God of the Christian confession; the marker of the difference is the doctrine of the Trinity. Without an operative doctrine of the being and action of the triune persons in their unity, a theology of the divine attributes will be incapable of achieving the right sort of Christian determinacy. It will misconstrue both the character of God's immanent life and the manner of his relation to the world; God's life *in se* will most naturally be thought of as causal will, and his works *pro nobis* will be reduced to remote providential governance, with the divine attributes expounded accordingly. A trinitarian account of God's being, acts and perfections, on the other hand, will be concerned at every point to indicate the fellowship which God is in his own limitless majesty and which he establishes with his creatures. As Father, Son and Spirit, God is and acts out of holy love.

A trinitarian account of the divine perfections will be especially alert to the need to coordinate the 'immanent' and the 'operative'. 'Every clarity (*Klarheit*) of God is to be understood as a *clarity of*

---

6. Barth, *Church Dogmatics* II/1, p. 260.
7. Barth, *Church Dogmatics* II/1, p. 260.

the trinitarian God. That means that it must speak of God not only in relation to the world but also in *relation to himself.*[8] Dogmatics must avoid any separation of 'absolute' from 'relative' attributes for exactly the same reason that it must avoid any separation of the immanent from the economic Trinity, namely that only in their full integration can the specific freedom and movement of God's being be conceived. God's aseity is the plenitude in which he turns to his creation; his turning to his creation is rooted in the unoriginate perfection and abundance of his life. Because God relates to and acts upon his creatures as the one he is, too sharp a distinction must not be drawn between *attributa immanentia* and *attributa operativa* – especially one in which the *attributa immanentia* are considered to be 'absolute' properties whose content can be determined without reference to the biblical-historical representation of God's acts. Thus the holiness which God is *in se* is active in the election and purification of a people for himself, and the love of the triune persons abounds as loving mercy towards ruined creatures. Yet a proper distinction between immanent and operative ought not to be abandoned and the attributes collapsed without residue into economic operations. God's holy love for his creatures would be groundless if it were not the outworking in time and space of his eternal being as the holy and loving Father, Son and Spirit. We now turn to a description of that holy and loving being and of its work in the world.

II

God's holiness is the majestic incomparability, difference and purity which he is in himself as Father, Son and Holy Spirit, and which is manifest and operative in the economy of his works in the love with which he elects, reconciles and perfects human partners for fellowship with himself.

'There is none holy like the Lord, there is none besides thee; there is no rock like our God' (1 Sam. 2.2). God's holiness is his *majestic incomparability.* 'There is none holy like the Lord.' First and foremost, talk of God as holy simply betokens his utter uniqueness, his being as himself and not another. As the one who is holy as no other is holy, God is not to be considered the most consistent

8. Krötke, *Gottes Klarheiten*, p. 115.

instantiation of some quality called holiness, present elsewhere in lower degree but finding maximal exemplification in God. Talk of God's holiness, because it is nominal before it is predicative, says at its simplest: 'Holy is he!' and says it in such a way that 'he' determines the content of 'holy'. As with all the attributes of God, so here: language about holiness makes identifying rather than classificatory reference.

God's holiness is therefore his sheer *difference*. 'There is none besides thee.' 'God is holy as the one who is distinct from everything else.'[9] The act in which God fulfils his holy being as Father, Son and Spirit differentiates him from every other being; as God enacts his majestic identity, he is entirely himself. Like all God's acts, this act of personal self-differentiation is wholly effortless, uncaused and perfect, requiring nothing for its fulfilment beyond itself. God's 'otherness' is not something which God comes to have in rivalry between himself and others. The divine being is replete, and is involved in no agonistics. God's holiness is thus his transcendence of any possible relation in which he is merely one factor alongside another, even if it be the supreme or victorious factor. There is none besides the holy God; he simply *is*.

God's holiness is his incomparable and different majesty. In speaking of the holiness of God, therefore, we are seeking to listen to the name of the active personal being of God as it maintains itself in its absolute singularity and unrivalled difference. God is, however, this singular and unrivalled one in his thrice-holy being; his uniqueness is not some kind of substratum to his identity as Father, Son and Spirit, but is identical with his triunity. God is simple and singular in his threeness. In the completeness of the one divine essence and in the majesty of the three persons as the mutually determining subsistences of that one essence; in the consubstantiality and coinherence of the three persons; in their proper identities and acts as the one who begets, the one who is begotten and the one who proceeds; in their loving acts as the world's creator, the world's reconciler and the world's perfecter – in this unwearied and unbroken act of his triune life, God is the holy one without beginning and end.

Incomparable and different in his being and act as the three-in-one, God is *pure*. God's holiness is also *moral* holiness, for he is 'of

<hr>

9.   E. Schlink, *Ökumenische Dogmatik. Grundzüge* (Göttingen: Vandenhoeck und Ruprecht, 1983), p. 760.

purer eyes than to behold evil' (Hab. 1.13). God's holiness is *pure* majesty. It is unsullied by anything which is opposed to or outside his will; its difference includes its otherness from all that is polluted; it admits of no compromise or degradation of its perfection. But, crucially, moral perfection does not exhaust the notion of God's holiness, and is properly subordinate to holiness as God's incomparable identity. At this point, dogmatics must be particularly scrupulous not to allow an alien conception of moral purity to infiltrate its account of the divine attributes and disrupt what it says about God's uniqueness. God's moral purity is *his*; here, too, 'there is none holy *like the Lord*'.

God is not an archetype; his moral holiness is not simply his maximal possession of a virtue whose application is more general. In his *Lectures on the Philosophical Doctrine of Religion* from the first half of the 1780s, Kant remarks that '*[h]oliness* is the absolute or unlimited moral perfection of the will. A holy being must not be affected with the least inclination contrary to morality.'[10] This is because '[a] being who is to give objective reality to moral duties must possess without limit the moral perfections of *holiness, benevolence and justice. These attributes constitute the entire moral concept of God.*'[11] What is problematic in Kant's account (which is a commonplace of a good deal of analytical philosophy of religion) is not simply that the doctrine of the divine perfections is harnessed to a particular use of the doctrine of God as 'holy legislator'[12] to underwrite a theory of human ethical duty by giving 'objective reality to moral duties'. It is also that Kant collapses God's holiness into moral purity. Detached from God's *essential* holiness and no longer rooted in the distinctive identity of God, holiness is moralized. And cut adrift in this way from the triune essence of God, holiness can quickly be transformed into God's conformity to an abstract moral law. Divine holiness becomes virtue personified, and therefore it encounters us simply as moral imperative.

Thinking of God's holiness in isolation from God's identity means that a contradiction is inscribed deep into the doctrine of God: the contradiction between God's holiness and his love. This

10. I. Kant, *Lectures on the Philosophical Doctrine of Religion*, in A. W. Wood and G. di Giovanni (eds), *Religion and Rational Theology* (Cambridge: Cambridge University Press, 1996), p. 409.

11. Kant, *Lectures on the Philosophical Doctrine of Religion*, p. 408 (italics in original).

12. Kant, *Lectures on the Philosophical Doctrine of Religion*, p. 409.

consequence of the moralization of God's holiness becomes especially visible in the theology of atonement, where divine holiness can be presented as an ethical righteousness which is at variance with God's attitude of merciful love towards sinners. The contradiction between holiness and love often takes the form of an estrangement of Father and Son in the work of atonement: the Father is the source of holy wrath against sin, the Son its victim in the place of sinners. In modern theology, the contradiction is commonly eased by the eradication of holiness in favour of love. But a dogmatics of divine holiness must move beyond such abstractions. What is required by way of alternative is (1) the reintegration of God's purity into a more comprehensive conception of holiness as self-maintaining identity and difference, and (2) an understanding of God's moral holiness not as merely statutory or morally legislative but as intrinsic to God's loving purpose of fellowship with humankind. Holiness and love, that is, are mutually conditioning and mutually illuminative terms, which can only be expounded in relation to each other, and which both serve as conceptual indicators of the being and ways of the triune God.

God is holy in himself as Father, Son and Spirit. If God's triunity is not accidental but essential, if it is identical with the particular being which God is, then his holiness is also in every respect determined by the fact that it is the holiness of this one. Furthermore, the difference which is acknowledged in the church's trinitarian confession of God is visible in God's relation to his creatures, for the holiness which God is in himself *is manifest and operative in the economy of his works in the love with which he elects, reconciles and perfects human partners for fellowship with himself.*

In developing this theme, we may begin by completing the sequence of thought in 1 Sam. 2.2. There is none holy like God – that is, God's holiness is his incomparability – for there is none besides God – that is, God's holiness is his absolute difference from all else that is. Yet, precisely as the God who is thus incomparable and different, God is holy in being the 'rock' of those who confess him: 'there is no rock like our God'. The holiness of God *in se* is the support and strength of the people of God, the unshakeable foundation of creaturely being and confidence. How is this to be understood?

To the sovereign act of God's holiness in which he maintains his own triune being in its integrity and distinctiveness there corresponds a further act of holiness in which God extends himself to maintain the being of his creature. God's self-consecration – the pure majesty with which he wills and establishes himself as who he is – includes his consecration of the creature, willing and establishing the creature as possessed of its own integrity and distinctiveness in relation to himself, destroying all that opposes his will for the creature, and so leading the creature to the perfect fulfilment of its being. The holiness of the triune God is not only the infinity and integral perfection of his being, but also that infinity and perfection in its turning to the creature. Holiness is manifest and operative in God's loving works of relating to the creature, taking up its cause and sanctifying it for life with himself.

As the holy one, God consecrates creatures for fellowship, so that his holiness is active in his covenant-creating and covenant-sustaining work as the creature's 'rock'. Isaiah repeatedly puts together the idea of God as the Holy One and God as Redeemer and Saviour (Isa. 41.14; 43.3; 48.17; 49.7): 'your Redeemer is the Holy One of Israel'. God's holiness is present as the active love in which he comes to the aid of his people, taking up their cause, bearing their sin, purifying them and binding them to his own life. The 'otherness' of the Holy Trinity may not be thought of as simple segregation. God does not 'hallow' his being – that is, maintain himself in full integrity as the one he is – by isolating himself; he maintains his holy being in freedom and sovereign power by fulfilling his will to fellowship. It is in this will to fellowship, not in utter seclusion, that God's holiness is operative. God is the Holy One. But he is 'the Holy One *in your midst*' (Hos. 11.9). The self-election of the holy God includes his election and sanctification of the creature.

> The holy God ... acts as the one who elects, *the one who draws to himself*, the one who establishes fellowship – as the one who brings salvation and gives himself ... The wholly Other of the divine holiness finds its most potent expression in the reality that fellowship with him is only possible on the basis of the fact that out of himself and in free love he took to himself the enslaved Israelite tribes.[13]

Or, as Barth puts it, '"holy" ... clearly means primarily and fundamentally that which singles out, helps, blesses and restores'.[14]

God is holy as he loves the creature; his love for his creature is holy love. Once again, everything depends on giving the right sort

---

13. Schlink, *Ökumenische Dogmatik*, p. 761.
14. Barth, *Church Dogmatics* II/1, p. 361.

of specificity to the conception of holiness, which must not be allowed to become separated even by a hair's breadth from attention to the triune God and his loving ways in the world. Aulén, for example, is quite correct to speak of holiness as God's 'unconditional majesty';[15] but his account remains wedded to an abstract notion of separation: 'That God is called the Holy One implies primarily that there is a definite line of demarcation between the divine and the merely human, and that God is God and man is man.'[16] This stands in need of correction by consideration of the directedness of God's triune holiness towards fellowship. Again, like Aulén, Brunner fails to catch the full scope of God's holiness by speaking of a 'dialectic of Holiness and Love';[17] even Martensen (whose presentation of the divine attributes contains much that is worthy of praise) assumes that in God's relation to creatures holiness indicates separation, whereas love indicates proximity: 'The holy God testifies to us in conscience, that love is not an indefinite flowing over of the nature of man into that of God, but a community of *persons*, the purity of which depends upon a strict regard being paid to the *limits* separating the one from the other.'[18] Many of the same problems arise in a theology of the divine attributes when holiness is expounded on the basis of a supposed contrast between clean and unclean, sacred and defiled, unapproachable and proximate. Thus Tillich:

> The unapproachable character of God, or the impossibility of having a relation with him in the proper sense of the word, is expressed in the word 'holiness'. God is essentially holy, and every relation to him involves the consciousness that it is paradoxical to be related to that which is holy. God cannot become an object of knowledge or a partner in action. If we speak, as we must, of the ego–thou relation between God and man, the thou embraces the ego and consequently the entire relation. ... Ultimately, it is an insult to the divine holiness to talk about God as we do of objects whose existence or non-existence can be discussed. It is an insult to the divine holiness to treat God as a partner with whom one collaborates or as a superior power whom one influences by rites and prayers. The holiness of God makes it impossible to draw him into the context of the ego-world and the subject–object correlation.

15. G. Aulén, *The Faith of the Christian Church* (London: SCM, 1954), p. 123.
16. Aulén, *The Faith of the Christian Church*, pp. 120f.
17. E. Brunner, *Dogmatics*, vol. 1 (London: Lutterworth, 1949), p. 163.
18. H. Martensen, *Christian Dogmatics* (Edinburgh: T&T Clark, 1898), p. 100.

He himself is the ground and meaning of this correlation, not an element within it.'[19]

This protest against the reification of God is, doubtless, justifiable; but it comes at cost to holiness as a mode of God's relation. Moreover, even in stating the relational character of divine holiness, it is of capital importance that the relation be conceived concretely, that is, historically and personally, on the basis of the events in which Father, Son and Spirit are at work to create and preserve fellowship. God's triune acts of relation are not simply the outworking of a prior ontology of the 'true Infinite' in which holiness transcends its own antithesis in the profane.[20] They are, irreducibly and not merely nominally, the work of the Father, the Holy One in our midst, of the Son, the Holy One of Israel, and of the Holy Spirit.

God's loving holiness is operative in the work of election. 'Blessed be the God and Father of our Lord Jesus Christ, who has blessed us in Christ with every spiritual blessing in the heavenly places, even as he chose us in him before the foundation of the world, that we should be holy and blameless before him' (Eph. 1.3f.). Election is an act of God's holiness because it is an act which segregates, that is, which marks out a specific creaturely being as the recipient of a specific blessing. In the act of election, the being of the creaturely object of election is established, in that it is demarcated from all that is not and from all other creatures who are not the recipients of this divine benefit. Election is that operation of the holiness of God in which God wills that there should be a counterpart to his consecration of himself, a further reality which is the object of his good pleasure. As God maintains himself in his self-election ('I am who I am') so also he upholds the being of the creature in his election of the human correspondent to himself. In this sense, election is a blessing for which God the Father is to be blessed, one in which the creature is dignified by appointment to be the specific being which it is. God's 'choosing' of the creature is,

    19.   P. Tillich, *Systematic Theology*, vol. 1 (Chicago: University of Chicago Press, 1951), pp. 271f.

    20.   W. Pannenberg, *Systematic Theology*, vol. 1 (Edinburgh: T&T Clark, 1991), p. 400: 'The Infinite that is merely a negation of the finite is not yet truly seen as the Infinite (as Hegel showed), for it is defined by delimitation from something else, i.e., the finite ... The Infinite is truly infinite only when it transcends its own antithesis to the finite. In this sense the holiness of God is truly infinite, for it is opposed to the profane, yet it also enters the profane world, penetrates it, and makes it holy.'

moreover, not simply the establishment of a static, invariant reality. It is appointment to active assumption of destiny in relation to God. The purpose of the will of the holy God is that we should be God's 'sons and daughters' (Eph. 1.5); his choosing has as its *telos* that we should be 'holy and blameless before him' (Eph. 1.4). And because God's holiness is active in this way, choosing the creature for participation in a specific destiny in relation to himself, then the work of holiness is at the very same time and in the very same measure a work of God's love. 'He destined us *in love*' (Eph. 1.5); and in this act of his there is operative the grace which is bestowed on us in 'the Beloved' (Eph. 1.6). Just as God's holiness *in se* cannot be conceived in isolation from his operations in consecrating creaturely being for fellowship, so also God's holiness cannot be grasped without attending to its loving extension of itself into the creaturely realm in the works of holiness which establish the creature by setting it apart for himself.

This loving 'economic' holiness is the enactment of the eternal will of 'the Father of our Lord Jesus Christ' (Eph. 1.3) and so may be appropriated to the first person of the Trinity. As the holy Father, God purposes that his holiness become actual in his loving work. The Father's will is, of course, indissolubly bound up with the persons and operations of Son and Spirit: the Father's purpose is 'set forth in Christ' (Eph. 1.9), and it is brought to completion and made an object of creaturely knowledge through the work of the Holy Spirit (Eph. 1.13f., 1.17f.). Nevertheless, there is that which is proper to the Father: the lordly determination of a holy people for himself.

God's holiness is love because it is actual in the Father's unshakeable determination that the creature should *be* and should be held in life, and thereby enact its destiny. God's loving holiness is known in the acts which mark out the creature for participation in a history with God. The counterpart to God's self-consecration is not a mere involuntary and inert quantity but a living being, destined to be God's son or daughter. The 'You shall be holy' which corresponds to 'I am holy' is not simply the indication of a state; it is a life-giving imperative which bids the creature to inhabit and act out the role to which the creature has been appointed by the Father's purpose. God is holy as the creature's Lord, and it is in just this way that he *loves* the creature, willing that the creature should exist in accordance with its created nature and so have life. God the Father is the holy one in our midst who establishes the creature for life and fellowship, and loves what he has made.

This loving holiness, setting the creature apart for the blessing of life, is an undefeated purposiveness. God will not be turned aside from 'the purpose of his will'; his holy love wills to be triumphant. Having singled the creature out, giving the creature a specific being and form and consecrating the creature for a particular history in which it will find its fulfilment, God's holiness remains at work to ensure that the end of the creature will be attained. As the holy God elects, so he is lovingly faithful to what he chooses for covenant with himself. Part of that loving faithfulness is what might be called God's 'negative' holiness (corresponding to the 'positive' holiness which wills the creature into being). This is God's holiness as opposition to and destruction of all that is unholy. The unholy is that which lies beyond the will of God. In particular, it is the absurd history of human defiance in which the creature tries to be in a way other than that which has been purposed by God. Along this path, precisely by attempting to cease to be a creature and instead to determine its own destiny, the creature undermines and destroys its own being. And to this unholiness, the holiness of God is implacably opposed. But what is meant here by 'opposition'? Everything hangs on the fact that this opposition of God to creaturely infidelity and pollution must not be extracted from the larger scope of God's loving dealings with his creatures. God's holiness figures itself in the will of the Father for the creature which is embodied in the Son's work of sin-bearing and reconciliation, and it is extended into us by the Holy Spirit's sanctification of the reconciled. Only within the terms of that wide, inclusive history can God's 'negative' holiness be understood for what it is – the love of the holy God for the creature, a love which wills that the creature be held in life and which therefore must obliterate all that thwarts the creature's entering into life and fellowship.

In its purposiveness as love, therefore, the holiness of the Father includes *jealousy*. 'I the Lord your God am a jealous God' (Exod. 20.5). God's jealousy is his creative will in its singularity and exclusiveness. But as such it is not mere self-assertion (what Brunner calls 'an active self-differentiation, the willed energy with which God asserts and maintains the fact that He is Wholly Other against all else').[21] It is the energy of God's good will with which he directs himself in all his works and ways towards us. The jealousy of the triune God is his purposiveness; it is his refusal to negotiate

---

21. Brunner, *Dogmatics*, vol. 1, p. 160.

away the creature's good by allowing the creature itself to set the terms on which it will live. The holy God overcomes and destroys all that opposes his will, and in so doing loves us. Ezekiel puts it thus: 'I will restore the fortunes of Jacob and have mercy on the whole house of Israel; and I will be jealous for my holy name' (Ezek. 39.25). The Holy One in our midst is thus the one whose holy jealousy is restorative, and whose love is operative in the eradication of wickedness so that that to which we are destined may come to be. What we are powerless to destroy – our perverted, self-destructive versions of ourselves – God himself undertakes to destroy, to the immense dismay and terror of the sinful creature, and in just this way God fulfils his purpose by protecting and upholding us. 'The burning bush ... cannot be consumed. But the unconsumed bush must burn. This bush is Israel. And the flame which burns it but does not consume it is the God of Israel, the holy God.'[22]

God's loving holiness is active in the world. It is at work in the history of holy love in which God consecrates and defends the creature. God's holy love stands between the creature and its self-destruction. This history of holy love, the economy of God's works, is *divine* history (and therefore really is holy, really loving, really the creature's rock of defence) because it is willed by God the Father, rooted in his eternal act of self-consecration. Moreover, it is a history of comprehensive scope, gathering up all of God's acts towards the creature. Yet at the centre of this all-embracing series of divine acts lies a particular history, the history of Israel, and – as the centre of the centre, so to speak – the history of Jesus, the Son of God in whom God's holy love overcomes its opposite and in whom, therefore, holiness is perfectly triumphant.

God's consecration of the creature for fellowship faces the creature's defiance. This refusal of God's benefit is both an affront to the divine majesty and a mortal threat to the creature, which can only be what it is called to be in fellowship with the holy God. In opposing God's holy purpose, the creature opposes itself and enacts its own destruction. There can, certainly, be no possibility that this opposition on the part of the creature will somehow constitute a genuine threat to the consecrating will of God. God's will is wholly antecedent, 'before the foundation of the world' (Eph. 1.4) and cannot be deflected by anything which the creature does to elude it.

22. Barth, *Church Dogmatics* II/1, p. 366.

In his love and holiness God has destined us to be his children, and
what God determines will be. But how will it be? In what way are
the purposes of the Father brought to bear on the defiant creature?

God's loving purpose of holy fellowship is accomplished in Jesus
Christ. In him there takes place definitively the consecration,
conservation and glorification of creaturely being which God the
holy Father wills. 'He destined us in love to be his sons through
Jesus Christ, according to the purpose of his will, to the praise of his
glorious grace which he freely bestowed on us in the Beloved. In
him we have redemption through his blood, the forgiveness of our
trespasses, according to the riches of his grace which he lavished
upon us' (Eph. 1.5–8). 'In him' here is a movement; it is his *coming*
to us. The holy God does not abandon his creature, but comes to us
in the person and work of the incarnate Son. God's holy will –
which we must learn to see as his will to fellowship, his
determination to consecrate the creature as part of his divine self-
consecration – is not set aside or held in abeyance when he comes to
us and enters into the creature's pollution. Quite the opposite: here
in this history, God's holy will is accomplished in love. As sin
abounds, God's determination to single out the creature for
blessing abounds all the more. It abounds in the fact that God
the Son takes flesh and dwells among us. Entering into estrangement and facing hostility, rejected by his own (those whom he
possesses with jealous love), God the Son is the embodiment of the
divine self-declaration: 'I am the Holy One in your midst' (Hos.
11.9).

In this coming, God's holiness is at work as consecrating mercy.
The Son of God, the Holy One of God as he is acclaimed in terror
by the demons (Mk 1.24), comes to the aid of the sick and sinful
and polluted creature. In its wickedness, the creature can pretend to
no claim upon the mercy of the Holy One, can hope, indeed, for
nothing other than judgement and destruction. Yet the coming of
God the Son is the fulfilment of the divine promise: 'I will not come
to destroy' (Hos. 11.9). His coming as the Holy One, that is to say,
is wholly to the creature's benefit, an act of fellowship and therefore
of blessing. In what does this blessing consist?

The Holy One takes up our cause. The creature's rejection of the
holy purpose of God leaves a void: because of sin's pollution, there
is no longer an active creaturely counterpart to God's consecrating
purpose. All that there is is the ruined creature, dead in trespasses
and sins, incapable of any act by which fellowship with God might
be restored. But in the person of his Son, the holy God himself

undertakes for the creature, acting on the creature's behalf and in the creature's place, both representative and substitute. His history enfolds our own within itself, consecrating us as it were from within our accursed existence. He assumes our evil situation in all its squalor and deprivation, making it his own. 'For our sake [God] made him to be sin' (2 Cor. 5.21). The blessing of the creature purposed by the holy Father is effected precisely in the fact that Jesus Christ, the Holy One who 'knew no sin', becomes the sin-bearer. He carries our sin, and so does indeed bear God's holy wrath against our pollution. But this pouring out and receiving of divine wrath by God himself in his unified work as Father and Son is not simply a destructive act, an eradication. The negative work of exclusion only has meaning within the creative and loving work of God's holiness, which is to confirm the creature in life. In the person of his Son, the holy God destroys sin in order that what he wills from all eternity – a people for himself – will come to full fruition.

'Our great God and Saviour Jesus Christ ... gave himself for us to redeem us from all iniquity and to purify for himself a people of his own who are zealous for good deeds' (Tit. 2.13f.). That is God's holiness operative as love. God the Son 'gave himself', entering the situation of human ruin in love and grace. He did this 'for us', in order to bless, restore and bring the creature to its proper glory in the purpose of God. In so doing 'he redeemed us from all iniquity' and 'purified' us, separating us from the world of unrighteousness and unholiness which we had made for ourselves and which poisoned our well-being. And acting in this way in holy love, he re-established the divine purpose, bringing into being a consecrated people, purifying 'for himself a people of his own' who are characterized above all by zeal for holiness of life.

This, then, is the second moment of God's holy love: God the Son re-establishing the creature's cause, holiness operative in reconciling love. This is the centre of the centre. Like the Father's work of election which it effects, the Son's work of reconciliation is complete in itself, requiring no creaturely element as a cooperating cause. If it were otherwise, then reconciliation would not be *mercy*, for it would require of the creature what the creature simply cannot be and do. Election and reconciliation are both alike perfect. But in that very perfection they are full of transformative power. Their perfection – their character as a wholly achieved work of grace – is an *inclusive* perfection, a perfection whose glory includes the glorification of the creature. Election and reconciliation are not a closed circle; they are the acts of the holy love of God, and so they stretch out towards their goal, which is the fulfilment of God's self-consecration by the consecration of creatures for fellowship with himself. And they do this in the third work of God's holy love, the work of the Holy Spirit.

The Holy Spirit completes the trajectory of God's self-sanctification in the sanctification of the creature, in that the Spirit is the 'perfecting cause' of creaturely reality. The Spirit, that is, is the agent of those divine acts through which the creature really does become in full integrity what it is destined to be. The Spirit gives *life*, acting in and upon the creature in such a way that the creature attains its full stature, filling out its history in completion of the divine purpose. This gift of life is also the gift of holiness, as the Spirit makes actual and effective in the creature the blessing for which the creature has been lovingly singled out and reconciled. That blessing is fellowship between the holy God and his holy people.

No less than the works of election and reconciling grace, the work of the Spirit is a work of God's holy majesty. The Spirit is *holy* because he is intrinsic to God's self-consecration, not merely a force in the economy. With Father and Son, the Spirit is within the sphere of deity; he is Lord, and only as such is he the lifegiver. In his work in and upon the creature, the Spirit is no mere immanent principle, a cause which disappears into that of which it is the cause. As the Holy Spirit of God he is incomparable; besides him, there is no spirit who is holy. Furthermore, the Spirit's work is inseparable from the works of Father and Son. As the work of the Father looks ahead to reconciliation and sanctification, and as the work of the Son gathers up election and points to perfection, so also the work of the Spirit completes what has been willed by the Father and effected by the Son. The sanctifying work of the Spirit is not a 'new' divine work in the sense that it might be thought to complete what has been left unfinished by the Son of God. The holiness of the church and of the Christian rest on the sufficiency of Christ. It is the office of the Holy Spirit to extend this sufficiency as the agent through whom it stretches out in its power. 'You were washed, you were sanctified, you were justified in the name of the Lord Jesus Christ and in the Spirit of our God' (1 Cor. 6.11): the 'and' here is consequential, the Spirit's work being the full effectiveness of the 'name' (the enacted identity) of Jesus Christ who in this as in all things is to be acknowledged as Lord. But at the same time this 'consequence' is not accidental but utterly necessary; without it, washing, sanctification, justification – the entire alteration of the creature's situation before God – would not be present as determinations of creaturely existence. That they are so present is to be explained only by confession of this third work of the holy God.

The Spirit generates a form of human life which corresponds to election and reconciliation. An adequate dogmatic description of that form of life would require a full account of ecclesiology and of sanctification, as well as an ethics of holiness. Here we may only hint that undergirding such an account of the active common life of the *sanctorum communio* and of the individual saint in Christ must be the work of the Spirit in establishing fellowship with God. Fellowship with God is, crucially, not only status or appointment but history and task. Those who are 'sanctified in Christ Jesus' are in the very same movement 'called to be saints' (1 Cor. 1.2). The sanctifying Spirit singles out and empowers the creature for active holiness, and this active holiness is 'partnership with God'. This does not, of course, mean that by the Spirit the saints are made into cooperating or supplementary agents alongside God. To speak in such terms erodes the proper distinction between the creature and its Lord in a way which both takes away from the creator's sovereignty and robs the creature of its genuine creaturely integrity. Over against this, the partnership with God which the Holy Spirit bestows is a fellowship in which the creature is consecrated *as creature*, called to hallow God's name by echoing in its creaturely acts the great divine act of self-consecration. Sanctification is not a matter of participation in God's work but rather of the restoration of creaturely vocation. The Holy Spirit makes creatures holy and therefore makes them human. And in that is fulfilled the love of God for what he has made for himself.

With this we complete this sketch of the movement of God's holy love, *in se* and *propter nos homines et propter nostram salutem*. It is all, doubtless, well known to the colleague whose Christian courage and theological testimony we celebrate today. For the inseparability of holiness and love is one of the many clarifications which his theology offers to church and theology, and for which we are in his debt.[23] When it is in its right mind, theology counts among its tasks

---

23. See, for example, *Gottes Klarheiten*, p. 116: 'God's holiness is so closely related to, indeed immanent within ... the event of his δόξα that it is to be understood as a characteristic of δόξα itself *in all its concretions*. The clarities of truth,

the service of the worship of the saints. At the centre of that
worship is a cry of praise: *sanctus sanctus sanctus, Dominus Deus
Sabaoth*, a cry which may form a fitting summary of what has been
suggested here. God is the thrice Holy One, endlessly moving and at
perfect rest in full and limitless glory. And as this one he is the Lord
of hosts, the one who has purposed from all eternity to make the
common life of his holy people into his dwelling place, and who acts
as saviour and sanctifier to come to his people's aid and, in bringing
many to glory, to glorify himself.

> There is a river whose streams make glad the city of God,
> The holy habitation of the Most High.
> God is in the midst of her, she shall not be moved;
> God will help her right early.
> The nations rage, the kingdoms totter;
> He utters his voice, the earth melts.
> The Lord of hosts is with us,
> The God of Jacob is our refuge. (Ps. 46.4–7)

love, power and eternity can thus be regarded in every way as *holy clarities*. Christian
talk about God has anchored this irrevocably in its concept of God by confessing
God to be the *Holy* Spirit.'

6

PROLEGOMENA TO CHRISTOLOGY: FOUR THESES

I

Antecedently present in his effulgent majesty as the eternal Son of God, Jesus Christ is known by virtue of the movement of his being in which as Lord and reconciler he freely gives himself to be known by us, and not otherwise.

In Christology, at least, the method may not be arbitrary, for Christology is determined in a fundamental way by the fact that its 'object', that towards which its attention is turned and by which it is led, is the personal presence of Jesus Christ. Jesus Christ is present; his identity is not simply past. His identity, that is, is not located in a temporally remote sphere, nor is it 'finished' in the sense that it can be docketed as a closed, achieved reality which does not initiate active encounter with us, but possesses only the passivity of a past reality which we summon into our presence. He is and is present. Jesus Christ's identity as one who is present to us is, of course, inseparable from his past, a past which has a definite, unalterable sequence and shape, summarized in the church's confession through the key moments of birth, suffering, crucifixion, death, burial, resurrection and ascension. But, as the last two events in that sequence indicate, the trajectory of Jesus Christ's identity stretches inexorably into the present, his past being gathered into his present identity as one who cannot truthfully be spoken of only in the past tense. His past is not mere contingency, but an integral part of his identity as the one who was and is and is to come. He is risen from the dead; and his resurrection is not simply a retrospective declaration – an indication, perhaps, of the unity of purpose between Jesus and his heavenly Father signalling the Father's vindication of his cause – but rather the actuality of his participation in the aliveness and comprehensive presence of God. Moreover, as the present one Jesus Christ is not absent. His temporal 'presentness', that is, is not only actual in a sphere remote from us. He is our contemporary, not in the sense that his time as it were runs parallel to ours in some other region but does not enter into our own and remains inaccessible, but in the sense that he is *with* us. Risen from the dead, he ascended into heaven and sits at the Father's right hand in glory. But though his presence is no longer in bodily fashion, he is not thereby separated from us: ascension and enthronement are not mere withdrawal, but express the lordly freedom with which he enters into relation with and, indeed, freely binds himself to those to whom he presents himself in the power of the Holy Spirit.

The 'matter' of Christology is this present one. How is his presence to be characterized? He is present *antecedently*. His presence precedes our self-presence, and fashions it into a counter-part to itself. That is, the presence of Christ is not an extension or modification of our presence to ourselves; it is not some presence-to-hand towards which we are entitled to dispose ourselves as we will. The presence of Christ is divine self-presence, and as such becomes a human present autonomously, in spontaneous fulfilment of its own determination, by virtue of the action of the Holy Spirit, and not by human acts of projection or reconstruction. Accordingly, our presence to ourselves is not a stable and settled disposition of ourselves by which all other presences are measured, and before which Jesus Christ may be summoned to appear as a further object for our attention. It is 'eschatological': our human self-presence is a function of the fact that as Jesus Christ presents himself to us in the Spirit's power, he creates a human present as the auxiliary of his presence, overcoming our pretended self-sufficiency, and making us into the new creatures of God who confess that he is before them. The paradigm of his antecedent presence as the risen one is thus the effortless, unfettered and wholly effective coming of Jesus Christ: 'Jesus came and stood among them' (Jn 20.26).

Jesus Christ is present as God is present, and so *present in his effulgent majesty as the eternal Son of God*. As the *eternal* Son, he is not Son by adoption or annexation, drawn into the life of the godhead from outside and ennobled, but ingredient within the immanent life of God. No less than the Father, he is in the beginning; were he not, the Father would not be who he is. The Son is God from God, light from light, sharing in the substance of the Father, and so fittingly praised as God. He does not merely symbolize God or present a particular concentration of the divine presence; he is divine person and agent, to be confessed as Lord. As such he is God's *only* Son. His sonship is wholly unique: he does not exemplify some more general relation of creatures to God, but as the 'only-begotten' Son of the Father he is distinguished from all creatures because his origin lies wholly within the inner life of the godhead; 'begotten of his Father before all worlds', he is the repetition of the being of God, antecedently God's Son. As true God and only Son of the Father, in short, he is Lord, intrinsic to the divine essence, sharing in its might, majesty, dominion and power. And for this reason the Son is – as the *Te Deum Laudamus* puts it – *venerandus*, worthy of all worship, the fit object of the creature's praise of God because he shares in the eternal glory of the divine nature.

The presence of this one is his presence in *effulgent majesty*. It is a majestic presence, because in his presence he is and acts as one who is infinitely superior, disposing himself in utter liberty. As he comes to us, he does not place himself in our hands, ontologically or noetically; he cannot be converted into a function of our intention, thought or action, but comes as the one he is, in boundless majesty. His presence, though it is real, reliable and constant and not merely asymptotic, has the character of proximity, of a coming to be near rather than of that which can be held and manipulated.[1] Yet this majestic presence is not dark, something whose form we cannot discern. It is radiant; in it the divine glory is manifest (Heb. 1.3; 2 Cor. 4.4). God is in himself glorious and therefore resplendent. His glory is not self-enclosed but self-diffusing, a light which, because it is *light*, sheds itself abroad, freely and majestically imparting and disclosing itself. The presence of Jesus Christ is this divine effulgence: radiant presence, presence which enlightens and so establishes knowledge of itself.

Once again, this radiance may be characterized more closely. The light which Jesus Christ is, his effulgent majesty, is not simply a state but an action and *movement*. In his majesty as the eternal Son, he is not inert and passive, resting in a separate and secluded glory. Rather, the majesty of Jesus Christ is known in and as the action or movement in which he imparts himself. He himself moves towards

---

1.   In this connection, Hans Frei's worry that talk of the presence of Christ – at least in its nineteenth-century idealist exposition – almost inevitably subjects Christ to the believer to whom he is present might be countered by a more dogmatically robust articulation of the freedom of Christ's presence – something which Frei's alternative concept of 'identity' does not fully succeed in doing because of its formality. See H. Frei, *The Identity of Jesus Christ* (Philadelphia: Fortress Press, 1975), pp. vii–x.

us; he *comes* to us; his being is a being-in-coming which is equiprimordially a being-in-giving. This movement is the movement of the one who is *Lord*. It is a free movement, not an action under constraint; in his self-bestowal, Jesus Christ does not give himself away. To be accosted by this movement of his presence is not to encounter an accidental reality, a process wholly within the economy of human temporal causality and sequence, but rather to encounter that which is the fulfilment in time of the eternal resolve of God. The origin, energy and mobility of this movement all derive from the divine purpose which is 'set forth in Christ' (Eph. 1.9), and so that which is to be discerned in Christ's presence is 'the purpose of him who accomplishes all things according to the counsel of his will' (Eph. 1.11). Further, this movement is the movement of one who is *reconciler*. The particular path of this movement, that is, is one along which the Lord faces and overcomes the creature's opposition. As he moves along this path, he directs himself to the evil reality of creaturely defiance and repudiation of the human vocation to live in the presence of God, defiance and opposition which trap the creature in ignorance and idolatry. The presence of Jesus Christ as reconciler simply abolishes this human hostility; it outbids it by its sheer radiance, scattering the darkness and restoring creatures to fellowship, and so to knowledge.

In sum: the movement of the being of Jesus Christ is presence, radiance, reconciling self-bestowal. In this movement is the *Sache* of Christology. What are the consequences of this for the knowledge of Christ and therefore for the manner in which the Christological task is to be approached? Our proposition states it in these terms: *Jesus Christ is known by virtue of the movement of his being, and not otherwise.*

Knowledge of Jesus Christ flows from the movement of his self-presentation which we have just described in summary form. What is the fundamental ground of the knowledge of Jesus Christ? The judgement of some dominant strands of modern theology has been that knowledge of Jesus Christ is subject to a dynamic which is immanent to the human knower, and which can be formulated in general, content-neutral principles of human cognition. Christology is therefore to be preceded by an epistemology, a hermeneutics or a phenomenology of human knowing and interpreting as modes of being in the world. If such a procedure is Christologically problematic, it is because it entails a basic compromise of the character of the object of Christology: it cannot be shown to be fully coherent with the church's confession that Jesus Christ is

Lord. If Christology is erected on this basis, that is, at some point or other there will become visible the fact that this strategy regards the knowing or interpreting human subject as the *fundamentum inconcussum veritatis*. This coheres ill with intellectual deference to the lordly movement of Jesus Christ's own being, since it involves a fatal exchange of subjects in which knowledge of his presence is subordinated to the conditions of the knower. Tucked inside this strategy there is often an assumption about creaturely competence in the matter of knowledge of Christ. This may be a prideful assumption that Jesus Christ, like everything else, is subject to the dictates of universal reason, or it may be a very insecure and anxious assumption that we can rely on nothing other than our fragile selves. But both pride and fear construe acts of knowledge as lying outside the sphere of Christ's lordship; and it is precisely into this construal that Christology must at all costs not betray itself. The lordship of Christ is his non-comparable, self-grounded and axiomatic sovereignty. In the matter of the knowledge of himself, the corollary of his lordship is that there is no access to him other than that which he himself affords. If there were any such access, if parallel to the movement of his self-presence there were a creaturely movement which could anticipate, evoke or even compel Christ's appearance, then Christ would no longer be Lord, for he is not Lord if he is not the agent of his own becoming known. This is simply the extension of the principle *solus Christus* to the *ordo cognoscendi*. In formal terms, what is spoken of here is 'revelation'. But to speak of revelation is to indicate how knowledge of Jesus Christ is rooted in the teleology of his being, his turning to us in which he is known, not because we can draw him into our sphere but because he himself reaches out, anticipating us by being already on the way to us as the risen one in the Spirit's power. Only he can do this; only he has authority and competence to establish knowledge of himself; and only he has the mercy and the determination to act with such authority and competence. Moreover, to speak of revelation is at the same time to speak of reconciliation. Revelation is a term for Jesus Christ's merciful outreach in which he creates fellowship with lost sinners, and 'revealed' knowledge is that knowledge which occurs in the course of the reconciliation of sinners to whom it has been given to perceive the glorious self-movement of the reconciler.

As a result of this free, gracious movement of his, Jesus Christ is *known by us*. He bestows himself, bridging the gulf (historical,

moral, experiential) between himself and us, and thereby granting a
specific permission and establishing a specific prohibition.

The permission is permission to know him. Knowledge of Jesus
Christ is possible and legitimate because of his antecedent,
gratuitous and utterly real self-presence. Setting himself forth,
expounding himself as the present one who encloses and orders all
things, Jesus Christ makes himself known, and thereby excludes the
possibility of legitimate, well-founded ignorance of himself. He is,
and therefore he is present, and therefore he is known. There is a
negative inference to be drawn here, namely that this given presence
of Christ excludes ways of approaching the task of Christology in
which there lurks the assumption that Jesus Christ is not, or may
not or cannot be present to us. Jesus Christ's givenness sits ill with,
for example, those Christologies which make historical scepticism
or probabilistic reasoning into the first principle of the knowledge
of Christ. More seriously, it cannot be made to cohere with ascetical
or negative Christologies which so fear making Jesus Christ into a
possessed object that he is pushed into extreme transcendence.
Scruples along these lines may be motivated ethically (a desire to
counter ideological abuse of a theology of Christ's presence) or
metaphysically (a desire to extract Christology from ontotheology).
But the diagnosis is incorrect, in that it assumes that the Christian
confession of *Christus praesens* is an instance of a degenerate
ideology or ontology; and the cure – an assertion of the elusiveness
of Christ as the first principle of Christology – kills the patient.

Jesus Christ can be known, and known *by us*. The knowledge
which is authorized by the self-presence of Jesus Christ is a genuine
human knowing. What his risen presence creates are forms of
thought and speech which are a human counterpart to his self-
declaration. The gift of his presence is thus not simply an utterly
objective and self-enclosed *perfectum*, but a matter for human
knowing and language. Alongside and in strict subordination to
'revelation' there is 'revealedness', the human fruit of the Spirit's
regeneration of the work of creaturely knowing in which Christ is
not only glimpsed from afar but also genuinely known by those
whom he illuminates with his presence. Because this creaturely
work can at no point be considered in abstraction from the work of
the Spirit, it has a particular character; both the identity of the
knower and the activities of knowing are transformed as they are
subject to the Spirit's realization of the regenerative work of Christ.
This knowing and its human subjects are in Christ, and therefore
they are a new creation. Their newness is especially visible in that

the knowledge of Christ which the Spirit realizes is not an act of *positing* but of *confession*. There is certainly a genuinely human knowing which can properly be characterized as a knowing *by us*. But 'by us' does not entail 'put forward by us': we are not authorized or competent to make any such proposal, once again because that which is the matter of our knowing is Jesus Christ's reality as Lord, the one whose majesty and spontaneous freedom wholly precede us. The deity which is his and in which he presents himself to us is antecedent (otherwise it would not be deity). As such, it cannot be ascribed to him, perhaps as the fruit of some process of theological deduction; nor can it be an evaluation of him reached as the terminus of a consideration of his moral or experiential impact. He is Lord, and therefore knowledge of him is underivable from anything other than his own being and action. But this does not disqualify knowledge of him as authentic human knowledge; it simply specifies it as confession – as an act of hearing, obedience and allegiance in which the church bows before the presence of the one by whom it has been found, and gives voice to his sheer prevenience.

In the sphere of reality whose resplendent centre is Jesus Christ himself, God the Father has willed a knowledge of the Son of God which God the Holy Spirit has effected. The God of our Lord Jesus, the Father of glory, has given to his church a spirit of wisdom and of revelation in the knowledge of him (cf. Eph. 1.17). This permission carries with it a prohibition: the fact that *Jesus Christ is known by virtue of the movement of his being* entails *not otherwise*. The fact that in the Spirit's power Jesus Christ gives himself to be known in this way, creating this very specific reality and the corresponding capacity, entails an exclusiveness of access. The rule by which Christology must be governed is: he is Lord in the knowledge of his lordship, and can therefore be known only as he moves towards us. Only as the one he is and in the movement of his being can he be known. Because he is who he is, and because he acts as he acts in his majestic self-presentation, he cannot be 'sought'. That is, he cannot be approached as if he were an elusive figure, absent from us, locked in transcendence or buried in the past, and only to be discovered through the exercise of human ingenuity. Christology cannot creep up on him and catch him unawares. Nor is it at liberty to decide that his self-presence is so indefinite or fogged over by the distortions and incapacities of his human witnesses that theology must run its own independent checks in order to reassure itself that he really is able to present himself. All such strategies, whether in biblical scholarship or philosophical and dogmatic theology, are in the end methodologically sophisticated forms of infidelity. Their assumption is that he is not present unless demonstrably present – present, that is, to undisturbed and unconverted reason. But to such demonstration he will not yield the mystery of his person.

II

'God sets among men a fact which speaks for itself.'[2] We may sum up what has been indicated so far by saying that, as there is a sphere of reality over which Jesus Christ presides as the enthroned Lord who is before all things and in whom all things hold together, so there is also a sphere of knowledge of him. He establishes that sphere in the act of his self-bestowal; his reconciling presence sets aside the estrangement and hostility of mind of corrupt creatures, and brings into existence a place in which he makes himself known. The knowledge which he creates is legitimate; it is not wholly imperilled by the vacillation and pride of all human projects, but calmly, soberly and lawfully constituted as true, reliable knowledge of Christ. Its legitimacy, truth and reliability do not derive from its human subjects (whether in the form of epistemological sophistication, critical awareness, historical learning or experiential finesse), but solely from the turning of Jesus Christ. That movement of his being is always gracious; it cannot be arrested, or considered to be a movement which is complete and can be set behind us. As a consequence, there is always a measure of human insecurity in this knowledge. But what is humanly fragile is divinely secure, authoritative and lawful, because of the self-giving of Jesus Christ. In that movement of his, he is supremely indifferent to human ignorance, unbelief and anxiety; he does not remain at a distance or keep silence, but he simply comes and speaks (cf. Mt. 28.18), declaring the promise which is the unshakeable basis of knowledge of himself: 'I am with you always' (Mt. 28.20). Before proceeding to discuss the character of the sphere of the knowledge of Christ – the sphere of the church and, more particularly, of the church's hearing of Holy Scripture – we pause to consider the consequences of the cognitive ground of Christology for the understanding of the Christological task as positive science.

2.   K. Barth, *Church Dogmatics* IV/2 (Edinburgh: T&T Clark, 1961), p. 221.

Within the sphere of knowledge established by Jesus Christ's self-bestowal, Christology is a joyful and reverent positive science whose prolegomena perform a didactic but not demonstrative task.

Christology is a positive science, in that it is the repetition, elucidation and explication in human words and concepts of the axiomatic reality of Jesus Christ. Because of this, Christology may not proceed as *a priori* inquiry into the creaturely conditions for knowledge of Jesus Christ: such inquiry cannot but subvert Christology's attention to its object by treating it as a possible state of affairs, so holding at bay its lordly actuality. Rather, as a positive science the task of Christology is *a posteriori* depiction of that which has been given. Certainly both terms, 'positive' and 'science', are stretched when deployed in a Christological context. This *positum* has its own determinate character as the presence and action of Jesus Christ in which by the power of the Holy Spirit he sheds abroad the knowledge of his reconciling person and work. His 'givenness' is not that of a worldly entity but of a history of willed divine activity: only in this sense is Christology positive. Moreover, this givenness determines the mode of *scientia* which is appropriate to itself: the operations of Christological science are at every point determined by the lordly movement of Christ, and Christology will always in some way struggle against the confines of existing conceptions of science. Christology is a special science of a special object. However, the designation 'positive science' can still serve to indicate how in the circle of knowledge established by reconciliation and revelation, questions of the existence and availability of its *Sache* have already received an answer in the church's confession of the mystery of Christ's presence.

Christology is a *joyful and reverent* science. Such terms are not merely accidental descriptions of the subjective states of its practitioners; rather, they identify Spirit-generated dispositions which are properly 'objective', that is, fitting and necessary if the work of theological reason is to act in conformity to its given matter. Joy and reverence are not simply ways of talking of the atmosphere of piety in which Christological thought is undertaken. They determine the operations of theology in a direct way, shaping its procedures by enabling it to construe its object appropriately, to adopt a proper posture before that object, to pursue certain modes of activity and to refrain from others, to articulate goals, and to establish criteria by which judgements of adequacy can be made.

Christology is a *joyful* science because thought and speech about Jesus Christ really are made possible by his presence. Finding itself in the sphere of knowledge which he brings into being and maintains, Christology is not harassed by anxious scruple. It is not, for example, overwhelmed by concerns that talk of 'presence' can slide into all manner of idolatry, or that it may be tied to a leaden metaphysics of substance, or that it requires some foundation other than that of the sheer self-presentation of Christ as Lord. Christology can be joyful in the face of these anxieties, not because it fails to register that there are real threats to its purity, still less because it considers itself amply equipped to overcome them. Christology's joy derives instead from the fact that it is undertaken in the sphere of Christ's presence and promise. Only in abstraction from that sphere does Christian thought and speech seem a joyless task, condemned to an unending search for reassurances which can never be had in the manner in which they are sought. Yet the joy which is to characterize positive Christological science is *reverent* joy: not brash confidence but the astonished gratitude of the reconciled at the goodness of the one into whose presence they have been called. Joy may be displaced not only by anxiety or irony, but also by a very human and ungodly assertion (orthodox or unorthodox) which replaces the spiritual *positum* of the presence of Christ. A Christology in which this is the case will betray lack of reverence, because it will be forgetful of the movement of mercy which is its founding condition and constant accompaniment. If Christology is to guard itself at this point, however, it will not do so by adopting more strategies of self-inspection, more mechanisms to regulate trust. What is required is a certain spiritual vigilance, that fear of the Lord which fastens on the very specific calling and hope given to theology by the presence of Christ, and which looks to him not only to judge but also to sanctify and perfect its work.

In the light of this characterization of the positive science of Christology, what is to be said of the task of formal prolegomena? Positive Christology requires no prolegomenal demonstration of its viability, because what such a work of demonstration seeks to achieve is already accomplished by its object, Jesus Christ himself in his lordly self-demonstration.

In more detail: Jesus Christ is comprehensively Lord and therefore Lord in the knowledge of his lordship. Because of this, Christology proceeds illegitimately if it attempts to deduce Jesus Christ as a conclusion from some premise other than his own luminous reality, from something supposedly anterior to him and more firmly established or evident. Jesus Christ is only and always the beginning, not the end, of a process of thought; his reality is analytic, not synthetic; basic, and never derivative. Thought and speech about him may not be set within some more comprehensive context or considered from some higher vantage-point – a theory of history or religion, some sort of philosophical theism, an ethics of justice. He is not a conclusion to be drawn from some other reality; we cannot look behind him to discover something more fundamental. Christology, therefore, does not labour towards him, but moves easily and freely in the light of the fact that he has already posited himself and established the sphere in which he can be known.

Accordingly, prolegomena conceived as independent *demonstratio* of the reality of Jesus Christ is not a defence of him but a narrowing of the range of his effectiveness, even, perhaps, a covert attack on his sovereignty. To defend his majestic self-presence by some prolegomenal strategies is to risk standing against the free clarity, power and truth of his giving of himself, by acting as if we had competence to tender our assistance to complete his self-manifestation and render it persuasive. Why press this point? The ground for this refusal of prolegomenal demonstration is not a principled rejection of apologetics or foundations: theology is unlikely to be served by over-interest in such issues of general epistemology. What calls into question independent demonstration of positive Christological science is not epistemological theory but an ontological matter: Jesus Christ is the embodiment of the divine omnipotence. He has no ground of reality except in himself, the Son who proceeds from the Father; and there is, therefore, no ground of the knowledge of him except his own spontaneous and effective self-exposition in the Holy Spirit. Put formally: the law of thinking must be the law of the object. The object is 'law' in that it is a formed and self-communicative reality, an authoritative presence which commands, empowers and directs our acts of recognition. Prolegomenal demonstration subjects that object to an alien law (epistemological, phenomenological, metaphysical). In so doing, it has to evade the fact that the object of Christology is, indeed, *in se* formed, self-communicative, authoritative and present, and has to operate as if form, communication, authority and presence were bestowed on Jesus Christ by a reality more fundamental than himself. This a well-ordered Christology will not allow.

In this light, Christological prolegomena has a more modest, *didactic* task. Its aim is to outline basic characteristics of

Christological thought and speech, and to indicate something of the requirements under which Christology stands by virtue of its subject matter. In an important sense, it is retrospective, in that it seeks to draw attention to that which is already established, namely Christ in his self-demonstration, and to trace what that self-demonstration entails for the intellectual activity of Christology. Its limited concern is with the character and modes of operation of Christology in the face of the given reality under whose tutelage it stands. It is a low-level undertaking, presenting a preliminary map of the Christological terrain and offering guidance on how best to move through it. It orients Christology to the nature of its object (Jesus Christ's majestic self-communication); it indicates the sphere of his presence in the fellowship of the saints; and it identifies the instrument of his self-communication (Holy Scripture) and speaks of the manner in which that constitutes the norms of Christological thought and speech. In this way it serves orderly instruction. Beyond this – in prefacing Christology by some pre-theological discussion of methods, norms and sources, or in articulating a better rationale for confession of Christ than that known to the confession itself – it will be reluctant to go.

III

Christology is a positive science in the church, the fellowship of the saints which knows Jesus Christ.

Christology is church science, the orderly explication of the knowledge of Jesus Christ which is already present in the church because Jesus Christ is present to the church. It has, therefore, a twofold 'positivity'. It is a positive science because of its object, Jesus Christ, who presents himself to the church in lordly freedom. But it is also a positive science because, as Jesus Christ presents himself by the power of the Holy Spirit, he posits a sphere in which he can be and is known. As he presents himself, he establishes a domain and gathers a community which he authorizes and empowers for knowledge of himself. Theology is the positive science of that fellowship.

These two aspects of the positivity of Christology – that which derives from its object, and that which derives from its social locale – exist in strict and irreversible sequence. Christology is positive church science because and only because it is the positive science of Jesus Christ; its churchly positivity is wholly derivative from the positivity which it has by virtue of its object. This is so for two reasons. (1) The churchly positivity of theology is not an instance of a general rule that *scientia* is always embedded within particular forms of common life. Application of this rule has been standard in criticism of modern ideals of universal reason and their purported elision of the local or traditional character of rational practices; as such, it has often found a welcome from those who have sought to recover the churchly character of theological work. One of the weaknesses into which these theologies may be betrayed, however, is that of slipping into an immanentist ecclesiology in which churchly positivity far outweighs Christological positivity. Appealing to general principles of sociality, the accounts of churchly existence which are produced are often only secondarily theological. Frequently lacking in much by way of direct deployment of language of Jesus Christ's self-presentation, and frequently giving prominence to the historical visibility of the church, they construe the churchly positivity of theology primarily in terms of its existence within this social domain. This is often coupled with a view of the church as a stable, consistent set of practices which it is the task of theology to describe. But the church is not simply a visible form of common life: as the fellowship of the saints it is in a very important sense 'invisible', that is, visible and knowable only by virtue of the act of Christ's eschatological self-presence in the Spirit. Only as such is it a *positum*, and only as the science of such a community is Christology a positive churchly science. (2) The churchly positivity of Christology does not entail a claim that Jesus Christ attains to wholeness of being in the sphere of the church, or that the church bodies forth or completes him. Such a claim is both Christologically and ecclesiologically inadequate. Its Christological inadequacy is that only with difficulty can it cohere with a sense that Jesus Christ is *a se*, and that he is an ontological *perfectum*. It construes his giving of himself to the church as in some way his generating of himself. His sufficiency, his majestic repose at the Father's right hand in which he is head over all things, is not easily coordinated with any affirmation of the coinherence of Christ and the church. Certainly he is 'head over all things for the church' (Eph. 1.22); certainly the church is his 'body' and 'fullness' (Eph. 1.23): but always and only because of his immanent and sovereign power as the one who 'fills all in all', who alone is properly and in himself 'fullness'. Furthermore, the ecclesiological inadequacy of talk of the church as bodying forth Christ is that its expansiveness misconstrues the character of the church as *creatura verbi divini*, failing to catch the passivity of the church's existence as elect fellowship, called, justified and made holy for praise, confession and testimony. That is, any account of churchly positivity has to respect the fundamental ontological law of the church, namely that as God's 'workmanship' (Eph. 2.20), the church is what it is by virtue of 'the immeasurable greatness of his power in us who believe' (Eph. 1.19).

With this qualification, we turn to explicate how it is that Christology is church science.

First, the church of Jesus Christ is the fellowship of the saints, the holy church. The church's holiness is its election by God. Holiness is not a property which the church has in and of itself, but a relation into which it has been adopted, and a summons which it is called to obey. The church's holiness is alien: it is holy, not because of any inherent worth or dignity, or on the basis of moral or religious performance, but because of the absolution which it has received from the work and word of Christ. He makes the church holy, calling it into fellowship with himself, cleansing it from its sins by his death and resurrection, and through the Spirit uniting it to himself so that it becomes the gathering of those who are 'saints in Christ Jesus' (cf. Eph. 5.25b–27). The church's holiness consists, therefore, in the fact that it is set apart by the triune God. By the will of God the Father, the church is destined to live in holiness – from all eternity, 'before the foundation of the world', the church is chosen to be 'holy and blameless' (Eph. 1.4). The Father's will is acted out in the saving mission of God the Son, in whom the holy church has 'redemption' and 'forgiveness' (Eph. 1.7). And the church is renewed in holiness by the action of God the Holy Spirit, whose work it is to bestow God's life upon 'the saints who are also faithful in Christ Jesus' (Eph. 1.1). Holiness is thus the gift of the Holy Trinity. It is precisely this which prohibits theology from developing an account of the church's life (and of the churchly character of its Christology) primarily in terms of its visible sociality, for the fellowship of the saints is first of all vertical, and only by derivation horizontal; the saints' *koinonia* is defined by its object (Jesus Christ in his active self-presence) and only thereafter by the co-presence of social actors.

Second, this fellowship of the saints is, *inter alia*, a sphere of knowledge. The acts of the Holy Trinity in electing, reconciling and sanctifying the community continue in the work of enlightening the church about the truth of its existence. The church is therefore a fellowship in which it makes good sense to pray 'that the God of our Lord Jesus Christ, the Father of glory, may give you a spirit of

wisdom and of revelation in the knowledge of him, having the eyes
of your hearts enlightened, that you may know ...' (Eph. 1.17f.).
The saints' knowledge may variously be described. It is (1) a triune
work. It is not the hesitant or bold self-reflection of the community,
but knowledge which must be talked about by speaking of the God
of our Lord Jesus Christ, the Father of glory and the Spirit who
bestows understanding. Such knowledge is, therefore, (2) knowledge by gift. It is Spirit-derived wisdom, the fruit of revelation and
enlightenment in which human folly, ignorance and darkness are set
aside in order that the church may know. And it is (3) knowledge
which has a definite object, namely the condition in which the
church stands. It is knowledge of 'the hope to which he has called
you ... the riches of his glorious inheritance in the saints, and ...
the immeasurable greatness of his power in us who believe'
(Eph. 1.18f.). It is not exploratory or arbitrary knowledge, but
the cognitive repetition of the divine work which engenders and
upholds the church. In a culture for which historical process is
axiomatic, the immediacy of the way in which Ephesians describes
the church as a sphere of knowledge is startling. Are we committed
thereby to describing the saints' knowledge of Christ as somehow
'pure' – non-contingent, unsullied by time and the processes of
learning, segregated from other spheres and acts of knowing, simply
given? The commitment of a good deal of historical theology to
deny that the church's knowledge of Christ is uncontaminated has
certainly sometimes been a wholesome affirmation that creaturely
knowledge of Christ is just that – *creaturely*, and therefore not
independent of creaturely modes of reception. But more needs to be
said: the church's knowledge of Christ, because it is the knowledge
of the *holy* church, of the saints, is a sphere in which human
knowing is in transformation. It is not simply caught up in the tide
of human process, but is also set under the sign of Christ's victory.
That victory includes his victory in the sphere of knowledge. In him,
there is given to the saints not an indefinite word overlain with all
manner of accretions, but 'the word of truth' (Eph. 1.13). And
because of him, the apostle's prayer 'that you may know'
(Eph. 1.18; cf. Col. 1.10) is a prayer which looks towards a very
real possibility, one for which the saints are authorized and
empowered, and one under whose promise the work of Christology
is to be undertaken.

IV

As an exercise of sanctified reason in the fellowship of the saints, Christology assists in the Spirit's work of edifying the church by orderly explication of the knowledge of Christ which is already present in the church because he himself is present to the church. Jesus Christ is present to the church as the Word of God. As the eternal divine Word he is in himself eloquent, and he now addresses himself to the church, setting himself in the midst of the fellowship of the saints clothed with his gospel. The instruments of his self-presentation as Word are Holy Scripture and the sacraments. Through these creaturely auxiliaries he bears witness to himself and so edifies the community. The theological work of the church has a particular relation to the canon of Scripture, because through Holy Scripture Christ exercises his governance of the church's intellectual acts, moulding the saints' thought and speech into conformity with himself by reproving invention and arbitrariness, and enabling truthful articulation of the gospel. Hence a final proposition: *The norm of Christology is Holy Scripture, the sanctified and inspired instrument through which Christ speaks his gospel to the church and which, as the sufficient and clear attestation of the reality of Christ and as the subject of ever-fresh exegesis, is to direct the church's Christological thought and speech.*

As a positive science, Christology is a normed science. Because it does not posit itself but is posited in and with Jesus Christ's self-presence, Christology derives its law *ab extra*, and is legitimate and edifying to the degree to which it does its work in submission to that law. Christological *ratio* is subordinate to *lex Christi*. Jesus Christ is himself the proper and final norm of Christological science; all other norms (credal, confessional, traditional) are relative to him. His direction of the thought and speech of the church is, however, exercised through the creaturely auxiliary of Holy Scripture.

To put the matter in telegraphic form: Holy Scripture is a fitting servant of the self-presentation of Jesus Christ because it is sanctified and inspired in order to perform this service. The sanctification of Scripture – that by virtue of which it may be called holy – is the work of the Spirit whereby this collection of creaturely texts is, without forfeit of its creaturely integrity, so ordered, shaped and preserved that it becomes capable of the task to which it is appointed. As a sanctified reality, Holy Scripture is not divinized; rather its course – from pre-literary tradition through authorship, redaction, reception and canonization – is overseen, and it is made sufficient for its calling. Inspiration is a more restricted category, a way of indicating the work of the Holy Spirit with regard to the words of Scripture. Scripture is inspired, not simply because its authors or readers are illumined, but because – again without prejudice to the integrity of creaturely occurrence – the Spirit generates a *text*: not simply a 'message' within a text, or a response from its readers, but a fitting linguistic form of the substance of the gospel in which Christ addresses himself to the saints. The viability of such an account depends, of course, on a variety of other factors: a non-dualist, non-competitive understanding of the relation of divine and creaturely activity, a carefully constructed account of divine self-mediation, a direct and operative theology of resurrection, ascension and Spirit. Here, however, these matters must remain unexplored, and the main point secured, namely that, so construed, Holy Scripture is the means through which Christ speaks his gospel to the church, so attesting his own reality and presence. This complex though unified collection of texts serves the presence of Jesus Christ by indicating or bearing testimony to his address of the saints.

This event – Jesus Christ's act of eloquence – through this instrument – the canon of Scripture – is the norm for the church's Christology. Christology is a normed science; because it is church *science*, knowledge in accordance with the inherent law and movement of its object, it is not an arbitrary but a ruled exercise of the church's mind. This means, consequently, that Christology has a definite subject matter about which it is required to think and speak. That subject matter is not something which the church's theology is free to create or manipulate *ad libitum*, perhaps in response to the demands or limitations of its culture. Jesus Christ presents himself in this definite form, through the testimony of the prophets and apostles; he is radiant *here*, in a way which requires Christology to discover in Scripture the clarity which he already has, rather than to cast around for some other kind of clarity (such as the clarity of historical evidences or philosophical foundations). And in the light of this very definite subject matter which presents itself in Holy Scripture with radiant force, Christology is subject to very definite limits beyond which it is prohibited to go. To the *clarity* of the gospel of Christ in Scripture there corresponds its *sufficiency*: the thought and speech of the church in the matter of Jesus Christ do not require some supplements to Scripture, for the instrument through which Jesus Christ announces himself is, by

virtue of the Spirit's work, adequate for the task which it is
appointed to undertake.

Normed in this way by the canon in its clarity and sufficiency,
Christology is required to make a definite act of submission. Holy
Scripture is Christology's norm. But respect for that norm involves
a good deal more than formal acknowledgement of its authority;
Scripture's normativeness is not abstract, but a concrete directive,
namely, a requirement that Christological statements both derive
from and promote attention to the biblical attestation. The
seriousness with which Christology takes up its position beneath
the canon will be shown less in formal statements of biblical
authority (and still less by efforts to establish Scripture's veracity
through historical apologetics) and more by constant exegesis. This
is because the normativity of Scripture is not merely statutory,
something which can be accorded recognition but then left to one
side, to be invoked only in cases of transgression. Scripture is
normative because it is the *viva vox Christi*, a movement of
revelation requiring not merely acknowledgement but a corresponding movement of active subordination. How is that subordination demonstrated in the work of Christology? Christological
science attempts to explicate the self-presence of Christ to which
Scripture testifies. That explication has characteristically involved
the fashioning and refinement of a (relatively small) number of
concepts such as substance, person, nature and their corollaries,
mostly borrowed from the vocabulary of late antique metaphysics.
Those concepts have acquired authority in the church by
incorporation into its confessions, which act as a further,
subordinate norm for Christology. The fruitfulness of this
conceptual equipment, its capacity to act as a fitting norm, depends
upon its being deployed in such a way that it demonstrates
deference to the biblical testimony. This deference requires a careful
employment of abstraction. Abstract concepts such as those created
in the dogmatic tradition of the church are not intended to replace
or improve upon what is set out in Scripture, but simply to gather
together what Scripture articulates to assist its orderly explication.
The concepts are valuable only to the extent to which they are
lightweight, informal and transparent to the biblical witness which
they serve to indicate. The conceptuality of Christology must
therefore emerge from and promote attention to Scripture; its end is
to demonstrate exemplary submission to the canon and so assist in
the church's hearing and speaking of the gospel of Christ.

V

Christology is a special science of a special object. Hegel's worry – that such a theology condemns itself to become the last relic of pre-critical realism, busily portraying a world of timeless supersensible objects – has by now acquired canonical status. Critical theology sought to dispose of the danger by refusing to allow that there are any special-status sciences: if coherent claims to knowledge of Jesus Christ are to be advanced, they must be defensible as instances of a more comprehensive science. More recent deconstructive theology has sought to dispose of the danger by a more extreme measure, namely abandoning both 'science' and 'objects'. What is attempted here is certainly closer to the tradition for which Kant had only contempt, and over which Hegel lingered before making a final rejection; but there are some important differences. It places much emphasis on the divine 'movement' or 'turning', and so its understanding of the fit between concepts and reality is historical, not static. It sees this movement as one of reconciliation, a history of repentance, rebirth, justification and sanctification, and not as abstract coordination of minds and objects. And its idiom is that of the personal presence of Jesus Christ in the power of the Spirit and in fulfilment of the Father's resolve. Christological science is the science of this movement. To trace that movement is not to busy oneself with a comfortable science of being, but to be brought into crisis – not the pretentious crisis of dissonance from cultural norms, but the crisis which derives from the fact that to encounter Christ in thought is to be encountered by one before whose feet we fall as though dead (Rev. 1.17). Yet the one who slays also addresses us: 'Fear not': and in that is the promise under which Christology may stand.

Church and Christian Life

7

ON EVANGELICAL ECCLESIOLOGY

I *The Church and the Perfection of God*

1. The task of evangelical ecclesiology is to describe the relation between the gospel and the church. It is charged to investigate the sense in which the existence of a new human social order is a necessary implicate of the gospel of Jesus Christ, asking whether the life of the Christian community is internal to the logic of the gospel or simply accessory and accidental. Are gospel and church extrinsically or internally related? The answer proposed here can be described summarily in the following way: the matter of the gospel is the free majesty of the triune God's grace in his works of creation, reconciliation and completion. Out of the plenitude and limitless perfection of his own self-originating life as Father, Son and Spirit, God determines to be God with his creatures. This directedness of God to creatures has its eternal origin in the purpose of the Father. The Father wills that *ex nihilo* there should come into being a creaturely counterpart to the fellowship of love which is the inner life of the Holy Trinity. This purpose is put into effect by God the Son, who is both maker and remaker of creatures, calling them into being and calling them back into being when they have fallen into estrangement from the one through whom and for whom they are made. And the divine purpose is perfected in the Spirit. The Spirit completes creatures by sustaining them in life, directing their course so that they attain their end, which is fellowship with the Father, through the Son and in the Spirit. Fellowship with God is thus the mystery of which the gospel is the open manifestation (Col. 1.26).

This manifestation does not simply take the form of an announcement. As the manifestation of God's purpose for his creatures, it is limitlessly potent and creative; it generates an assembly, a social space (we might even say: a polity and a culture). In that space, the converting power of the gospel of reconciliation becomes visible in creaturely relations and actions. That visible form is not a straightforward natural quantity, but is possessed of a special kind of visibility, created by Christ and the Spirit and so perceptible only at their behest. Yet there is a form of creaturely assembly to which the gospel necessarily gives rise, and that form is the communion of saints.

The Christian faith is thus ecclesial because it is evangelical. But it is no less true that it is *only* because the Christian faith is evangelical that it is ecclesial; that is to say, its ecclesial character derives solely from and is wholly dependent upon the gospel's manifestation of God's sovereign purpose for his creatures. The church is, because God is and acts *thus*. Consequently, an especial concern for evangelical ecclesiology is to demonstrate not only that the church is a necessary implicate of the gospel, but also that gospel and church exist in a strict and irreversible order, one in which the gospel precedes and the church follows. Much of the particular character of evangelical ecclesiology turns upon articulating in the right way the relation-in-distinction between the gospel and the church. 'Relation', because the gospel concerns fellowship between God and creatures; 'distinction', because that fellowship, even in its mutuality, is always a miracle of unilateral grace. It is this particular modality of the encounter between God and creatures – what Christoph Schwöbel calls a 'fundamental asymmetry'[1] between divine and human being and action – which is to characterize both the church's constitution and its continuing existence.

Evangelical ecclesiology is concerned to lay bare both the necessary character of the church and its necessarily derivative character. Two consequences follow. (1) An account of the gospel to which ecclesiology is purely extrinsic is inadequate. Much modern Protestant theology and church life has been vitiated by the dualist assumption that the church's social form is simple externality and so indifferent, merely the apparatus for the proclamation of the Word or the occasion for faith conceived as internal spiritual event. Among some strands of evangelical Protestantism, assimilation of the voluntarism and individualism of modern political and philosophical culture has had especially

---

1.   C. Schwöbel, 'The Creature of the Word: Recovering the Ecclesiology of the Reformers', in C. E. Gunton and D. W. Hardy (eds), *On Being the Church: Essays on the Christian Community* (Edinburgh: T&T Clark, 1989), p. 120.

corrosive effects, not only inhibiting a sense of the full ecclesial scope of the gospel but also obscuring much that should have been learned from the magisterial Reformers and their high Protestant heirs. 'So powerful is participation in the church', wrote Calvin, 'that it keeps us in the society of God.'[2] (2) Nevertheless, ecclesiology may not become 'first theology'; the ecclesiological minimalism of much modern Protestantism cannot be corrected by an inflation of ecclesiology so that it becomes the doctrinal *substratum* of all Christian teaching. In mainstream Protestant theology of the last couple of decades, this inflation has been rapid and highly successful: among those drawing inspiration from theological 'postliberalism',[3] among Lutherans who have unearthed a Catholic Luther and a catholic Lutheranism,[4] or among those who describe the church through the language of 'practice'.[5] The attempted reintegration of theology and the life of the church which stimulates such proposals is, of course, of capital importance, as is the emphasis upon the church as ingredient within the economy of salvation. Yet the very density of the resultant ecclesiology can sometimes become problematic. Ecclesiology can so fill the horizon that it obscures the miracle of grace which is fundamental to the church's life and activity.

2. J. Calvin, *Institutes of the Christian Religion* IV.i.3 (London: SCM, 1960), p. 1015.

3. A sort of ecclesiology is primary in much 'Yale school' theology, though often in somewhat secularized, social scientific or ethnographic versions: see, for example, G. Lindbeck, *The Nature of Doctrine* (London: SPCK, 1984); G. Lindbeck, *The Church in a Postliberal Age* (London: SCM, 2002), esp. pp. 1–9, 145–65; H. Frei, *Types of Christian Theology* (New Haven: Yale University Press, 1992).

4. Paradigmatically, R. Jenson: see *Systematic Theology*, vol. 2 (Oxford: Oxford University Press, 1999), pp. 167–305; 'The Church as *Communio*', in C. Braaten and R. Jenson (eds), *The Catholicity of the Reformation* (Grand Rapids: Eerdmans, 1996), pp. 1–12; 'The Church and the Sacraments', in C. Gunton (ed.), *The Cambridge Companion to Christian Doctrine* (Cambridge: Cambridge University Press, 1997), pp. 207–25. On the larger context, see the important essay of D. Yeago, 'The Church as Polity? The Lutheran Context of Robert W. Jenson's Ecclesiology', in C. Gunton (ed.), *Trinity, Time and Church: A Response to the Theology of Robert W. Jenson* (Grand Rapids: Eerdmans, 2000), pp. 201–37.

5. Notably R. Hütter, *Suffering Divine Things: Theology as Church Practice* (Grand Rapids: Eerdmans, 2000); M. Volf and D. Bass (eds), *Practicing Theology: Beliefs and Practices in Christian Life* (Grand Rapids: Eerdmans, 2001); J. Buckley and D. Yeago (eds), *Knowing the Triune God: The Work of the Spirit in the Practices of the Church* (Grand Rapids: Eerdmans, 2001).

The required alternative to this ecclesiological hypertrophy is not the atrophied evangelical ecclesiologies which have (not without justice) been the object of Catholic critique. The task is not that of putting the church in its place so much as recognizing the place which is proper to the doctrine of the church in an orderly unfolding of the mighty works of God. What follows is a preliminary sketch of such an account, focused on two related themes: (1) the relation of the church to the divine perfection, in which it is shown that the church is the communion of saints, the assembly of those whom God has consecrated for fellowship with himself through his works of election, reconciliation and consummation; (2) the relation of the visible life and activity of the church as human society to its invisible being as creature of Word and Spirit. Genuine attentiveness to gospel verities entails recognizing distinctions – between God and humankind, between Christ and the church, between the works of the Holy Spirit and the testimonies of the sanctified. Such distinctions are not to the taste of most modern ecclesiology, and are sometimes maligned as the sour fruit of what de Lubac called a 'separated theology' of nature versus supernature.[6] But some deeper account of them is surely needed. Such an account would show that – made well, under the discipline of the gospel – these distinctions can reflect the proper order of creator and creatures, restored in Christ and consecrated to blessedness by the Spirit, and gathered now into the communion of saints as they hasten to the courts of God's glory.

2. A doctrine of the church is only as good as the doctrine of God which underlies it. This principle – which is simply the affirmation of the primacy of the doctrine of the Trinity for all Christian teaching – means that good dogmatic order prohibits any moves in ecclesiology which do not cohere with the church's confession of the triune God and of the character of his acts. In terms of the task of constructing a theology of the church, therefore, this means that in its ecclesiology Christian theology must be especially vigilant to ensure two things: (1) that the full scope of the Christian confession of God is operative, and not merely a selection of those divine attributes or acts which coordinate with a certain ecclesiological proposal; (2) that the norm of ecclesiology is the particular character of God as it is made known in revelation, rather than

---

6. H. de Lubac, *Catholicism: A Study of Dogma in Relation to the Corporate Destiny of Mankind* (London: Burns, Oates and Washbourne, 1950), p. 166.

some common term in ecclesiology and theology proper (such as the term 'relation', which is almost ubiquitous in contemporary discussion). Theology must pause before beginning its ecclesiology to ensure a proper demarcation of duties between the doctrine of God and the doctrine of the church; impatience at this point will return to haunt us (indeed, it already has).

It is for this reason that I propose to start from a theological conception of God's perfection. The prevailing voices in ecclesiology would bid us begin elsewhere, most often in a doctrine of the economic Trinity; that they are mistaken in doing so, and that adoption of this starting point can lead to misconstrual of the relation-in-distinction between the gospel and the church will, I hope, become evident as the argument proceeds.

What is meant by God's perfection? In this context, God's perfection refers to God's metaphysical rather than his moral greatness. God's perfection is not only God's maximal moral goodness; it is the repleteness of his life, the fullness or completeness of his being, the entirety with which he is himself. As the perfect one, God is utterly realized, lacks nothing, and is devoid of no element of his own blessedness. From all eternity he is wholly and unceasingly fulfilled. Conceived in this way, God's perfection stands in close proximity to such divine attributes as his infinity – that is, the unrestricted character of his being and of his presence to creatures – or to his sovereignty – that is, the entire effectiveness of God's righteous rule over all things. As the sum of the divine attributes, however, 'perfection' is a more comprehensive concept, indicating the full majesty in which God is who he is.

The perfection of God is not primarily a formal but a material concept; it speaks to us of his life and activity. The perfection of God's *life* is the fullness of unity and relation – that is, of love – which God immanently is as Father, Son and Spirit. In that perfect circle of the unbegotten Father, the Son who is eternally begotten, and the Spirit who proceeds, God is unoriginate and therefore supremely alive with his own life. He does not receive his life at the hand of any other, and no other can modify or extend his life, for he *is* incomparably alive. The perfection of God's *acts* is the pure completeness of the divine work. Like God's life, God's acts are self-derived and therefore self-directed and self-fulfilling. There is no hiatus or insecure pause between God's purpose and its accomplishment in his work, no point at which God must call upon the assistance of other agents to bring his work to its completion. In his freedom, God may choose to consecrate other agents for his service. But such consecration does not indicate some lack in God, but rather the mercy with which, in his fullness, he chooses to dignify creatures by electing them for his service. And God's work is wholly spontaneous and wholly effective, setting aside all resistance and reaching its end with effortless potency.

Although this conception of God's perfection may initially appear rather remote from the doctrine of the church, the ecclesiological implications are ready to hand. God's perfection is the repleteness of his life and act. But within that life and act there is a movement or turning *ad extra*, in which out of his own perfection God wills and establishes creatures. How are we to conceive the relation between God's perfection and the creaturely realm? More particularly: is God's perfection an *inclusive* or an *exclusive* perfection? To speak of inclusive perfection would be to say that the fullness of God includes as an integral element of itself some reality other than God – that, because creatures are in some way called to participate in God's life, his life is co-constituted by their participation. To speak, on the other hand, of exclusive perfection would be to say that the fullness of God is *a se* and *in se*. God's relations to that which is other than himself are real; but they are the expression of God's freedom, not of a lack, and in those relations creatures do not participate in God but are elected for fellowship and therefore summoned into God's presence. To put the question in terms of ecclesiology: is the church, as the assembly of redeemed creatures in fellowship with God, intrinsic to God's perfection, or externally related to God's perfect being and work? Does God's perfect being include the being of the church?

3. In order to open up these ecclesiological dimensions, we may begin by considering what has been the most important trajectory in the theology of the church over the last forty years, namely 'communion ecclesiology'.[7] The use of the language of *koinonia* to

---

7. .The literature is vast, multilingual and spans the fields of biblical and historical theology, dogmatics and ecumenics. Following J. A. Möhler's 1825 *Unity in the Church* (ET Washington: Catholic University of America Press, 1996), the foundational modern text is de Lubac's *Catholicism* – surely one of the enduring ecclesiological essays of its century. The most searching Roman Catholic account is J.-M. R. Tillard, *Church of Churches: An Ecclesiology of Communion* (Collegeville: Liturgical Press, 1992); the most uncompromising account from a Protestant theologian is to be found in the second volume of R. Jenson, *Systematic Theology*. The influence of J. Zizioulas, *Being as Communion: Studies in Personhood and the Church* (New York: St Vladimir's Press, 1985) is pervasive. The ecclesiology of

speak of the nature of the church, its relation to God and its place in the mystery of salvation is now pervasive. The theology of *koinonia* is generally judged to have proved itself potent in inter-confessional dialogue – Anglican and Roman Catholic enthusiasm has been a decisive factor – especially because of its apparent capacity to provide a comprehensive account of the nature of the church on the basis of which particular confessional divisions (about eucharist, ministerial order or justification, for example) can be reconceived. Moreover, its rooting of ecclesiology in a particular theology of revelation and salvation has offered to a range of Christian traditions the resources to develop a richer ecclesiology untrammelled by inherited inhibitions. For Roman Catholics, it has offered a context in which juridical concepts of the church can be related to the life of the church as saving mystery; for many Anglicans, it has enabled a fresh articulation of the theology of the historic episcopate as a (even *the*) 'sign' of unity; for a significant body of Lutherans it has made possible a move away from the externalism of inherited Lutheran doctrines of the church and a reintegration of the theology of the church and the theology of salvation.

Communion ecclesiology is not so much a consistent set of doctrines as a diverse collection of approaches to topics in ecclesiology, sacramental theology and ecumenics, all bearing some strong family resemblances. For our present purposes, two aspects of communion ecclesiology call for attention: its dogmatic arrangement and its metaphysical substructure. Both turn on a key question: what is the relation of the church as creaturely communion to the perfection of the divine communion of Father, Son and Spirit?

Vatican II's *Lumen Gentium* is of central significance; on this, see W. Kasper, 'The Church as Communion: Reflections on the Guiding Ecclesiological Idea of the Second Vatican Council', in *Theology and Church* (New York: Crossroad, 1989), pp. 148–65. On ecumenical materials, see the reports by S. Wood, 'Ecclesial Koinonia in Ecumenical Dialogues', *One in Christ* 30 (1994), pp. 124–45; H. Schülte, *Die Kirche im ökumenischen Verständnis* (Paderborn: Bonifacius, 1991); G. R. Evans, *The Church and the Churches: Toward an Ecumenical Ecclesiology* (Cambridge: Cambridge University Press, 1994), pp. 291–314; and especially N. Sagovsky, *Ecumenism, Christian Origins and the Practice of Communion* (Cambridge: Cambridge University Press, 2000). More generally, see J. Hamer, *The Church is a Communion* (New York: Sheed and Ward, 1964); D. M. Doyle, *Communion Ecclesiology: Vision and Versions* (Maryknoll: Orbis, 2000); C. Schwöbel, 'Kirche als Communio', in *Gott in Beziehung. Studien zur Dogmatik* (Tübingen: Mohr, 2002), pp. 379–435.

In terms of its dogmatic arrangement, we may begin from a summary statement of communion ecclesiology from one of its finest expositions, Jean-Marie Tillard's *Eglise d'Eglises*:

> *Communion* with God (himself trinitarian *communion*) in the benefits of Salvation acquired by Christ (whose incarnation is a realistic *communion* between God and humanity) and given by his Spirit, the fraternal *communion* of the baptised (recreating the connective tissue of torn apart humanity), all of it made possible by *communion* in the once-and-for-all (irreversible) Event Jesus Christ which *communion* in the apostolic witness guarantees throughout the centuries and which the Eucharist celebrates (sacrament of *communion*). There is the Church in its substance.[8]

From this, three interlocking doctrines can be teased apart. First, the doctrine of God. The Christian doctrine of God is the doctrine of the Trinity, conceived as a *koinonia* of divine persons. God's unity is thus not undifferentiated homogeneity but the rich life of communion between Father, Son and Spirit, a communion which is mutual and open. Second, the doctrine of salvation. Made in the image of God, the end of the human creature is to participate in communion with God and all other creatures. Sin is a turn against this creaturely finality, a breach of communion with God and therefore with others (the language of sin as individuality is pervasive). The end of salvation is the reintegration of human persons in communion, both with God and with others. And this end is not attained simply in an extrinsic or declaratory fashion – as it were by a divine announcement of the end of hostilities – but intrinsically: by the incarnational union of God and humanity in Jesus Christ. The Word's assumption of humanity is thus not merely a device to secure a divine sin-bearer, but the resumption of communion between God and creatures. Third, the doctrine of the church. The incarnational communion is savingly extended in the church, for the church is intrinsic to the Christological mystery of the union between God and humanity. Christology and ecclesiology are mutually implicating. That is, the church is not simply an external assembly around the saving action of God, or an arena in which the benefits of salvation are distributed: rather, as communion it is ingredient within the mystery of salvation. In the church's communion, salvation is not so much confessed as bodied forth; the

8.   Tillard, *Church of Churches*, p. 319.

church *is* saved humankind, the social reality of salvation. Consequently, as the gathering of the new humanity into communion with God in Christ, the church is essentially visible as a form of common life and a part of the world's historical and material economy.

> [I]t is precisely as a polity – a people joined in a common life animated by the expectation of God's kingdom – that the church is the body of Christ, and vice-versa. An immediate implication of this is that it is precisely as a *public* phenomenon – an 'outward', 'bodily', and 'visible' community – that the church is an eschatological reality, participating in the newness of the resurrection; likewise, in so far as the church bears eschatological predicates, it is precisely as a public phenomenon, as a polity, that it does so.[9]

In eucharistic theology, this means that the eucharist cannot be thought of as a retrospective memorial of an absent event, or an illustration of an inner spiritual transaction; rather, it *is* communion: participation in Christ, salvation present and operative and not simply indicated. In terms of the order of the community, this means that – minimally – office is indispensable to the public shape of communion in the apostolic gospel. In terms of the church's relation to the world, further, this means that the common life of the church is constitutive of the perfection of human life and culture, and hence that an ecclesiology of communion lies at the centre of a comprehensive account of human social goods.[10] In short: 'our faith should never make separate what God from the beginning has joined together: *sacramentum magnum in Christo et in ecclesia*'.[11]

With this we move to the second aspect of communion ecclesiology, namely its metaphysical substructure. The key text here is Henri de Lubac's (still untranslated) work *Surnaturel*.[12] Like most of the *ressourcement* thinkers, de Lubac was not a

9.   D. Yeago, 'The Church as Polity?', p. 203.

10.   Most vividly articulated by D. L. Schindler, *Heart of the World, Center of the Church: Communio Ecclesiology, Liberalism, and Liberation* (Edinburgh: T&T Clark, 1996); see also R. Jenson, 'Christ as Culture 1: Christ as Polity', *International Journal of Systematic Theology* 5 (2003), pp. 323–29, and (more distantly) J. Milbank, *Theology and Social Theory: Beyond Secular Reason* (Oxford: Blackwell, 1990).

11.   de Lubac, *Catholicism*, p. 28.

12.   H. de Lubac, *Surnaturel* (Paris: Aubier, 1946). For useful background here, see F. Kerr, *After Aquinas: Versions of Thomism* (Oxford: Blackwell, 2002), pp. 134–48.

philosophical theologian but an exegete of the tradition. In *Surnaturel*, however, he gave sustained attention to the borderlands of doctrine, spirituality and philosophy, and the work has had an extraordinarily wide impact on Roman Catholic theology and beyond in the last fifty years: the work of figures as diverse as von Balthasar and Milbank is unthinkable without the possibilities which de Lubac opened. For de Lubac, an ecclesiology of communion – in his parlance, 'catholicism' – stands opposed not only to a 'separated theology' but also to a 'separated philosophy' – that is, a metaphysics constructed around a systematic separation of nature from supernature. Like its more dogmatic counterpart *Catholicism*, *Surnaturel* attempts to dismantle the edifice of neo-Scholastic dogmatics and apologetics which de Lubac believed had been erected on the foundation of a duality between nature and grace, a duality absent both from the fathers and from Thomas, and which led inexorably to the secularization of nature and its alienation from the reality of God. Nature considered on its own comes to acquire an immanent finality, having purely natural ends, and so as 'pure' nature can be conceived apart from any transcendent ordering towards participation in God. The resultant dualisms – between supernatural and natural, between eternity and history, between material form and inner substance – not only render impossible a Christian ontology of creatureliness; they also have destructive ecclesiological effects. Christ as supernature and the church as nature are placed in a purely extrinsic relation. Corresponding to the invention of natural philosophy, natural law and natural theology, that is, we have in effect a natural ecclesiology, shared by both Trent and the Reformers. In Catholic form, this natural ecclesiology abstracts the church's hierarchical and juridical institutions from the incarnational and eucharistic self-communication of God in Christ; in Protestant form, the result is a drastic internalism, in which the visible forms of the church can never be anything other than secular occasions for the occurrence of unmediated grace.

In terms of our theme, the central question raised by both the dogmatics and the metaphysics of communion ecclesiology is this: does an ecclesiology which starts from a theology of the perfection of God have built into it from the beginning the corrosive dualisms which de Lubac sought to expose and which lead inexorably to an ecclesiological extrinsicism? Put the other way round, as a question to communion ecclesiology, the matter becomes: does an ecclesiology centred on communion of necessity compromise the imparticipable perfection of God's triune life, and so disturb the fundamental asymmetry of Christ and the church? The issues can be introduced by some critical observations on the ecclesiology of communion.

The most pressing questions to be asked concern the distinction between God and creatures. It would be entirely improper to interpret communion ecclesiology as a systematic attempt to subsume God and creatures under a single reality of 'communion'. Nevertheless, the confluence of two factors – a mistrust of the category of 'pure nature', and a potent doctrine of the church's relation to God as both participatory and mediatorial – makes communion ecclesiology rather uneasy with at least some ways of speaking of the 'originality' of God, that is, of God's utter difference from creatures even in his acts towards and in them. In a telling passage, de Lubac suggest that 'nowhere within our world is there any absolute beginning of any kind, and if, *per impossibile*, everything could be destroyed it would be impossible to create all afresh.'[13] At the very least, it is not self-evident that such an account can be coordinated with an account of *creatio ex nihilo*, still less with a theology of incarnation and atonement, resurrection, Spirit, justification and sanctification. For what are such acts if not absolute beginnings, the introduction into creation of an absolute *novum*, unconditioned and unexpected?

A test case here is, of course, Christology, and especially the perfection of Christ. Because communion ecclesiology is heavily invested in a theology of the ontological union between Christ and the body of the church, it is characteristically insecure (even casual) about identifying Christological boundaries: it is not possible to determine the point at which Jesus stops and the church begins. A maximal instance is Milbank's rendering of the person and work of Christ as wholly resolvable into the church. The motive of this 'ecclesiological deduction'[14] of incarnation and atonement is (presumably) the avoidance of a merely external Christology and soteriology, on the principle that 'the only thing that will really remove us from extrinsicism is the primacy of ecclesiology'.[15] But the result is an account of Christ and the church as co-constitutive,

13. de Lubac, *Catholicism*, p. 145.

14. J. Milbank, 'The Name of Jesus', in *The Word Made Strange: Theology, Language, Culture* (Oxford: Blackwell, 1997), p. 159.

15. Milbank, 'The Name of Jesus', p. 165.

even, perhaps, of Christ as ecclesially constituted, and so having no substantial subjectivity proper to him. Milbank is an extreme example; but similar patterns of thought can often be found elsewhere. Thus Robert Jenson proposes that the church as the body of the risen Christ is the sole means of his presence:

> That the church is the body of Christ ... means that she is the object in the world as which the risen Christ is an object for the world, an available something as which Christ is there to be addressed and grasped. Where am I to aim my intention, to intend the risen Christ? The first answer must be: to the assembled church, and if I am in the assembly, to the gathering that surrounds me.[16]

Or again:

> The church with her sacraments is the object as which we may intend Christ because she is the object as which he intends himself. The relation between Christ as a subject and the church with her sacraments is precisely that between transcendental subjectivity and the objective self ... the church is the risen Christ's Ego.[17]

Jenson does offer a qualification to this startling statement of the identity between the church and the risen Christ in these terms:

> Within the gathering we can intend the identical Christ as the sacramental elements in our midst, which are other than us ... [T]he church as community is the object-Christ for the world and her own members severally, in that the church as association is objectively confronted within herself by the same Christ.[18]

But it is very doubtful if the distinction between Christ and the church is adequately secured by reference to the eucharistic elements as a transcendent presence of Christ to his body: much more is needed by way of specification of Christ's personal will and action ('availability' is a curiously passive term for Christ's gratuitous and authoritative presence). And it will not do for Jenson to gesticulate at potential critics by saying that they are merely repeating 'the metaphysics of Mediterranean antiquity ... Therefore they are in error':[19] traditions of Christian thought surely

---

16. Jenson, *Systematic Theology* vol. 2, p. 213.
17. Jenson, *Systematic Theology* vol. 2, p. 215.
18. Jenson, *Systematic Theology* vol. 2, p. 213.
19. Jenson, *Systematic Theology* vol. 2, p. 215.

deserve a bit more pondering? De Lubac is a good deal more measured.

> If God had willed to save us without our co-operation, Christ's sacrifice by itself would have sufficed. But does not the very existence of our Saviour presuppose a lengthy period of collaboration on man's part? Moreover, salvation on such terms would not have been worthy of the persons that God willed us to be. God did not desire to save mankind as a wreck is salvaged; he meant to raise up within it a life, his own life. The law of redemption is here a reproduction of the law of creation: man's cooperation was always necessary if his exalted destiny was to be reached, and his cooperation is necessary now for his redemption. Christ did not come to take our place – or rather this aspect of substitution refers only to the first stage of his work – but to enable us to raise ourselves through him to God. He came not to win for us an external pardon – that fundamentally was ours from all eternity and is presupposed by the Incarnation itself; for redemption is a mystery of love and mercy – but to change us inwardly. Thenceforth humanity was to cooperate actively in its own salvation, and that is why to the act of his sacrifice Christ joined the objective revelation of his Person and the foundation of his Church. To sum up, revelation and redemption are bound up together, and the Church is their only Tabernacle.[20]

Yet even here all is not well. 'Christ did not come to take our place': just possible as a rejection of pure soteriological extrinsicism; but the emphasis on collaboration and cooperation, on raising ourselves through Christ, and the hostility to 'sufficient sacrifice' and 'external pardon' all suggest a porous Christology, one which is a function of 'the leavening of the Gospel within the Catholic community'.[21]

Much more could be said along these lines: the negative effects upon Christology of an over-elaborated theology of the spousal union between Christ and the church;[22] the elevation of the church beyond creaturely status;[23] an apparent transference of agency from Christ to the church.[24] All of this, it should be remarked, is not

----

20. de Lubac, *Catholicism*, pp. 111f.

21. de Lubac, *Catholicism*, p. 111.

22. Exemplified in Schindler, *Heart of the World*, pp. 18ff.

23. See here S. K. Wood, 'Robert Jenson's Ecclesiology from a Roman Catholic Perspective', in C. Gunton (ed.), *Trinity, Time and Church*, pp. 178–87.

24. Thus de Lubac: 'If Christ is the sacrament of God, the Church is for us the sacrament of Christ; she represents him ... she really makes him present. She not only carries on his work, but she is his very continuation': *Catholicism*, p. 29.

unconnected to a decidedly thin theology of the cross. At the end of
Catholicism, de Lubac has a tantalizingly brief section on
'Mysterium Crucis': 'There is', he writes, 'no smooth transition
from a natural to a supernatural love. To find himself man must
lose himself, in a spiritual dialectic as imperative in all its severity
for humanity as for the individual.'[25] But the cross, we should note,
is quickly assimilated into the church's spirituality or ethics of self-
loss; it is not explicated in terms of *solus Christus* or *sola fide*; and
the eucharistic representation of the cross is not so much a figure of
the divine '*ephapax*' as of the enduring communion between creator
and creature.

To criticize the ecclesiology of *koinonia* along these lines is not
simply to regress to the polarities of nature versus supernature: the
theology of Christ's perfection surely transcends any such duality.
But for evangelical ecclesiology – that is, for an account of the
church which tries to sit under the governance of the gospel – the
options are not restricted to either a theology of *koinonia* or the
drastic dualism which de Lubac and others rightly sought to scour
out of modern Christianity. A fresh set of possibilities are opened
for us by a dogmatics of the mutuality between God and creatures.
Such a dogmatics attempts to articulate the difference between God
and his human partners, not because it is infected by naturalism or
extrinsicism, but because the theology of creation and of
reconciliation alike require us to conceive of the relation of God
and creatures as a relation-in-distinction, that is to say, as *covenant
fellowship*.

4. The doctrine of the church may not be developed in such a way as
to compromise the perfection of God and Christ; but theology
cannot protect itself from the compromise by the draconian
measure of eliminating the church from the economy of salvation.
What is required is not a reduction of ecclesiology to vanishing
point, but a more precise specification of God's perfection, out of
which an ecclesiology of fellowship can be generated. We must
return, therefore, to the doctrine of God.

God is perfect; but his perfection includes a movement outwards,
a turning to that which is not God, as its lordly creator, reconciler
and consummator. Of this turning – wholly miraculous, beautiful
beyond expression – we need to say at least three things. (1) It is not

25.   de Lubac, *Catholicism*, p. 206.

the first but a second movement of the being of God. The first movement is the eternally mobile repose of the Holy Trinity, the life, peace and love of Father, Son and Spirit. This is the movement of God's majestic repleteness. To this movement there corresponds a further movement in which the fullness of God is the origin and continuing ground of a reality which is *outside* his own life: 'outside', not in the sense of unrelated, but in the sense of having its own integral being as a gift rather than as an extension of God's own being. This second movement, in which God wills and provides for free creaturely being, is a necessary movement. It is not *externally* necessary, for then it would not be a divine movement but a divine reaction (and therefore not divine); rather, it is internally necessary, because it flows from the eternal divine counsel to be himself also in this second movement. (2) This movement is a movement of holy love. God's holy love is the perfect integrity with which he consecrates creatures for fellowship with himself. He consecrates first by willing the creature, then by creating, by preserving the creature, by reconciling it to himself, and by directing it to its perfection. God's holiness is loving because it is not mere divine self-segregation but God's self-election for integrity in loving fellowship with what is not God; God's love is holy because it sanctifies creatures for fellowship with the Holy One. (3) This movement is, therefore, most properly and fundamentally a movement of God's grace. Grace is sovereignty directed to the creature's well-being. The perfection of God's lordship – his unbroken, effortless rule – is wholly to the creature's good. Through it, God wills, allows and nourishes the creature's being and so gives it life.

In this second movement of holy love and grace, then, God's perfection is actual as his determination for fellowship. It is this movement which is the ground of the church. The basis of the church's being is the very simple and entirely unfathomable divine declaration: 'I am the Lord your God'. Expressed dogmatically: ecclesiology is a function of the election of the saints, and the first statement in ecclesiology is thus *credo sanctorum communionem*. Accordingly, *communio* is a derivative ecclesiological concept, a function of the twin notions of election and holiness. What is gained in this way is the retention of a sense of God's perfection, and thus of the distinction of the church from God, a distinction which is the primary condition for fellowship.

In deploying these doctrines, however, we need to extricate them from some of their more familiar uses in the context of ecclesiology.

Though holiness has an established place as a credal mark of the church, it has attracted relatively little modern discussion, especially in ecumenical ecclesiology, where unity, catholicity and apostolicity have commonly been at the forefront of the discussion, because they act as markers of confessional divergences. Where the holiness of the church is discussed,[26] it is usually in the context of sanctification. However, holiness as ecclesial sanctity is properly a subordinate aspect of the church's holiness; primarily, to speak of the church as holy is to indicate that it is the assembly of the *elect*. To be the saints is to be those summoned by the divine call: 'You will be my people'. This association of the church's holiness with its election entails, in turn, a refocusing of the ecclesiological consequences of the doctrine of election. The near-exclusive association of election with the inscrutability of divine choice in high Protestant orthodoxy meant that in ecclesiology, election served to emphasize that mere membership of the visible 'mixed' church is no guarantee of eternal security. The consequence which was ready to hand was a moralization or subjectivization of election, its enclosure within the drama of Christian selfhood. This 'concealed naturalism'[27] is deeply distorting, because it converts an affirmation about God into a knot of anxiety. Most properly, election concerns the sovereign directedness of the being of God to us, the divine self-determination to summon, protect and bless a people for himself. In short: the church 'stands by God's election'.[28] As with holiness, the ecclesiological force of the doctrine of election is to emphasize the twofold truth of the divine originality of the church's fellowship with God, and the directedness of the ways of God to the church as 'God's own people'.

What, then, is meant by the church's confession: 'we believe in the communion of saints'? (1) In theological talk of the church we are in the realm of the confession of faith. Truthful apprehension of the church's existence and nature cannot be derived from consideration of its natural history in and of itself, but only from the knowledge of the electing and consecrating work of God. The church exists by virtue of that work, having no naturally spontaneous source of life and no immanent capacity to sustain

---

26. Authoritatively in *Lumen Gentium* 39–42.

27. K. Barth, *The Theology of the Reformed Confessions* (Louisville: WJKP, 2002), p. 142.

28. Calvin, *Institutes* IV.i.3 (p. 1015).

itself as a spiritual company. The church's nature as the creaturely sphere in which we are in the society of God derives wholly from God's electing and consecrating presence. And so it is only in faith's knowledge of the works and ways of God that the church can be seen for what it is: the fellowship of the saints. In formal terms: the concept of 'church' is not deducible from or resolvable into the concept of 'sociality' (even Christian sociality). Though the life of the saints necessarily is a social form, it is this only by God's choice and calling. In a sense, therefore, to confess the communion of saints is simply to repeat the confession of God, Father, Son and Spirit. (2) The object of the confession is the communion of *saints*. God's saints are God's elect. God's elect are a human assembly which has its existence solely on the basis of a divine decision, not on the basis of creaturely prestige. 'It was not because you were more in number than any other people that the Lord set his love upon you and chose you, for you were fewer than all peoples; but it is because the Lord loves you ...' (Deut. 7.7f.). God's election is enacted in the work of salvation, which gathers a people by extricating them from absolute jeopardy (bringing the people out of the land of Egypt, out of the house of bondage (Deut. 5.6); being summoned out of the condition of being 'no people' into the condition of being 'God's people' (1 Pet. 2.10; Hos. 2.23)). That divine saving work sets the newly created people of God apart from all other possibilities, for consecration closes off any other avenues along which the people might stray: to depart from this God is simply to revert to the non-state of being 'not my people'. In so doing, election places this people in the sphere of God's blessing, since it is determination for life. And blessed in this way by its election, the church is summoned to obedience, to live in accordance with the law – that is, the given shape – of its nature as the people of the covenant. To sanctity as consecration there corresponds sanctity as active holiness. (3) The object of the church's confession is the *communion* of saints. Election generates a polity, a common life. Yet it is a common life of a distinctive kind, not just a modulation of sociality in general. It is the communion of the saints, and so determined at every point of its life by the shock-waves which flow from God's reconciling work. It is regenerate, eschatological communion, common life transfigured. At the heart of its polity is an event and presence which cannot be assimilated, of which the community is no extension, and in which it may not participate. That event and presence is the perfect being and work of the community's Lord, the Holy One in its midst.

But what is meant by a human common life which has the Holy One in its midst? In particular: how does this common life relate to its Lord? What is the relation between the Holy One and the saints? Because the relation is most properly conceived as a relation-in-distinction, the 'communion' between the church and its Lord is best articulated as *fellowship* rather than *participation*. Here much may be learned from Calvin's account of the union of Christ and the church. That there is such a union is for Calvin a deep truth of the gospel:

> that joining together of Head and members, that indwelling of Christ in our hearts – in short, that mystical union – are accorded by us the highest degree of importance, so that Christ, having been made ours, makes us sharers with him in the gifts with which he has been endowed. We do not, therefore, contemplate him outside ourselves from afar, in order that his righteousness may be imputed to us but because we put on Christ and are engrafted into his body – in short, because he deigns to make us one with him. For this reason, we glory that we have fellowship of righteousness with him.[29]

But this 'fellowship of righteousness' is utterly different from the *crassa mixtura*, the gross mixture of deity and humanity which Calvin abhors in Osiander.[30] It is 'spiritual bond'[31] rather than 'essential indwelling'.[32] That is, the church's relation to Christ is a fellowship in which distance or difference is as essential as union, for it is a mutuality ordered as precedence and subsequence, giving and receiving, and so one from which any identification is excluded. Later in the *Institutes*, Calvin gives this exquisitely condensed trinitarian statement of the matter: '[A]ll those who, by the kindness of God the Father, through the work of the Holy Spirit, have entered into fellowship with Christ, are set apart as God's property and personal possession; and ... when we are of that number we share that great grace.'[33]

---

29. Calvin, *Institutes* III.xi.10 (p. 737). For a somewhat different account of Calvin's theology of 'non-substantial participation' in Christ, see recently J. Canliss, 'Calvin, Osiander and Participation in God', *International Journal of Systematic Theology* 6 (2004), pp. 169–84.

30. Calvin, *Institutes* III.xi.10 (p. 737).

31. Calvin, *Institutes* III.xi.10 (p. 737).

32. Calvin, *Institutes* III.xi.10 (p. 737).

33. Calvin, *Institutes* IV.i.3 (pp. 1015f.). See further G. C. Berkouwer, *The Church* (Grand Rapids: Eerdmans, 1976), pp. 77–102.

There are Christological ramifications here to which we will shortly turn; but before doing so, we should not fail to note that more is at stake than establishing the precise nuances of the term *koinonia*. At its core, the matter concerns the right relation of God and creatures; and so, as often in fundamental ecclesiology, the ontological dimension has once again to claim our attention. Ecclesiologies which make much of the notion of communion commonly assume a particular understanding of the ontological difference between God and creation. 'The patristic concept of *theosis* is the most precise and compendious possible evocation of the end for which God creates us. The difference of Creator and creature is indeed absolute and eternal, but precisely because God is the infinite Creator there can be no limit to the modes and degrees of creatures' promised participation in his life.'[34] From such a vantage-point, to lay emphasis upon fellowship (rather than mutual participation) between the Holy One and the saints is simply to repeat an ontological error, one in which God and creatures are conceived in extrinsicist and therefore competitive fashion, such that they are considered to be inversely rather than directly proportional. But this collapses too much together. For, on the one hand, it is a basic entailment of the doctrine of *creatio ex nihilo* that God and creatures are in a certain sense inversely proportional. Yet, on the other hand, this is not to deny *any* relation between God and creatures. Rather, it is to say, first, that at key moments in the drama of God's ways with the world – in establishing his covenants, in taking flesh, in the Son's glorification, in the outpouring of the Holy Spirit – God acts alone. And it is to say, second, that even in God's uniting himself to the communion of the saints and in his acting through the church, there is no transgression of the boundary between the Holy One and his saints. God may choose to act through creatures; in doing so, he elevates the creature but does not bestow an enduring capacity on the creature so much as consecrate it for a specific appointment. And in its acts, the creature remains wholly subservient, ministerial and ostensive. The ontological rule in ecclesiology is therefore that whatever conjunction there may be between God and his saints, it is comprehended within an ever-greater dissimilarity. That, in brief, is what is meant by the saints' communion with the Lord who is the Holy One.

34.   Jenson, 'The Church as *Communio*', p. 3.

To sum up so far: a theology of the church needs to be undergirded by a theology of divine perfection; this is accomplished by tying ecclesiology to election, thus generating an account of the church as differentiated, asymmetrical fellowship with God. We turn finally to the Christological dimensions of God's perfection in relation to the church.

5. In his extraordinary early book *The Gospel and the Catholic Church* – with de Lubac's *Catholicism*, one of the magisterial ecclesiological texts of the last century – Michael Ramsey argued with characteristic economy and cogency that 'the meaning and ground of the church are seen in the death and resurrection of Jesus and in the mysterious sharing of the disciples in these happenings'.[35] But can this notion of the church's sharing in Christ be coordinated with an affirmation of the perfection of God? Can we say with Ramsey that 'the history of the Church and the lives of the saints are acts of the biography of the Messiah'?[36]

A first line of reflection concerns the manner of the Word's becoming flesh. The Incarnation is a wholly unique, utterly non-reversible divine act; in it the Son of God unites himself to the man Jesus. It is an instance of itself; it is not a figure in some more general union of divinity and humanity. Its origin lies wholly outside creaturely capacity, and there is no pre-existing creaturely coordinate of its occurrence. The humanity of Jesus is thus not a creaturely quantity which is annexed or commandeered by God, for then it would precede the Incarnation as its creaturely condition. The Incarnation is unilateral; it rests on the unqualified freedom of God to be and do this. Moreover, because it is irreversible, the Incarnation is not extensible. It is categorically dissimilar from (for example) the providential presence of God in and through creatures, and has no analogies or repetitions in other realities. Nothing can qualify its insistent singularity. It is for this reason that the incarnational union is a *personal* or *hypostatic* union, not a union at the level of the natures in some general conjunction of deity and humanity. Only as such can its perfection be grasped. This is not, of course, to deny the genuineness and integrity of the humanity of Christ, but simply to specify the conditions of its occurrence. Nor is it to deny the consubstantiality of the incarnate

35. A. M. Ramsey, *The Gospel and the Catholic Church* (London: Longmans, Green, 1936), p. 6.
36. Ramsey, *The Gospel and the Catholic Church*, pp. 35f.

one with us. In Christ God unites himself to us; but he does so only in this one person, and this one person is not the symbol of some more general communion or identity. He is the one mediator; he alone is the place of union between God and creatures. But what kind of union? It is a union in which he elects to share with us the benefits of fellowship with God. He acts as our reconciler, taking upon himself our alienation from God, and so taking it away. He assumes our humanity; but he does not do this by absorbing it into his own and so enabling us to partake of his union with the Father. Rather, he assumes our humanity by freely taking our place, being and acting in our stead. His humanity only gathers all others into itself as substitute; it includes all in itself only as it also excludes them. Whatever else may be meant by speaking of the mystery of the church as the marital union between Christ and his body, it cannot mean any subtraction from the Incarnation's uniqueness.

Second: Christ's perfection is enacted in his death and resurrection. To the incarnational *filius unicus* there corresponds the soteriological *solus Christus*. In the mystery of salvation, Christ acts alone, and acts with finality and sufficiency. Of that action, no ecclesial repetition is possible, because none is needed. That the incarnate Son's death and resurrection constitute the baptismal figure of the church's existence is, of course, indisputable. But the church's dying and rising are wholly contingent upon the non-representable death and resurrection of its Lord. To talk of the church 'entering into the movement of his self-offering' is possible only if by that we mean that the moral life-act of the church is a faint analogy to Christ's saving intervention; as a eucharistic motif it undermines the *alien* character of Christ's person and work, and so compromises their perfection and grace.

Third, therefore, great ecclesiological significance is to be attached to the resurrection and ascension. In an important way, those events indicate the proper distance between Christ and his saints, even as the saints are 'in' him. Christ's exaltation at Easter and after the forty days enacts his over-againstness to the church. The church is risen with Christ; but it is not risen as Christ. He himself is properly withdrawn at the ascension, which marks his transcendence as the enthroned Lord who is the object of the saints' worship. The saints, to be sure, are made alive together with him, and raised up to sit with him in the heavenly places (Eph. 2.5f.). But the undergirding principle here is: 'by grace you have been saved' (Eph. 2.5); even as the church is raised with him and sits with him in heaven, it is only as the creature of resurrection mercy and as the subject of his lordly rule. 'Christ is indeed properly called the sole Head', says Calvin, 'for he alone rules by his own authority and in his own name.'[37] Calvin makes the point against the trespass of the redeemer's rule which can attend some views of ministerial order in the church; but beneath it lies a theology of Christ's perfection in which, as the risen and ascended Lord who in the Spirit exhibits his benefits, he transcends the church even as he enters into intimate fellowship with it.

All this, then, amounts to a cumulative suggestion that the notion of the *totus Christus* – of Christ's completeness as inclusive of the church as his body – will be impermissible if it elides the distinction between Christ and the objects of his mercy: impermissible on the grounds of the doctrines of incarnation, salvation and the exaltation of Christ. Christ, says de Lubac, bears 'all men within himself ... For the Word did not merely take a human body; his Incarnation was not a simple *corporatio* but ... a *concorporatio*.'[38] At this point, a responsible evangelical ecclesiology must beg to differ: any attempted synthesis of Christology and ecclesiology must be broken by 'the all-shattering truth of *unus solus creator*'.[39] Christ's perfection is not integrative or inclusive, but complete in itself, and only so extended to the saints in the work of the Spirit who shares 'the immeasurable riches of his grace towards us' (Eph. 2.7).

But does not this leave us with an essentially negative ecclesiology, a church without enduring, active form in the world? Is there a real ecclesial horizontal which corresponds to the incarnational and soteriological vertical? Is there a visible history of the saints?

II *'The Visible Attests the Invisible'*

1. 'The Body of Christ takes up physical space here on earth.'[40] Thus Bonhoeffer at the beginning of a remarkable set of reflections on 'the visible church community' in *Discipleship*. The consensus of much recent ecclesiology has been to confirm the correctness of Bonhoeffer's judgement: no ecclesiology can be adequate which

---

37. Calvin, *Institutes* IV.vi.9 (p. 1110).
38. de Lubac, *Catholicism*, p. 8.
39. Barth, *The Theology of the Reformed Confessions*, p. 80.
40. D. Bonhoeffer, *Discipleship* (Minneapolis: Fortress Press, 2001), p. 225.

does not give primacy to the church's *visibility*. Here I propose an evangelical *sed contra*: rather than focusing on the church as a visible community of practices, contemporary ecclesiology would do well to recover a proper sense of the church's *invisibility* – that is to say, of the 'spiritual' character of its visible life. And as a corollary the active life of the church is best understood, not as a visible realization or representation of the divine presence but as an attestation of the perfect work of God in Christ, now irrepressibly present and effective in the Spirit's power. This combination of emphases, on the 'spiritual visibility' of the church and on the character of its acts as 'attestations' of God, reflects an orderly account of the relation between God's perfection and creaturely being and activity, neither separating nor confusing the divine and the human. The church is the form of common human life and action which is generated by the gospel to bear witness to the perfect word and work of the triune God.

Like the concept of communion, that of visibility is pervasive in contemporary ecclesiology.[41] They are, of course, correlative notions, for both are rooted in a rejection of the inherited dualisms which separate the natural history of the church from its life in God, and both therefore refuse to sever the church as the sphere of divine grace from the public existence of the church as 'political' community in time. The church's essence is participation in the divine communion; but this does not in any way entail its removal from the negotiations of temporal, social and material existence, precisely because it is as such – as a visible social form – that the church is in God.

---

41. For a recent expression of contemporary sensibilities on the issue, see O. Tjørhom, *Visible Church – Visible Unity*: *Ecumenical Ecclesiology and 'The Great Tradition of the Church'* (Collegeville: Liturgical Press, 2004). On ecumenical developments, see M. Tanner, 'The Goal of Unity in Theological Dialogues involving Anglicans', in G. Gassmann and P. Nørgaard-Højen (eds), *Einheit der Kirche* (Frankfurt/M: Lembeck, 1988), pp. 69–78; M. Tanner, 'The Ecumenical Future', in S. W. Sykes *et al.* (eds), *The Study of Anglicanism* (London: SPCK, 1998), pp. 427–46; M. Root, '"Reconciled Diversity" and the Visible Church', in C. Podmore (ed.), *Community – Unity – Communion* (London: Church House Publishing, 1998), pp. 237–51; J. Webster, 'The Goals of Ecumenism', in P. Avis (ed.), *Paths to Unity: Explorations in Ecumenical Method* (London: Church House Publishing, 2004), pp. 1–12. From the earlier literature, see the notable essay by M. Thurian, 'Visible Unity of Christians', in *Visible Unity and Tradition* (London: Darton, Longman and Todd, 1964), pp. 1–49.

Bonhoeffer reflects twice on the church's visibility in *Discipleship*,[42] and on both occasions what he has to say betrays his profound mistrust of the way in which the notion of the invisibility of the church can be used to resist the church's calling by assimilating itself to or hiding itself within the civil order.[43] Unlike contemporaries such as Althaus, Hirsch or Brunner, or later existentialist Lutherans like Ebeling, Bonhoeffer insists that the church's distinction from the world necessarily takes visible, bodily form. 'The followers are the visible community of faith; their discipleship is a visible act which separates them from the world – or it is not discipleship ... To flee into invisibility is to deny the call. Any community which wants to be invisible is no longer a community that follows him.'[44] Returning to the same themes later on in the book, Bonhoeffer grounds the church's visibility in a theology of incarnation, for 'the incarnation does entail the claim to space on earth, and anything that takes up space is visible. Thus the body of Jesus Christ can only be a visible body, or else it is not a body at all.'[45] Why? Because 'a truth, a doctrine, or a religion needs no space of its own. Such entities are bodyless. They do not go beyond being heard, learned, and understood. But the incarnate Son of God needs not only ears or even hearts; he needs actual, living human beings who follow him. His community with them was something everyone could see.' And '[t]he body of the exalted Lord is likewise a visible body, taking the form of the church-community'.[46] Bonhoeffer's use of spatial imagery is especially significant: in its acts of proclamation, sacrament and order, the church assumes a specific set of contours, and so claims a particular territory. The church's authority in the world, its representation of a commendable mode of human existence, does not take the form of a doctrine only but of a communal enactment in space, what Bonhoeffer calls (pointedly) 'the living-space [*Lebensraum*] of the visible church-community'.[47] 'The bodily presence of the Son of God demands bodily commitment to him and with him throughout one's daily life. With all our bodily living, existence, we belong to

42.   Bonhoeffer, *Discipleship*, pp. 110–15, 225–52; both sections have the same title, 'The Visible Church-Community'.

43.   For background, see D. Yeago, 'The Church as Polity?'

44.   Bonhoeffer, *Discipleship*, p. 113.

45.   Bonhoeffer, *Discipleship*, p. 225.

46.   Bonhoeffer, *Discipleship*, p. 226.

47.   Bonhoeffer, *Discipleship*, p. 232.

him who took on a human body for our sake. In following him, the disciple is inseparably linked to the body of Jesus.'[48] Whereas for most of his contemporary Lutherans, Christian difference was radically internalized, for Bonhoeffer the church's public, territorial character is essential to its witness, for in its visibility before the world, the church 'gains space for Christ'.[49]

Thus Bonhoeffer; many of the same themes can be picked up in recent theological interest in the concept of 'practice' as it has been developed in social and cultural theory. Some of the discussion has concentrated on epistemological issues, above all, on how theological knowledge emerges out of the practices of the church[50] – a move not unrelated to explorations of the relation of knowledge and virtue which have preoccupied some recent philosophical writing.[51] Here it is important to note that speaking of knowledge of God as carried by Christian communal activity tends to favour a certain theology of the church, one in which the 'communion of the church' is to be identified in terms of its forms of life, that is, 'the specific practices that make it distinctive among human communities'.[52] This stress on practices, it should be noted, is not simply empiricist, a way of getting some kind of descriptive purchase on the actualities of church life. It is, at heart, an ontological proposal, undergirded by resistance to what are taken to be modern assumptions about the dialectical relation of inner and outer, and about the way in which the 'spiritual' is always tainted by being brought into association with the embodied and public. Controverting these assumptions entails refusing to separate the church as – say – pneumatological reality from its distinctive habits of discourse, its routines of practice and its shape as a temporally extended human polity.

48. Bonhoeffer, *Discipleship*, p. 232.

49. Bonhoeffer, *Discipleship*, p. 236.

50. See, for example, B. Marshall, *Trinity and Truth* (Cambridge: Cambridge University Press, 2000).

51. See L. Zagzebski, *Virtues of the Mind* (Cambridge: Cambridge University Press, 1996);
A. Fairweather and L. Zagzebski (eds), *Virtue Epistemology: Essays on Epistemic Virtue and Responsibility* (Oxford: Oxford University Press, 2001); A. MacIntyre, *Dependent Rational Animals: Why Human Beings Need the Virtues* (London: Duckworth, 1999).

52. J. Buckley and D. Yeago, 'Introduction: A Catholic and Evangelical Theology?', in Buckley and Yeago (eds), *Knowing the Triune God*, p. 8.

All this is clearly companionable to de Lubac's interpretation of the plight of modern ecclesiology: marred by the segregation of natural from supernatural history, it almost inevitably ends up in one or other version of ecclesiological monophysitism – the church is either purely divine or merely human. Worries like these often surface in analysis of Barth's ecclesiology.[53] Barth's doctrine of the church is generally accorded a rather cool reception. If it fails (and many of its interpreters are disposed to think that, for all its glories, it does in some measure fail), it is because Barth will not allow that the church itself is the medium or form of the gospel in the world, and so presupposes the fatal separation of the divine work of reconciliation from the human and the temporal. By thinking of the church as external to the work of the Spirit, Barth leaves himself on the one hand with a pneumatology which lacks a sufficiently concrete historical referent, and on the other hand with a doctrine of the church in which the only significant ecclesial act is that of self-transcending indication of the word and work of God, which exist in their perfection in another, non-churchly realm. As von Balthasar put the point (his criticism has all the more substance because of his superbly attentive and sympathetic rendering of Barth's intentions): 'The greatest doubts surround what Barth means by Church ... Does this space, considered as a concrete reality in the world, suffice to bear witness to the presence of faith and revelation in the world?'[54] Now, it is by no means self-evident that the criticism of Barth stands. Barth took very seriously the 'horizontal', ethical-political interests of the Reformed tradition, and had a deep commitment to the historical and ecclesial character

53.   See, for example, N. Healy, 'The Logic of Karl Barth's Ecclesiology', *Modern Theology* 10 (1994), pp. 253–70; J. Mangina, '"Bearing the Marks of Jesus": The Church in the Economy of Salvation in Barth and Hauerwas', *Scottish Journal of Theology* 52 (1999), pp. 269–305; J. Mangina, 'The Stranger as Sacrament: Karl Barth and the Ethics of Ecclesial Practice' *International Journal of Systematic Theology* 1 (1999), pp. 322–39; R. Hütter, *Evangelische Ethik als kirchliche Zeugnis* (Neukirchen: Neukirchener Verlag, 1993); R. Hütter, 'Karl Barth's "Dialectical Catholicism": *Sic et Non*', *Modern Theology* 16 (2000), pp. 137–58; J. Buckley, 'Christian Community, Baptism, and the Lord's Supper', in J. Webster (ed.), *The Cambridge Companion to Karl Barth* (Cambridge: Cambridge University Press, 2000), pp. 195–211; S. Hauerwas, *With the Grain of the Universe: The Church's Witness and Natural Theology* (Grand Rapids: Brazos, 2001); J. Yocum, *Ecclesial Mediation in Karl Barth* (Aldershot: Ashgate, 2004).

54.   H. U. von Balthasar, *The Theology of Karl Barth: Exposition and Interpretation* (San Francisco: Ignatius, 1992), p. 245.

of Christianity; to think of him as espousing a docetic ecclesiology is, at the very least, counter-intuitive. Nevertheless, Barth has often served as an example of where ecclesiology ought not to go if it is to give attention to the enduring shape and active forms of the church as a human, historical reality.

This 'turn to the visible' – whether in ecumenical concern for *visible* unity, or in the deployment of notions of 'social practice' to describe the church – clearly raises large questions for the ecclesiological sketch offered here, with its orientation to the perfection of God. The most pressing issue is this: does an account of the church which is governed by a theology of God's perfection inevitably underplay social and historical materiality, above all by rooting the ontology of the church in pre-temporal election and in the imparticipable person and work of the incarnate Son? Is not the inevitable result a 'spiritualization' of the church, in which the church's social form is extrinsic to its being, and its public life is secularized or naturalized as just so much accumulated debris? And does this not lead to an overwhelming emphasis on the *passivity* of the church, segregated as it is from the acts of Christ, of which it is always and only a recipient? Does the church then not become simply a void created by the incursion into time of pure grace as an alien power? In short: what becomes of the church's visibility?

2. We must be clear from the outset: the issue is not *whether* the church is visible, but what *kind* of visibility is to be predicated of the church. Nothing of what has been said so far about the perfection of God, about election or about the unique efficacy and sufficiency of the person and work of Christ should be taken as a denial of the church's visibility. What is required, however, is careful dogmatic specification of a notion of visibility, to ensure that it is demonstrably coherent with the Christian confession of God. This specification will entail both an account of the church's visibility as 'spiritual' visibility, and an account of the acts of the church as attestations of the word and work of God.

How is the visibility of the church to be conceived? The primary concern of this piece of Christian teaching is not with discriminating between true believers and hypocrites. Along with the corresponding notion of 'invisibility', the notion of visibility has often been used (especially in the Reformation tradition) to address the question of how to distinguish the church as the – invisible – community of believers from the – visible – church as a mixed body of saints and false professors. Thus Calvin:

> Often ... the name "church" designates the whole multitude of men spread over the whole earth who profess to worship one God and Christ ... In this church are mingled many hypocrites who have nothing of Christ but the name and outward appearance. There are very many ambitious, greedy, envious persons, evil speakers, and some of quite unclean life. Such are tolerated for a time either because they cannot be convicted by a competent tribunal or because a vigorous discipline does not always flourish as it ought.[55]

In the present context, however, I use 'visible' in a different, though not unrelated, sense. The 'visible' church is the 'phenomenal' church: the church which has form, shape and endurance as a human undertaking, and which is present in the history of the world as a social project. The church is visible in the sense that it is a genuine creaturely event and assembly, not a purely eschatological polity or culture. It is what men and women do because of the gospel. The church is a human gathering; it engages in human activities; it has customs, texts, orders, procedures, possessions, like any other visible social entity. But how does it do and have these things? It does and has these things by virtue of the work of the Holy Spirit. Only through the Holy Spirit's empowerment is the church a human assembly; and therefore only through the same Spirit is the church visible.

The Holy Spirit is the one who brings to completion the work of reconciliation by generating and sustaining its human correspondent; in this way, the Spirit perfects creatures so that they attain that for which they were created. The work of reconciliation is triune. It has its deep ground in the eternal purpose of the Father, who wills creatures for fellowship. This purpose is established by the Son, against all creaturely defiance and in mercy upon creaturely distress, overcoming alienation and reconciling us to God. The office of the Holy Spirit is then to apply to creatures the benefits of salvation, in the sense of making actual in creaturely time and space that for which creatures have been reconciled – fellowship with God and with one another. In perfecting creatures, sanctifying them so that they come to take the form purposed by the Father and achieved for them by the Son, the Spirit is, according to the credal confession, the 'giver of life', for creatures can only 'have' life in relation to God who creates and defends life. But as the life-giver, the Spirit is also confessed as 'Lord'. He

---

55. Calvin, *Institutes* IV.i.7 (pp. 1021f.).

perfects creatures through acts of transcendent freedom; he cannot be folded into creaturely causality as a kind of immanent life-force. Always he is *Spiritus creator*, renewing creaturely existence by the event of his coming, rather than simply being some sort of continuous substratum to created being. The Holy Spirit is the church's God.

This rooting of the doctrine of the church in the doctrine of the Spirit has one crucial effect. It makes clear that the third element of the economy of salvation – the making real of reconciliation in human life and history – is as much a divine work as the first element (the Father's purpose) and the second (its accomplishment by the Son). In ecclesiology we are within the sphere of the perfection and sovereignty of God. There can be no sense in which, whilst God's first and second works are pure grace, his third work involves some kind of coordination of divine and creaturely elements. The history of the application within the creaturely realm of God's reconciling will and deed – that is, the history of the church – is the history of the new creation, the history of the resurrection of the dead. 'You he made alive' (Eph. 2.1,5). This sheer gratuity is fundamental to the church's being: the church is what it is because in the Holy Spirit God has completed the circle of his electing and reconciling work, and consummated his purpose of gathering the church to himself. The church, therefore, is natural history only because it is spiritual history, history by the Spirit's grace. And so also for the church's visibility: it is through the Spirit's work alone that the church becomes visible, and its visibility is therefore a 'special' or 'spiritual visibility', created by the Spirit and revealed by the Spirit.[56]

More closely described, the church's visibility has its centre outside itself, in the ever-fresh coming of the Spirit. The 'phenomenal' form of the church is therefore the phenomenal form of the *church* only in reference to the Spirit's self-gift. The phenomena of church life – words, rites, orders, history and the rest – do not automatically, as it were *ex opere operato*, constitute the communion of saints; rather, the church becomes what it is as the Spirit animates the forms so that they indicate the presence of God. But if visible phenomena are not in and of themselves the final truth of the church, that is not because they are phenomena and therefore

---

56. See here K. Barth, *Church Dogmatics* IV/1 (Edinburgh: T&T Clark, 1956), pp. 656–58; IV/2 (1961), p. 619; IV/3 (1962), p. 726.

unspiritual, secular, pure nature. It is because of the kind of phenomena that they are: they are indications of the presence of the Spirit who bears Christ to the church and the world and so fulfils the Father's purpose. And so if the phenomena of the church really are the church's visibility, this is not because they constitute a 'true epiphany of God's reign in the flesh-and-blood community of the faithful'.[57] It is because through the Spirit they are consecrated, taken up into God's service as the witnesses to his presence and act.

Accordingly, knowledge of the church cannot be derived in a straightforward way by deduction from its visible phenomena and practices. Only through the Spirit's agency are the phenomena to be grasped as phenomena of the *church*. The church is known as God is known, in the knowledge which comes from God's self-communicative presence, of which the human coordinate is faith. Only in this spiritual knowledge is the church known and its phenomena seen as what they are. Faith does not, of course, perceive a different, 'hidden', set of phenomena, behind the natural-historical realities of the church's visible acts. It sees those acts as what they are: attestations of God. '[We] need not ... see the church with the eyes or touch it with the hands', writes Calvin.[58] Why? Not because behind dead nature there lurks the real, supernatural, invisible and intangible church. Indeed, it is only in the church's visible human instrumentality, in the voice of its teachers, for example, that God chooses to be heard. Calvin is very far indeed from any principled separation of the sensible from the spiritual. Rather, the church is visible to the perception of faith, for it is to faith that the church steps out of the obscurity and indefiniteness of an historical phenomenon and becomes fully and properly visible as the creature of the Spirit. '[T]he fact that it belongs to the realm of faith should warn us to regard it no less since it passes our understanding than if it were already visible.'[59]

The visibility of the church is thus spiritual event, spiritually discerned. This is not to espouse an ecclesiological occasionalism, as if the church lacks a durable identity and is simply a string of discrete moments in which the Spirit from above seizes dead forms and gives them temporary animation. That would be to deny that the Spirit really is promised and really is given to the church. But

57. Yeago, 'The Church as Polity?', p. 229.
58. Calvin, *Institutes* IV.i.3 (p. 1015).
59. Calvin, *Institutes* IV.i.3 (p. 1015).

how promised, and how given? Not in a way which is convertible into something immanent to the church, or something which the church fills out or realizes in its action. The Spirit is promised and given as Lord and giver of life. And as Lord and giver of life he is other than the church, the one in whom the church has faith, to whom the church is obedient, and for the event of whose coming the church must pray: *Veni, creator Spiritus*.

To sum up: the church is visible through the work of the Holy Spirit. Its life and acts are the life and acts of the communion of the saints by virtue of the animating power of the invisible Spirit, and are known as such by the revealing power of the invisible Spirit. Such an account of the church's visibility attempts to govern itself according to the fundamental norm of ecclesiology, namely the perfection of God in his works towards the saints. This perfection is as true in pneumatology as elsewhere; the outpouring of the Spirit, his gracious descent upon the community, is not a breach of the Spirit's integrity. But this norm does not assume a secularization of the church through a separation of inner from outer. It simply acknowledges that the Spirit's life-giving and revelatory agency is fundamental to the church's being, including its visibility in creaturely time and space.

3. If this is the way in which the church 'takes up space on earth', then what is to be said of the basic shape of the church's action? What *kind* of visibility does the church have? The suggestion I wish to explore is that the active visibility of the church consists in attestations of the word and work of the God who is its creator, reconciler and consummator.[60] In speaking of the acts of the church as acts of attestation or witness, we are trying to answer the question: what is the relation between the visible undertakings of the church and their ground in the perfect work of God? In view of the perfection of God's grace, and in view of the special visibility which the church has on the basis of the fact that it exists in that grace, the notion of witness tries to express the permanently derivative character of the work of the church.

---

60. The ecclesiological primacy of witness is pervasive in vol. IV of Barth's *Dogmatics*. See further C. Schwöbel, 'Kirche als Communio'; C. Schwöbel, 'The Creature of the Word'. See also T. F. Torrance's deployment of the somewhat similar notion of 'hypodeigma', in *Royal Priesthood: A Theology of Ordained Ministry* (Edinburgh: T&T Clark, 1993), pp. 94–97 – though Torrance envisages a good deal more continuity between divine and human action than I am suggesting here.

We may orient our explanation of this by returning to the doctrine of election. The church of Jesus Christ is a 'chosen race' (1 Pet. 2.9). It exists by virtue of the declaration of the Son in which the eternal resolve of the Father is realized: 'You did not choose me; I chose you' (Jn. 15.16). This being the case, the church is characterized by a particular dynamic or movement. This dynamic is its origin in the determination of God the Father, whose purpose is set forth in the Son and brought to human fruition in the work of the Holy Spirit. Its origin in the divine resolve is what gives the church its specific character and dynamic of *being chosen*. Divine election must not be thought of simply as a background or preliminary reality, perhaps the church's ultimate ground or origin but not an operative factor in giving an account of what the church actually does. Quite the contrary: the dynamic of being chosen determines the modes of common life and activity in which the church is visible. Its forms of life, its principal activities – all the ways in which it disposes itself in time and space – have to be such that they make reference to the election of God.

A number of demarcations follow from this. First, if the visible life of the church does have this definite and specific dynamic, then a general phenomenology of sociality will not prove particularly serviceable in setting out a doctrine of the church. Some recent ecclesiology has been (alarmingly) relaxed at this point, making free use of social or ethical or cultural theory to frame an account of the church to which talk of divine action is then rather loosely attached. But election and its outworking in the mighty acts of God through which the saints are gathered is not patent of ethnographic or pragmatic description. That is not because the life of the saints is not visible, but because it is spiritually visible, and therefore can be described only by reference to the work of God. Second, the application of the language of 'practice' is similarly restricted in a theology of the church, most of all because it can drift into immanentism, in which the doctrine of God threatens to become a function of the church. A representative account suggests that in an ecclesiology oriented to church practices, there is '*one single starting point*: in the Spirit, beginning with God's action and beginning with the Church and its practices are *one* beginning, in a unity in which the divine and the human are neither divided nor confused'.[61] But

---

61. Buckley and Yeago, 'Introduction: A Catholic and Evangelical Theology?', pp. 17f.

'Spirit' here becomes broadly identifiable with the acts of the church; the 'without confusion' can carry no real weight if Spirit and church together constitute 'one beginning'; and the referential objectivity of the church's acts is thereby in some measure threatened.[62] Third, even more directly theological language of the church's acts as epiphany, realization or mediation of the acts of God is not fully adequate to secure this reference. Such language certainly has a long tradition of usage across the confessions, and ought not to be discarded lightly. And it is genuinely theological, far from the easy pragmatic immanentism which can afflict some theologies of the visible church. But nevertheless it can unravel rather quickly (this often happens when it is used in the context of sacramental theology or the theology of ministerial order). Only with some real vigilance can it be used without some damage to the proper distinction between *opus Dei* and *opus hominum*. Otherwise, the purity and sufficiency of the work of God is in some measure broken down; divine agency, if not suspended, is at least relegated to background status and so in some measure inhibited.

What, by contrast, is involved in speaking of the church's acts as *attestations* of the word and work of God? Testimony is astonished indication. Arrested by the wholly disorienting grace of God in Christ and the Spirit, the church simply *points*. It is not identical or continuous with that to which it bears witness, for otherwise its testimony would be self-testimony and therefore false. Nor is its testimony an action which effects that which it indicates; the witness of the church is an ostensive, not an effective, sign; it indicates the inherent, achieved effectiveness which the object of testimony has in itself. Strictly subordinate to that which it is appointed and empowered to indicate, raised up not to participate in, extend or realize a reality which lies quite outside itself, the church lifts up its voice and says: Behold the Lamb of God who takes away the sin of the world. As Barth says of John the Baptist (probably his favourite biblical human character): 'for the very reason that he is a genuine witness [he] only makes reference to another. He has no subsistence of his own. He is without importance of his own. He only functions as he bears witness of another and points away from himself to another.'[63]

62. See here N. Healy, 'Practices and the New Ecclesiology: Misplaced Concreteness?', *International Journal of Systematic Theology* 5 (2003), pp. 287–308.
63. K. Barth, 'The Christian as Witness', in Barth, *God in Action* (Edinburgh: T&T Clark, 1936), p. 107.

Crucially, that to which the church's acts point is not something inert – locked in the past or in transcendence. The church points to the prevenient perfection of the triune God. It witnesses to God the Father's omnipotently effective purpose which in Jesus Christ has broken through the realm of deceit and opposition, which is now supremely real and limitlessly active in his risen presence, and which is unleashed with converting power in the Spirit of Christ. Of all this, the church is an attestation.

Developing a theology of the church's visible acts along these lines carries with it the considerable advantage of avoiding the transference of agency from God to the church. It ensures a conception of the church's action in which the work of God is not a reality awaiting completion, but a *perfectum* of unrestricted, self-realizing power. Yet this does not mean a reduction of the church to pure passivity, so that its only visible feature is emptiness, waiting upon the self-presenting Word of God. Attestation is human *activity* bent to the service of God. If the church takes with full seriousness that to which it bears witness, it is not indolent or irresponsible, precisely because the gospel is a summons. But it is a summons to act in particular ways which are shaped by the truth of the gospel. That means that the church is appointed to visible activity which is in accordance with the given fact that the world is the sphere in which the triune God's antecedent grace is wholly victorious and resplendent. To act in accordance with that given fact is, indeed, to *act*: think, speak, judge, assemble, celebrate, suffer, heal, share, bless. But such actions have no centre in themselves, no pure spontaneity. They are acts which arise from trust and hope in the action of God in Christ now present through the Spirit. They are wholly defined by the basic statement which underlies and conditions all other statements about the church: the Holy One is in your midst. The church *is* by virtue of the being and acts of another; and its acts are enabled by and witness to the one to whom the church owes itself and towards whom it is an unceasing turning.

4. The concrete forms of the church's attestation of the gospel are the proclamation of the Word and the celebration of the sacraments. In Word and sacraments, the church sets forth the presence and activity of the living Jesus Christ. Word and sacrament are not 'realizations' of Jesus Christ's work, for in the Holy Spirit he is self-realizing. They are, rather, a reference to his being and his work, a work which has been achieved with royal

freedom and full effectiveness, and which now sets itself before the church in its converting effect. Word and sacrament are the church's visible acts which let God act.

A full account of the theology of Word and sacrament cannot be attempted here. I restrict myself to some remarks about the ministry of the Word in the church. To do so is not to follow the sacramental minimalism which has attached itself to some bits of the evangelical tradition: often espoused as a reaction to what is perceived to be lush sacramentalism, this minimalism is deeply disruptive of the church's exposure to the gospel, and all too often goes along with a dreary moralization of the Christian faith. Rather, I concentrate on the ministry of the Word because modern ecumenical ecclesiology has shown surprisingly little interest in the topic and tends to have concentrated its energies elsewhere, on the sacraments (especially the eucharist) and on the theology of ministerial order. An effect of this has been to promote a theology of the church in which the ministry of the Word does not always play a determinative role in understanding the character of the church's action. Sacramental agency has usually been assumed to be paradigmatic of the church's action, and fundamental questions about the relation of God's work to the work of the church have commonly been approached by trying to sort out a number of issues in eucharistic theology (a good example is discussion of the 'sacrificial' character of the eucharist as the quintessential ecclesial act). The result is that 'eucharistic ecclesiology' presents itself as self-evidently normative; and it is not unimportant to redress the balance a little.

At the beginning of the Apocalypse, John writes thus:

> I was in the Spirit on the Lord's day, and I heard behind me a loud voice like a trumpet ... Then I turned to see the voice that was speaking to me, and on turning I saw seven golden lampstands, and in the midst of the lampstands one like a son of man, clothed with a long robe and with a golden girdle around his breast; his head and his hair were white as white wool, white as snow; his eyes were like a flame of fire, his feet were like burnished bronze, refined as in a furnace, and his voice was like the sound of many waters; in his right hand he held seven stars, from his mouth issued a sharp two-edged sword, and his face was like the sun shining in full strength. When I saw him, I fell at his feet as though dead. But he laid his right hand upon me, saying, "Fear not, I am the first and the last, and the living one; I died, and behold I am alive for evermore, and I have the keys of Death and Hades". (Rev. 1.10, 12–18)

What instruction might we receive here for an understanding of the church as the communion of saints which – like John the seer – bears witness to the Word of God (Rev. 1.2)?

Jesus Christ is alive: gloriously and resplendently alive, because alive with the life of God. He is risen from the dead, and so he is neither inert nor absent, neither a piece of the past nor one who possesses himself in solitude and remoteness: he is majestically and spontaneously present. And this presence of his is communicative or revelatory, in a way which is wholly free, self-originating and authoritative: he presents himself in royal power and glory, and with axiomatic certainty. He is life and therefore presence. There is no creaturely initiative here; his self-communication is prior to any human seeking. The 'loud voice' which John hears (v. 10) is 'behind' him, anterior to him; John 'turns' (v. 12) to the voice which is already addressing itself to him; the voice is not the voice of a creature but 'the sound of many waters' (v. 15); from the mouth of the speaker there issues no human speech but the 'sharp two-edged sword' of divine judgement. To see and hear this one is to be utterly overwhelmed: 'I fell at his feet as though dead' (v. 17). But the son of man does not slay; he *speaks*. And as he speaks, he declares himself: 'I am the first and the last, and the living one; I died, and behold I am alive for evermore, and I have the keys of Death and Hades' (vv. 17f.). He declares himself to be present to all times and places, catholically real because infinitely alive, spreading abroad the knowledge of himself and of his own repleteness.

Why begin here? Because what John describes is the fundamental situation of the church which seeks to testify to the Word of God. The church is the assembly which is addressed by this son of man. The situation in which the church speaks is, therefore, not one in which the church is as it were called upon to fill a silence, or to take some initiative in order to communicate Jesus Christ. It is a situation in which this son of man, undefeated and alive, is in the church's midst (v. 13), not on the periphery, and is already lifting up his voice and making himself known. The church speaks because it has been spoken to. Only because there is a word from this son of man – only, that is, because there is a Word of God – is there a word to be uttered by the church. And this word of the church is therefore nothing other than 'witness to the Word of God' (v. 2). In its word, the church does not activate, demonstrate or justify the Word which has already been spoken; it simply attests that Word in its inherent clarity and self-demonstration, announcing what has already been announced with kingly power.

This, then, is the fundamental dynamic of the Word in the church; this is what occurs when the church hears the announcement of the gospel in Holy Scripture and attests what it hears. For Jesus Christ announces himself to the communion of saints in the canon of Holy Scripture. In the words of the prophets and apostles, Jesus Christ declares himself. The crucial factor here is Jesus Christ's personal, non-transferable agency – that is, the fact that he *himself* declares himself. At his glorification to the Father's right hand, Jesus Christ does not resign his office of self-communication, handing it over to the texts of Scripture which are henceforth in and of themselves his voice in the world. Rather, in the texts of Holy Scripture, the living one himself speaks: Scripture is his prophet and his apostle. Holy Scripture is 'holy' because it is sanctified: that is, it is set apart by God for the service of his self-announcement. Scripture is the elect, consecrated auxiliary through which the living one walks among the churches and makes known his presence. For this reason, Scripture is a transcendent moment in the life of the church. Scripture is not the church's book, something internal to the community's discursive practices; what the church hears in Scripture is not its own voice. It is not a store of common meanings or a Christian cultural code – and if it engenders those things, it is only because Scripture is that in which Jesus Christ through the Spirit is pleased to utter the *viva vox dei*. Consecrated by God for the purpose of Christ's self-manifestation, Holy Scripture is always intrusive, in a deep sense *alien*, to the life of the church.

All this is to say that the church assembles around the revelatory self-presence of God in Christ through the Spirit, borne to the communion of saints by the writings of the prophets and apostles. This divine revelation is 'isolated'[64] – that is, it is a self-generating and self-completing event. God is known by God alone: this is central to a proper understanding of the church's relation to Scripture. Scripture is not to be thought of as one element of a movement of revelation which is completed by the church's acts of reception and interpretation. Scripture is not an initial stage of a process of divine communication which is only fully realized in the life of the church – whether that life be conceived through a theological notion of tradition or through hermeneutical notions such as readerly reception. Scripture bears witness to divine

---

64. The word is Barth's, from *The Theology of the Reformed Confessions*, pp. 48f., 56.

revelation in its perfection. It is for this reason that Holy Scripture is to be spoken of as possessing the properties of clarity and sufficiency. Both these ways of speaking of Scripture emphasize the completeness of Scripture, the fact that in Scripture the church encounters a fully achieved divine communication: in this sense, they are parallel to the sacramental notion of 'real presence'. Of course, neither 'real presence' nor scriptural clarity and sufficiency eliminate creaturely acts of reception. But they do reorder those creaturely acts. And so when, therefore, the church 'interprets' Scripture, it does not bestow upon Scripture a clarity which Scripture does not already possess, or bring about a completion of the event of revelation of which Scripture is only the precipitating occasion. Interpretation is not clarification or completion, but recognition, assent to the inherent clarity and adequacy of the prophetic and apostolic witness which bears to us the voice of the church's Lord.

The effect of this is clearly a rather drastic revision of some habitual ways of thinking of the church's relation to the Word. The Word is not *in* the church but announced *to* the church through Holy Scripture. The church is therefore not first and foremost a speaking but a hearing community. John the seer says that he turned to the voice that was speaking to him (Rev. 1.12); and there are few more succinct statements of the primary dynamic of the Christian assembly. The church *is* that turning. And, further, in making that movement, in fear and trembling, falling at the feet of the son of man, the church receives its appointment to a specific task: it is summoned to speech.

But what is the character of its speech? If Jesus Christ is the prophet of his own presence through the texts of the canon, then the speech of the church is an indication or attestation of what he himself says. The church's speech is a second, not a first, move, a responsive act whose aim is achieved when it draws attention, not to what it says itself, but to what it has heard. In concrete terms, this means that the primary public language of the church is the exegesis of Holy Scripture. Exegesis is the attempt to listen to the voice of the son of man who 'walks among the seven golden lampstands', to hear 'the words of him who has the sharp two-edged sword' (Rev. 2.1, 12). Christian exegesis of Scripture is neither textual archaeology nor hermeneutical revitalization, because the canon is not a lumber-room of obscure historical data or religious meaning which needs to be unearthed by exegetical or interpretative skill. Both these approaches make the mistake of naturalizing Scripture by extracting it from its place in the communicative economy of Christ and Spirit. Christian exegesis is, properly, listening to the address of Christ in his prophets and apostles, and trying to indicate what has been heard of him through their testimonies. '[A] holy exposition doth give a setting out to the Word of God, and bringeth forth much fruit to the Godly hearer', says Bullinger in *The Decades*.[65] His term 'setting out' catches exactly the way in which the church's public speech, rooted in its attention to the scriptural declaration, is an attestation of what has been spoken to the communion of saints. To 'set out' the Word is not to attempt to extend, enlighten or otherwise improve upon what has been said, as if it required to be made more manifest by some ingenuity on the church's part. Rather, it is simply to let the Word stand as what it is, and therefore to be placed beneath its governance.

My suggestion, therefore, is that as the visible community of the Word the church will be characterized in all its speaking by a deference to Holy Scripture. Of that deference, the primary expression is the church's act of reading so that it may bear testimony to what has been announced. Deferential reading of the Word – listening to and 'setting out' the words of Jesus Christ's apostles and prophets – is a paradigmatic instance of the church's activity as a community of attestation. This deference, it ought to be added, is not simply secured by a doctrine of scriptural authority. Such a doctrine is necessary; but it cannot be expected to bear the whole weight of the church's life in the Word of God. The church will demonstrate that it is a community of the Word not simply by formal affirmations about the nature of Holy Scripture, important though they are, but by setting itself beneath Holy Scripture as the law by which its mind and actions are ruled. The church's relation to Scripture cannot be settled once and for all by a theology of biblical authority and inspiration – and if we think that it can be so settled, we run the risk of arresting that movement in which the church has its being: that ceaseless turn to the voice of its Lord, and that echoing act of witness.

---

65. H. Bullinger, *The Decades* I & II (Cambridge: Cambridge University Press, 1849), p. 72.

III *In place of a conclusion*

1. Evangelical Christians need an ecclesiology, and the ecclesiology they need is an evangelical ecclesiology, for the gospel is ecclesial. But an ecclesiology has to be a good deal more than a set of inchoate instincts which grab hold of whatever bits of doctrine float in their direction. A properly evangelical ecclesiology has to take its place within the scope of doctrinal affirmations which spell out the Christian confession of God, Christ, the Spirit, election, reconciliation, sanctification and the rest. Evangelical Christianity nowadays is sometimes tempted to think that the remedy for its instinctive ecclesiological indifference or minimalism is to move upmarket. The evangelical tradition has latterly been alarmingly undiscriminating – in its very open attitude to socially immanent theories of atonement, for example, or in its enthusiasm for the concept of 'relationality' as a theological panacea. But the evangelical tradition surely has more to offer to catholic Christianity than a soft-focus version of the contemporary ecclesiological consensus. Is it too much to hope that the evangelical tradition will dig a little deeper into the theology of grace? Barth warned Roman Catholics around the time of Vatican II to beware lest they became liberal Protestants; should we perhaps worry lest evangelicals become catholicized Protestants who make the mistake of thinking that the only ecclesiological improvement upon individualism and 'soul liberty' is a rather ill-digested theology of the *totus Christus*?

2. In the present unreconciled state of the churches, evangelicals need to offer what they have received from their own traditions to the wider fellowship of the saints. They must do so without stridency or anxiety, with humble confidence and generosity, with attentiveness and a teachable bearing towards those from whom they find themselves separated by reason of confession. But these things can only happen if evangelicals take the time to reacquaint themselves with the deep exegetical and dogmatic foundations of the traditions to which they belong; and, more important still, they can only happen if evangelicals demonstrate the supreme ecumenical virtue of acknowledging that we also need to change. This, at least, the churches in the Reformation tradition ought to know: *ecclesia reformanda, quia reformata.*

3. Finally: ecclesiology is secondary; the life of the fellowship of the saints comes first, because it is in that fellowship that we keep company with God. The renewal of the fellowship of the church is

not a matter for dogmatics, but for the invocation of the church's
God. 'Almighty God, we beseech thee graciously to behold this thy
family, for which our Lord Jesus Christ was contented to be
betrayed, and given up into the hands of wicked men, and to suffer
death upon the cross, who now liveth and reigneth with thee and
the Holy Ghost, ever one God, world without end' (Collect for
Good Friday, *Book of Common Prayer*).

8

HOPE

I

Christian hope is a moral phenomenon; but it is so derivatively, and the derivation is one of the clues to its Christian character. For, on the one hand, to speak of Christian hope is most properly to speak of the object of Christian hoping, that for which the Christian hopes, namely the personal divine subject 'Jesus Christ our hope' (1 Tim. 1.1). Hope is this one, Jesus, before it is a set of attitudes or undertakings on the part of those who hope in him. And, on the other hand, hope shares with other Christian virtues – most of all, faith and love – the fact that its human exercise is at the same time a work of God the Holy Spirit, and so cannot be described in a comprehensive way simply by talking of creaturely operations. Nevertheless, the hope which Jesus Christ constitutes and which the Holy Spirit engenders is of necessity bound up with moral activities and moral judgements. To abound in hope by the power of the Holy Spirit (Rom. 15.13) is not only to look to a prospective benefit but also to receive appointment as a certain kind of agent. The presence of Christian hope is therefore visible in, amongst other things, the particular activities and abstentions by which members of Christ's fellowship dispose themselves in the world.

Christian hope is thus one of a cluster of spacious and internally complex theological realities which serve to provide moral orientation. The hope of Christian people is part of what is involved in envisaging the world in the light of the Christian gospel. Through this primary feature of Christian moral vision, the Christian agent is schooled into steady, disciplined knowledge of certain moral realities and ends, and is thereby instructed in action which is fitting, that is, action which is in accordance with the way in which the Christian gospel declares the world to be. In particular, hope enables the Christian moral agent to clarify and act out a way of life within the historical character of created existence – that is, to existence in time. To exist in Christian hope is to trust that in all its dissipation, complexity and misery, human history is by the mercy of God on the way to perfection. History is not random, unformed occurrence but an ordered reality moving towards the fulfilment of its given nature in the coming manifestation of the immeasurable greatness of Christ's power (Eph. 1.19ff.). The life and activity of the Christian fellowship is, therefore, life and activity in the knowledge of his coming reality, a reality of which the New Testament speaks in irreducibly personal terms as 'our blessed hope', namely 'the appearing of the glory of our great God and Saviour Jesus Christ' (Tit. 2.13). This knowledge is both the church's joy and its affliction: joy, because hope for coming perfection exalts; affliction, because to wait is to suffer imperfection. Further, hope is both prospective and retrospective. It is rooted in faith's trust in a *future* perfection which *has been* promised and secured. Hope arises from the divine promises, that is, from authoritative divine enactments and declarations in the past which are sufficiently commanding and persuasive in the present that they can direct the Christian fellowship's actions towards the future. Emerging from the promise of God, hope shapes the actions of the Christian fellowship by instructing it about its true condition. Hope sees the world as a particular kind of place, one which moves along a specific historical trajectory and which makes possible and necessary action in a particular direction.

Accordingly, an inquiry into Christian hope as a moral phenomenon asks a number of related questions. Are the world and its history such that hope is not a fantasy but a truthful estimation of our situation? What kind of person is the Christian who hopes, and in whose company does she live and act? Existing within that world and history, with a particular given identity and a particular set of companions, to what kind of hopeful action is the Christian summoned, equipped with what resources and for what ends? Taken together, answers to those questions would form an account of the conditions and modes of Christian hope. But they would only do so if they rested upon an answer to the fundamental question concerning Christian hope, namely the identity of God as the object and ground of Christian hope, the one by and towards whom all hopeful action is directed. A moral theology of Christian hope, that is, must start from the Christian confession of God.

Before turning to theology proper, however, three observations about this way of approaching the moral theology of hope ought to be recorded. First, one test of adequacy for a theological account of

Christian hope as a moral phenomenon will be whether it asks all those questions, and asks them in their proper sequence and order, in such a way that the range and structure of its account are shaped by the Christian confession. Thus, for example, answers to the question of the ethical forms of hope are derivative from answers to the question of the human historical condition, which are in turn dependent upon theological teaching about God. Second, a theological account of Christian hope will give priority to biblical and theological description, and will not invest heavily either in a phenomenology of hope as human attitude and disposition, or in the self-descriptions of contemporary culture. Often, indeed, it will find that the matter of its own inquiry requires a rather free and sometimes critical attitude to such preoccupations, believing that the persuasiveness of Christian hope is more satisfactorily demonstrated when it is allowed to emerge with its own inherent clarity and profile than when it is commended or defended comparatively. Third, a theological account of Christian hope is especially concerned with given moral nature and ends. This means that it is an exercise in moral ontology, though of a distinctively theological kind. Christian hope concerns the phenomenon of human action. But, as we shall see, it is not action as pure, spontaneous world-making, but action ordered to the world and its history as an *economy*, a shaped sphere in which God's creative, reconciling and perfecting acts precede, enclose, judge, vindicate and consummate the works of creatures.

With this in mind, we examine (1) theology proper, that is, the triune God as the object and ground of Christian hope; (2) a Christian understanding of the nature of creaturely history as the theatre of the works and promises of God which engender hope; (3) the nature of the human subject and agent of hope within the divine economy; and (4) the particular character of hopeful human action in relation to the coming perfection of all things in Christ.

II

Christian hope is hope in God, for the God confessed by the Christian fellowship is 'the God of hope' (Rom. 15.13). Christian hope and its activities have to be explicated out of faith's apprehension of God and God's ways with the world as its maker, reconciler and consummator. In formal terms, this is simply an application of the rule that Christian moral theology ought not to exist in independence of Christian doctrine. In material terms, it is an application of the rule that all Christian teaching, including teaching about the moral life, is an extension of the doctrine of the Trinity, which is the Christian doctrine of God. Christian hope is hope in this God; and the doctrine of the Trinity can therefore rightly be said to furnish 'the environment of Christian behaviour'.[1] How is this so?

The Christian confession of God as Trinity attempts to indicate that the sovereign majesty and perfection which is God's life is that of the eternal and perfect relations of Father, Son and Spirit. God is the relations of these three persons; his being is his eternal fullness as the Father who begets the Son, the Son who is begotten of the Father before all worlds, and the Spirit who proceeds from them. In these relations, fully achieved and lacking nothing, God is one; his unity is the repleteness and blessedness of the fellowship of the three.

This repleteness of God's life includes within itself, as an integral aspect of its perfection, a turn to that which is not God. In this turn there occurs a movement in which the fellowship of the immanent life of God creates a further object of love. This turn is free, self-caused, wholly spontaneous, original to the divine being; its necessity is purely the necessity of God's own self-determination to be in fellowship with that which is other than himself. As such, it is not a turn which completes or extends the divine life; it is a turning out of fullness, not out of lack. More simply: it is gift, love. This turning or act of love is the work of the triune God as the world's creator, reconciler and consummator. It takes historical form in the simple yet staggeringly complex work of God's majesty in the entire scope of the economy, as God brings creaturely reality into being, redeems it and ensures that it will arrive at its perfection.

As Father, God purposes that in its abundance, the divine love should be directed to bringing creation into being, bestowing upon it life, order and direction. Because it is rooted in the Father's will, this purpose is unshakeable. That is, God's relation to what he makes is not simply an act of origination, but an act which ensures the creation's *destiny*, and therefore one which oversees, directs and protects the creation so that it attains that destiny. As Son, God intervenes in the history of creation when by its own perversity the creature seeks to struggle free from the Father's purpose, refusing

---

1.   P. Lehmann, *Ethics in a Christian Context* (London: SCM, 1963), p. 117.

to be a creature, and in so doing exposing itself to mortal peril. Only as creature can the creature have life; and it is the work of the Son to reconcile and therefore to recreate what has brought destruction upon itself. Through the person and work of the Son, gathering created being to himself and bearing in himself its alienation from the source of its life and well-being, creation is reintegrated into the Father's purpose. Lastly, as Spirit, God acts to bring to completion that which the Father purposes and the Son secures against all opposition, namely the identity and integrity of the creation in fellowship with God. God the Spirit perfects, bringing creaturely being and history to their completion.

What is the significance of this for Christian hope? Hope is that creaturely disposition which corresponds to the fact that all occasions of human history, including its future, are caught up within the economy of the triune God's mercy. Because God is to the depths of his eternal being triune, and because he acts in the world as the one he is in himself, then the entire scope of human history and action is embraced by God's purpose. God is not simply originator (setting the creation in motion), nor simply end (tying up the loose ends of history at its terminus). Rather, as Father, Son and Spirit, God is infinite – no time or space is apart from or beyond his presence and action – and so steadfast – his purpose has been, is and will be at all times constantly and reliably at work. And it is as this one that God is the ground of hope, for hope trusts that, because the Father's purpose has been accomplished in the Son and is now at work in the world in the Spirit's power, then human history is God's economy. Within the space which the triune God creates, hope is neither a fantasy nor a gesture of defiance, but a fitting, truthful attitude and shape for action. In sum: hope rests upon God's faithfulness, and God's faithfulness is triune.

One immediate effect of rooting a theology of Christian hope in the doctrine of the Trinity is to prevent an exclusive orientation towards eschatology. Hope is not simply a correlate of the divine futurity or the coming of God; it is, rather, a disposition which is related to the entirety of God's dealings with his creature, past, present and future. Within this, hope undoubtedly has an especial regard for the future horizon of human history. But this future quickly becomes isolated when not adequately related to a theological account of God as the world's creator and as its reconciler in the person and work of Christ. An isolated eschatology accords little weight to created nature, and often functions with only a pale theology of incarnation and atonement, precisely because the preponderant doctrinal weight is placed in the future of God. This imbalance within the structure of Christian teaching orients hope, not to the fulfilment of God's eternal purpose but to an absolute eschatological *novum*. The corrective to the imbalance is achieved by relating hope not simply to the future but also to the triune eternity of God, that is, to God's sovereign and purposive presence to and action within all creaturely time. Christian hope, and therefore hopeful Christian action, rests not simply on what will be, but on what will be as the fulfilment of God's steadfastness as Father, Son and Spirit, his already-enacted, present and promised constancy to the creature. Hope is hope in God's steadfast love (Pss. 33.18, 22; 130.7; 131.3; 147.11).[2]

A Christian moral theology of hope begins thus with the perfection of the triune God. This suggests a further consequence, namely that because hope is hope in God, it has no grounds and no capacity in itself. Not only does this mean that hope is, as Aquinas puts it, *totaliter ab extrinseco*,[3] since it is that to which we have been 'born anew' (1 Pet. 1.3). It also means that hope relies upon the fulfilment of the promise of divine grace, and that only as such is it active engagement in the works of hope. 'The hoping person looks gladly, willingly, and joyfully beyond the present and away from himself', writes Barth.[4] And so:

> As faith is real faith only by being finally transcended in demonstration of the faithfulness of God, and as love is the good work of faith only inasmuch as we are loved by God before we ever love him ... so the question of whether we really hope can be answered with ultimate clarity and certainty only as we give up the dignity of being subjects and admit

---

2. Cf. C. Schwöbel, 'Last Things First? The Century of Eschatology in Retrospect', in D. Fergusson and M. Sarot (eds), *The Future as God's Gift: Explorations in Christian Eschatology* (Edinburgh: T&T Clark, 2000), p. 238: 'Christian hope has as its content the perfection of God's creation with his reconciled creation. In Christian theology the integrative framework for the understanding of God's action in creation, reconciliation and perfection is the doctrine of the Trinity. By understanding every form of divine action as an act of the triune God, creation, reconciliation and perfection are internally related by ascribing them all to the agency of the triune God. If we want to avoid the dangers of an isolated treatment of eschatology, the task consists in developing a Christian eschatology as a trinitarian eschatology.'

3. Aquinas, *Summa theologiae* IaIIae q63 a1.

4. K. Barth, *Ethics* (Edinburgh: T&T Clark, 1981), p. 515.

that we can hope only in and by God himself, and that the overwhelming certainty and clarity of Christian hope rests upon its being hope not at all on the basis of its own hope, but wholly and utterly for the sake of what is hoped for. ... Yet we do not plunge into an abyss here, for if we want to stand, then again we finally have to lose all ground beneath our feet save the one.[5]

Starting in this way from the doctrine of the Trinity shows how far back we must reach in inquiring into the practices of Christian hope. In order to reflect upon ourselves and our acts, we must talk of the perfection of God. But because God's perfection is his perfection as this one – the triune Lord, saviour and finisher of creation – then it is not a perfection indifferent to human history, absorbing it and robbing it of its proper substance; rather, God's perfection includes his perfecting of his creatures. The arena of this perfecting is human time; hope is among the virtues which correspond to God's perfecting work. Rightly to discern the character of Christian hope, therefore, we need to turn next to consider its historical conditions. In what kind of historical sphere do we exist? How does this condition shape the practices of Christian hope?

III

Christian hope requires for its exercise a particular sense of our historical condition; the explication of that condition is one of the tasks of Christian moral theology. As it elucidates the historical condition of Christian hope, theology seeks to develop a moral ontology. That is, it attempts to understand the kind of place the world is, and the kind of beings that we are; and what it says both about the world and about ourselves derives from what theology hears in the gospel about who God is. Christian moral theology thus depicts the historical situation of Christian hope by talking of 'natures' and 'ends'. It portrays, first, the given identities ('natures') of the agents in history – the triune God as the origin, ruler, sustainer, judge and redeemer of created time, and human persons as those created by God for fellowship with himself. And, second, theology depicts the historical situation of Christian hope by portraying the 'ends' of history, that is, the *telos* of created reality and persons in which their natures will be perfectly realized. Such a

5. Barth, *Ethics*, p. 515.

reflective portrait of the nature and ends of created history furnishes the frame for a Christian ethics of hope, offering a theological description of the moral field within which the practices of Christian hope take place.

Fundamental to such an account is an affirmation that it is possible to speak of history as a whole, as an integrated reality which has form and direction by virtue of the purpose of its creator and Lord. History is a field of hope because it is part of the divine economy, God's orderly administration of all things by which they are brought to fulfilment. History is not simply random, indecipherable, endlessly redescribable; it has shape, order. Shape and order are given; that is, they precede all our human attempts to bestow a unity upon history. Of course, history's shape and order are not given in such a way that history is from the beginning a finished product, established by a pre-temporal decree. History is real; its shape and order are acquired through an historical process of perfecting; they are that which history *comes to have* as it moves towards its end. Nevertheless, that which history becomes is in accordance with the divine purpose: it moves to its end.

To speak thus is certainly to invite reproach for ideological imposition, or for detaching hope from the broken miseries of time. The danger certainly exists, and protest against it is proper. But a gesture of protest, however necessary, ought not to be allowed to become a first principle; when it does, it inhibits thought, and may relieve theology of its responsibility to give an account of the Christian confession that our times are in the hands of God. Much will depend upon how theology sets about the task of giving such an account – whether it succeeds in avoiding heartless serenity, whether it retains a sense of its own corrigibility, whether it speaks of the end of history with fear and trembling. Yet not to speak of history as God's ordered economy is to fail to articulate a primary condition of Christian hope, for hope arises from discernment of our place in God's history with us.

What is it that hope discerns? It sees human history as the history of fellowship between the triune God and his human creatures. That history is a fellowship which is purposed by the eternal will of God the Father who creates and gives destiny to that which he creates. History is therefore embraced by 'the purpose of his will' (Eph. 1.5) or his 'plan for the fullness of time', namely 'to unite all things in [Christ], things in heaven and things on earth' (Eph. 1.9f.). By virtue of the Father's will, history has a destiny. Yet this history does not unfold flawlessly; the history of fellowship includes – and appears to be broken by – the contradiction of sin in which the creature refuses to be satisfied with its given nature and end as a creature made for fellowship, seeks to create its own destiny, and so unleashes the dreadful episode of human depravity. But it remains an *episode*; it may not be rendered absolute and all-consuming so as to annul the constancy of the creator. To the estrangement of creatures from their own good there corresponds the work of God the reconciler through whose saving work sinful, self-destructive creatures are reintegrated into the divine purpose, so that the Father's will to fellowship triumphs. 'In him we have redemption' (Eph. 1.8) – that is, human history is liberated from bondage to sin, falsehood and disorder and set free to attain its end. That it is even now moving towards perfection is the work of the Spirit, by whom history is pointed to its consummation in which the purpose of the Father will be vindicated and the creation glorified.

Christian hope knows itself to be in this historical condition. Grasping the fact that human creatures are caught up in the economy of God's grace, embraced by the Father's purpose, the Son's redemption and the Spirit's promised consummation, Christian hope is a stance within this history. Most of all it is a stance towards our future, which regards the incompleteness and imperfection and bleakness of history not with terror or resignation but with trust that, because God has made himself known as creator and reconciler, he will also demonstrate himself to be consummator. The triune God has been and is now for his creature, and so he will also prove himself to be in what is to come. This means, once again, that it is not quite correct to relate Christian hope only to the eschatological element of history. Christian hope is expectation; but it is expectation which is instructed by past and present mercy. Certainly it is oriented to 'the expected future of God's kingdom'.[6] But Christian hope anticipates the future as consummation, not only as contradiction of the present order; what is anticipated is the destiny purposed by God the Father and secured in the Son's reconciling work. The experience of Christian hope is not simply an intrusive 'sabbath' moment in which 'the laws of this world are suspended and only the righteousness of God

---

6.   J. Moltmann, 'The Liberation of the Future and Its Anticipations in History', in R. Bauckham (ed.), *God Will Be All in All: The Eschatology of Jürgen Moltmann* (Edinburgh: T&T Clark, 1999), p. 286.

counts'.[7] Rather, it is based on a judgement that the true 'law' of the
world is God's plan for the fullness of time, which is now at work
and which will receive its consummation in the future for which the
church hopes.[8]

As it takes stock of its circumstances, Christian hope does not see
itself situated in a history of decline, still less in a tragic situation in
face of which hope is simply protest or contradiction. It finds itself
in the time of grace, in that space in human history which follows
the death and resurrection of Jesus Christ and the outpouring of the
Spirit. Thus for the writer of Ephesians, knowing 'the hope to which
[God] has called you' (Eph. 1.18) is inseparable from knowing

> what is the immeasurable greatness of his power in us who believe,
> according to the working of his great might which he accomplished in
> Christ when he raised him from the dead and made him sit at his right
> hand in the heavenly places, far above all rule and authority and power
> and dominion, and above every name that is named, not only in this age
> but also in that which is to come; and he has put all things under his feet
> and has made him the head over all things for the church. (Eph. 1.19–22)

This is not to dismiss the reality of sin and suffering, nor to turn
from its victims: to wait in hope is to groan (Rom. 8.22f.). But the
situation in which hope finds itself remains – solely by the merciful
judgement of God – one in which grace is superabundant, and
therefore one in which the possibility of a tragic reading of our
history has been taken away. Jesus Christ rules, and Christian hope
finds in his rule the enactment of the Father's purpose which will be
fully manifest in the coming of 'our blessed hope, the appearing of
the glory of our great God and Saviour Jesus Christ' (Tit. 2.13).

To draw the threads together: a moral theology of Christian hope
generates a moral ontology, an account of hope's historical
condition. Looking back to God's work of creation and reconciliation, Christian hope also looks for the coming consummation of all
things. The present time is not an empty space to be filled with
dread, or perhaps with dread held at bay by projects of self-making

---

7.   Moltmann, 'The Liberation of the Future', p. 280.
8.   On the relation of hope to past and present as well as future, see J. Fischer,
'Zum Fürchten oder zum Hoffen? Die Wahrnehmung der Zukunft als Problem
theologischer Ethik', in J. Fischer and U. Gäbler (eds), *Angst und Hoffnung.
Grunderfahrungen des Menschen im Horizont von Religion und Theologie* (Stuttgart:
Kohlhammer, 1997), pp. 135–37; V. J. Genovesi, *Expectant Creativity: The Action of
Hope in Christian Ethics* (Washington: University Press of America, 1982).

and self-defence. It is the arena of promise. To hope is to exist in trust that God's constancy is such that the present is on the way to perfection.

This moral ontology finds both its norm and its content in the Christian gospel, from which it acquires its rather distinctive picture of human history and of the nature of hope. Beginning from the gospel and governed by it throughout its inquiry, a Christian moral theology of hope is not much disposed to take its bearings from prestigious readings of our cultural situation developed without the gospel's tutelage. Partly this is because the gospel outbids other interpretations of human history; partly it is because the gospel is the principle of its own explanation and defence. Little is to be gained (and a good deal may be lost) by expounding Christian hope as a counterpart to some philosophical or cultural-theoretical presentation of the human condition. Apologetic advantage is always short-lived, and frequently won by succumbing to the temptation to believe that our historical situation is transparent to us, that we know, as it were, what it is to be without hope, and need only to be furnished with the hope for which we long. Similar difficulties attend attempts to frame a theology of hope in terms of theodicy: how can we hope in face of this or that monstrous evil? But even – especially – our experience of evil is not self-interpreting: evil lies about itself. A theology of hope does not hang upon a satisfactory answer to the question of theodicy (satisfactory to whom, and to what ends?), but vice versa: only on the basis of faith's confession of the God of hope, of his ways with the world in the history of fellowship in which we now live and for whose consummation we wait, is it possible to develop anything like a responsible Christian theodicy.

IV

Having remarked on the God of hope and on hope's historical condition, we turn to the anthropological question: what kind of person is the Christian who hopes? By way of brief answer: the Christian who hopes is one who knows in faith that in the economy of God's grace, enacted in the resurrection of Jesus and the giving of the Spirit and lived out in the company of the saints, his or her future is secure; and so the Christian who hopes is one who turns to that future and acts in its light, confident because in the Spirit Jesus

Christ is our present help and the pledge of our coming consummation.

The question 'what kind of person is the Christian who hopes?' is an ontological question before it is an ethical one. The answer which it invites is a description of human nature formed by the purpose and action of God. The Christian who hopes is not engaged in an act of self-formation; he or she makes history only because in a deep sense history has already been made, and because only on that basis is it possible to be a hopeful person and agent. A Christian anthropology of hope is decidedly non-voluntarist. Hope is not a correlate of freedom (understood, degenerately, as radical self-government) but of nature (that is, of the reality which the work of the triune God establishes and which the gospel announces with joy). The Christian who hopes is one whose being is enclosed, determined and protected by Jesus Christ our hope.

Such an anthropology of hope is not readily available to us in late modernity. The disruptive effects of its absence can be illustrated from Rubem Alves' *A Theology of Human Hope*. 'Only as the creator of history does man find his authentic life; only where man is the creator of history is there hope for the world.'[9] By conflating hope with human self-actualization, the book falls victim to the agonistic habits of modern conceptions of freedom in which the primal form of free human consciousness is 'the consciousness of being dominated by a power which does not allow it to create its own history'.[10] On this account, hope is freedom and therefore power (not, note, trust in being helped). Hope is thus not to be set in the economy of grace, for any such economy could only be repressive and alienating: all perfection is at cost to human liberty. Rather, as Alves puts it, the person who hopes 'is experimentation':[11] 'when man's hope informs his action, man thrusts himself upon the world as power'.[12] The problem here is not simply that this remains entangled in modern dualities of freedom versus nature, divine versus human action, though they are ruinous enough and scarcely compensated for by a muddled theology of grace in which 'creation is a joint enterprise'.[13] It is more that Alves cannot conceive of a genuine anthropology of hope based on what he

9.   R. Alves, *A Theology of Human Hope* (Washington: Corpus, 1969), p. 141.
10.   Alves, *A Theology of Human Hope*, p. 10.
11.   Alves, *A Theology of Human Hope*, p. 137.
12.   Alves, *A Theology of Human Hope*, p. 138.
13.   Alves, *A Theology of Human Hope*, p. 144.

dismisses as 'a non-historical, dogmatic idea'.[14] And therefore he cannot satisfactorily distinguish his 'messianic humanism' from secular political humanism, since the entire metaphysical-theological apparatus of Christian anthropology has to be discarded in order to respect the basic principle for an account of the ethics of hope: 'When nature or any sort of order becomes the context which man elects for his life, history comes to an end. At least man loses his openness to the future since the future is to be the imitation of the values once given in the past.'[15] A Christian anthropology needs to move beyond this acute sense of historical responsibility, and allow the gospel to introduce us into a more spacious and relaxed world. It will do so by starting, not from human indeterminacy, but from faith's confession of God's works of creating and preserving persons for fellowship and therefore for hope. This (material) starting point will then be reflected in the order of exposition, so that the anthropology of hope is derivative, not fundamental. Here, too, it is a matter of removing 'the last possibility of a surreptitious resort to anthropology in Christian ethical reflection'.[16]

The Christian who hopes exists in an 'eschatological situation' defined not by self-realization but by the judgement of God. This is a matter of being

> a person under the promise and in the expectation of new life. Under this promise one is called, one is inserted into the new situation before God that is opened up by God's condemning and saving judgement. One is inserted into the hidden history of Jesus Christ in the world. That *is* the living space in which our human history is 'located' and 'takes place'. 'For you died, and your life is hidden with Christ in God' ... That is a categorical indicative, the content of the judgement of God upon our existence and at the same time the communication of new life.[17]

This new life determining the Christian is a life towards the future in which God's purpose will be completed. To hope as a Christian is to hope as a creature – one who has been formed and appointed by God to live a specific history, reach a specific destiny and so attain perfection. It is also to hope as a sinner who has been redeemed

---

14. Alves, *A Theology of Human Hope*, p. 87.
15. Alves, *A Theology of Human Hope*, p. 83.
16. Lehmann, *Ethics in a Christian Context*, p. 120.
17. G. Sauter, *Eschatological Rationality: Theological Issues in Focus* (Grand Rapids: Baker, 1996), pp. 197f.

from self-destruction – one whose evil tendency away from creaturely good has in Christ been authoritatively intercepted and put away. It is to hope as a saint – one who, because elect and redeemed, is also directed and empowered to live towards a certain perfection. And it is to be all this in a fellowship of persons gathered by God as the communion of the saints. Christian hope has its roots in our common participation in the reality of grace extended to us; to be a person of hope is to partake in this history in this company.[18]

All of this, however, rests upon the fact that God's merciful judgement upon lost creatures in which their human vocation is restored is the gift of *being*. God's judgement is not a conditional offer, contingent upon the completion of a task: it is a mighty work of creation. For the Christian who hopes, this is who she and her fellows are. Hope is thus an aspect of that 'conformity-to-being'[19] in which consists the goodness of our acts and our blessedness. To hope is to be the person one is and will be – a person for whom hope is 'natural', that is, a disposing of oneself in accordance with the nature and vocation bestowed by God. Two consequences follow.

First, the Christian who hopes is one who knows his or her future. Such knowledge comes from the 'spirit of wisdom and of revelation' by which 'the eyes of the heart are enlightened' and we come 'to know what is the hope to which God has called us' (Eph. 1.18). To the Christian who hopes there is revealed that we are reconciled creatures of God directed by him to our coming blessedness; and so hope includes knowledge. This knowledge, because it is the gift of the Spirit, is 'spiritual'. It is not sight or possession: 'who hopes for what he sees?' (Rom. 8.24). We have hope as we have God, as gift, not as material or psychological condition. Yet spiritual knowledge is for all that no less certain. Christian hope is 'fully assured' (cf. Heb. 6.11) of the coming perfection. Hope is not 'nescience' which fears to go beyond 'the

---

18.   On the social dimensions of eschatology, see K. Barth, *Church Dogmatics* IV/3 (Edinburgh: T&T Clark, 1962), pp. 930–34; W. Pannenberg, *Systematic Theology*, vol. 3 (Edinburgh: T&T Clark, 1998), pp. 177–80; M. Volf, 'The Final Reconciliation: Reflections on a Social Dimension of the Eschatological Transition', in J. Buckley and L. G. Jones (eds), *Theology and Eschatology at the Turn of the Millennium* (Oxford: Blackwell, 2001), pp. 89–111.

19.   R. Spaemann, *Happiness and Benevolence* (Notre Dame: University of Notre Dame Press, 2000), p. 79.

unfinished narrative of history'.[20] It is the knowledge of our future good given by the Spirit who is 'the guarantee of our inheritance until we acquire possession of it' (Eph. 1.14). And such knowledge is sufficiently robust, offering a sufficiently persuasive account of our condition and our identity, that it forms the basis for action which is not timid or calculative but a free, bold and generous move towards the future to which we have been appointed.

Moreover, because hope includes knowledge given in the Spirit's work of 'revelation in the knowledge of [Christ]' (Eph. 1.17), it is inadvisable to speak of the cognitive dimension of hope in terms of imagination.[21] 'Imagination' suggests something too projective or poetic, too little oriented to what has been accomplished and what is now being made known in the Spirit's revealing work. A natural counterpart of a strongly futurist eschatology, imagination is oriented more to possibility than to actuality; and it can make hope's envisaging of the future into a task to be undertaken rather than the hearing of an authoritative divine judgement which has already been announced.

Second, Christian hope is a mode of personal existence (though not *private*, since I hope in company with my fellow-members in the body of Christ) in which the Christian, having been turned by God to her future good, turns to that good. God's turning to his creatures, his self-communicative presence and promised constancy, evokes a corresponding turn on the part of the creature; Christian hope is an aspect of that turn. The creaturely movement of hope is entirely and astonishingly a matter of grace: 'It is very difficult to keep in mind the fundamentally incomprehensible fact that hope, as a virtue, is something wholly supernatural.'[22] The Christian turns to the future only because that future has already been secured, has already made itself our good and the condition of our being. Above

20. N. Lash, 'The Church's Responsibility for the Future of Humanity', in *Theology on the Way to Emmaus* (London: SCM, 1986), p. 195. For an (incomplete) corrective, see K. L. Hughes, 'The Crossing of Hope, or Apophatic Eschatology', in M. Volf and W. Katerberg (eds), *The Future of Hope: Christian Tradition amid Modernity and Postmodernity* (Grand Rapids: Eerdmans, 2004), pp. 101–24.

21. E.g. Genovesi, *Expectant Creativity*, and more recently R. Bauckham and T. Hart, *Hope Against Hope: Christian Eschatology in Contemporary Context* (London: Darton, Longman and Todd, 1999). Both make much use of W. F. Lynch, *Images of Hope: Imagination as a Healer of the Hopeless* (Dublin: Helicon, 1965). See also G. Green, 'Imagining the Future', in Fergusson and Sarot (eds), *The Future as God's Gift*, pp. 73–87.

22. J. Pieper, *On Hope* (San Francisco: Ignatius, 1986), p. 35.

all, that to which the Christian turns – this 'future good' – is Jesus Christ himself. Because he is not only the first but also the last, because he is alive for evermore (Rev. 1.17f.), then the Christian may – must – turn to him. To be without hope is for the Christian an impossibility, excluded by the promise of Jesus Christ; to turn to him in hope is the only way forward.

Yet hope is *hope*, not delight. The object of delight is 'a good that is present';[23] the object of hope is future: 'we do not hope for what is at present within our grasp'.[24] Further, the object of hope is 'something arduous, attainable only with difficulty'.[25] Hope is therefore a particular disposition which, in knowledge of our coming good, turns to that good. Hope lies between despair and the delight of possession. It is not despair, because Jesus Christ has already turned to us and secured our future; it is not delight, because our fellowship with him awaits consummation. Hope is, rather, confident longing for the full realization of life with Christ. The Christian who hopes is confident. Because hope is conformity to being, because it is knowledge, because it is active turning to the future which has already turned to us at the resurrection of Jesus Christ, then hope 'does not disappoint' (Rom. 5.5), and leads to boldness (2 Cor. 3.12) and steadiness (Heb. 6.19). Accordingly, the Christian who hopes is free and assured, and can venture what Paul Ramsey calls the 'immoderate life',[26] living and acting beyond the demonstrable and actual, with an intemperance grounded in the reality of the one who died, is risen and will come again.[27]

---

23.   Aquinas, *Summa theologiae* IaIIae q40 a8.

24.   Aquinas, *Summa theologiae* IaIIae q40 a8.

25.   Aquinas, *Summa theologiae* IaIIae q40 a8.

26.   P. Ramsey, *Basic Christian Ethics* (Louisville: WJKP, 1993), pp. 226–31.

27.   The lack of this note of boldness is a major weakness of J. Ellul's *Hope in Time of Abandonment* (New York: Seabury, 1977). The book's presentation is overshadowed by its insistence that what we have called the condition of hope is the divine *silence*, hope being the (quasi-absurd) confidence that, despite every indication, God might speak again. 'Hope is man's answer to God's silence' (p. 176); and 'If hope is indeed response to the silence of God, it has no place nor reason except when the situation is actually desperate' (p. 206). All this is intended by Ellul as an affirmation that Christian hope transcends every worldly possibility. 'It is the impossible which is the sole creator of true history. God's impossible is the only real … Hope … wants us to write another history, that of the impossible life, of the true life, which the mind of man never conceived' (p. 203). It is also a protest against making hope a matter of worldly calculation and efficacy ('As long as there is a chance to employ some kind of means … hope has no place in the venture', p. 197).

V

What has been offered so far is a sketch of the moral domain of Christian hope: Christian hope is part of the movement of reconciled life in which redeemed creatures look for and tend towards their end. But to exist in this moral domain, as this kind of person in covenant with this God, is to be quickened to action. The economy of grace is also *law* (that is, being in its imperatival force) to those who exist within its blessing. To what acts are we quickened? To what are we summoned by the law of our eschatological being?

In answering this question, moral theology has to guard against the drift towards either eschatological moralism or eschatological passivity. The first was much promoted by Kant: 'the Kingdom of Heaven can be interpreted as a symbolic representation aimed merely at stimulating greater hope and effort in achieving it'.[28] But eschatology is not mythological incitement to action; nor is that for which the Christian *hopes* identical with that which the Christian *makes*. Action is action in a field of reality and makes sense only as a response to a condition. Hope, courage and effort require a sense that the world has certain qualities which make such action possible and offer it a reasonable chance of success. 'Eschatology' – reflection upon the objects of Christian hope – is the attempt to depict these qualities; without them, Christian hope is moralistic and profoundly ungracious.

This does not, however, entail passivity. To hope is to act in conformity to being. 'Is hope a help or a hindrance to action?' asks

---

But this is an extreme moral ascesis; scouring out the *positum* of hope, it misjudges the condition of hope by neglecting the proper givenness of the Kingdom of God in which hope has its ground. 'Hope is that act whereby a person becomes aware of the distance of the Kingdom, and it clings to apocalyptic thinking. If the Kingdom is there, within easy reach, if the Kingdom is *quite naturally* within us, there is no need to hope ... Humanly speaking, it is not true that the Kingdom is present' (p. 207). Certainly the Kingdom is not an object of possession; but the negative will not do justice to the full scope of Christian hope and its modes. Ellul speaks of 'the pessimism of hope' (p. 227), of hope as 'a hazardous undertaking' (p. 229) and so reduces hope to 'pessimistic waiting' (p. 259), a kind of perverse, stubborn disengagement from the present. This is one mode of hope; but it is hardly the *parrhesia* which the gospel engenders and which sees itself, not in a time of abandonment, but in the era of grace.

28. I. Kant, *Religion within the Limits of Mere Reason*, in A. W. Wood and G. di Giovanni (eds), *Religion and Rational Theology* (Cambridge: Cambridge University Press, 1992), p. 161.

Aquinas.[29] It seems to be a hindrance, for 'hope brings a sense of security, but this feeling leads to carelessness, which frustrates action'. But

> of its very nature hope is an aid to action, intensifying effort in two ways. First, in terms of its object, which is difficult, possible and agreeable, awareness of difficulty calls forth concentration; the judgement of possibility certainly does not stifle effort. Hope, then, will inspire a man to earnest action. Second, in terms of its effect we have seen that hope causes delight, and that makes for more effective operation. Therefore hope is a help in acting.[30]

Hope does not generate *negligentia* but *operatio, conatus*. Because hope has this object and engenders delight, it leads to action. Put more concretely: hope is an aspect of the fellowship with God for which we have been created and reconciled and in which our perfection lies; and that fellowship is a differentiated fellowship of action. Elected to this end, we are summoned to hope in its direction. The divine Word which promises our end is also the divine command which summons us actively to move towards that which is promised. But with what kind of action?

Christian action is hopeful when it is oriented to the future consummation of all things in the Kingdom of Christ. Hopeful Christian action is undertaken in the trust that Christ's coming Kingdom is present and promised with such axiomatic certainty that it outweighs all discouragement, opposition and counter-testimony. In such trust (to which courage is closely akin) the Christian extends herself towards that which has been promised. Hope refuses a moral calculus based on what apart from the gospel is taken to be our present condition; it incites action which is obedient to the true law of our being, namely that the creation 'will be set free from its bondage to decay and obtain the glorious liberty of the children of God' (Rom. 8.21). Hopeful Christian action stems from the judgement which has been declared to the believer, namely that 'the sufferings of the present time are not worth comparing with the glory that is to be revealed to us' (Rom. 8.18). On the basis of that judgement, the Christian reaches towards the coming consummation and glorification, acting in and upon the world as the reality which it will be. That reaching towards – what Aquinas

29. Aquinas, *Summa theologiae* IaIIae q40 a8.
30. Aquinas, *Summa theologiae* IaIIae q40 a8.

calls magnanimity, *extensio animi ad magna*[31] – is action which seeks the fullest possible anticipation of our end.

Hopeful Christian action extends towards the world's coming judgement and vindication. The eschatological dimension of Christian action is sometimes stated by speaking of hope as essentially critical – oriented not to the present but to the overcoming of the present in the future. Hope thereby opens up a distance from the present which inhibits the kind of stasis in which history is considered to have already achieved its perfection. In his *Theology of Hope*, for example, Moltmann speaks of 'hope which sets about criticizing and transforming the present because it is open towards the universal future of the kingdom'.[32] In concrete terms, this means that hope engenders a highly mobile attitude to the orders of social existence: hope does not seek to preserve or stabilize but 'historify'.[33] This reaches towards one moral consequence of the last judgement. But Christian hope does not only look for the overthrow of present disorder, but also for the vindication of present righteousness. 'Hope', says Calvin, 'awaits the time when [God's] truth shall be manifested.'[34] The manifestation to which hope looks and towards which it acts will also be the vindication of present action, that is, the declaration that such action has been in conformity with the good order of God. To act in the light of that coming vindication is to trust that acts whose end is not yet evident, and which may therefore appear vulnerable, even futile, will bear fruit. Charity which receives little or no reciprocation, resistance to powers which oppose Jesus Christ, sponsoring forms of civic courtesy and respect for strangers: such things are hopeful, not simply because they 'historify' (which they do not always do; often they are caught in moral gridlock) but because they anticipate a coming revelation of their obedience to the law of our being. And in that lies their authority as hopeful actions which bear witness to the true end of the human world.

Hopeful Christian action is action which is both realistic and unafraid of its own limits. All action in history is necessarily limited – by lack of competence or knowledge, by the unavailability of

---

31. Aquinas, *Summa theologiae* IIaIIae q129 a1.
32. J. Moltmann, *Theology of Hope: On the Ground and Implications of Christian Eschatology* (London: SCM, 1967), p. 335.
33. Moltmann, *Theology of Hope*, p. 330.
34. J. Calvin, *Institutes of the Christian Religion* III.ii.42 (London: SCM, 1960), p. 590.

resources of time, energy, wisdom, political and economic power. Such limits do not undermine Christian action, however, because Christian hope confesses that we do not need to be infinite in order to act well now and to survive in the future: we are and will be *helped*. Incapacity and limitation do not inhibit, because Jesus Christ has undertaken for our future. And so the Christian agent, hoping in him, is relieved of final responsibility and called instead to steadfastness, alertness and expectancy.

Such are some of the characteristics of hopeful Christian action. If the description risks vagueness, it is because hope is primarily a matter of orientation or general moral policy. Hope is not so much a separate act as a quality of other acts; in one sense it is adjectival. The determination of the particular moral configuration of Christian hope will depend upon a number of factors: the depth and seriousness with which Christian agents have come to read themselves and their situation in the light of the gospel; a developed capacity for truthful attention to particulars; the existence of intelligent and worshipful forms of Christian common life to enable such training in Christianness. Above all, however, formation in hope, and discernment of which acts of hope are fitting and prudent, are the works of the Spirit; and prayer for his coming is the first and last act of the hopeful Christian.

9

EVANGELICAL FREEDOM

I

We are schooled by cultural convention to believe that freedom is self-determination. The convention is long-standing and pervasive. Its origins, largely hidden from us within our everyday dealings with the world until retrieved by critical historical reflection, lie in some deep mutations in the West's traditions of religious, philosophical and political thought and practice from the early modern period. Its presence is made known in a complex set of images of human selfhood which form our civic, economic and moral accounts of ourselves. Among its most enduring and culturally successful corollaries is the assumption that the existence of God and human freedom are necessarily antithetical.

One of the primary tasks of a theology of evangelical freedom is to bring that cultural convention to consciousness, and to show that it is both contingent and inhumane. That is, a theology of evangelical freedom has to demonstrate that the conventional conception of freedom as self-government is precisely that – a *convention*, an intellectual and practical strategy for negotiating certain problems which arose in the course of the history of the West's religious and political life. And it has also to demonstrate that the convention's claim to promote human well-being is untruthful, that it is, in fact, destructive of the very reality of liberty which it seeks to uphold and defend.

But this critical or polemical task of Christian theology can only be a secondary undertaking. Its primary task in the matter is descriptive, indeed celebratory: that is, the task of loving and joyful depiction of evangelical freedom. It is the claim of the Christian faith that the understanding and experience of evangelical freedom alone can illuminate, chasten and heal us of the convention which holds us in thrall and which is destructive of the peace and good order of our culture. What is evangelical freedom? Evangelical freedom is the freedom announced in the gospel. The gospel is the proclamation that in Jesus Christ, the risen one who is now present in the power of the Holy Spirit, God the Father's eternal decision to live in fellowship with his human creatures has been unshakeably secured. In fellowship with this God, creator, reconciler and perfecter, we have our freedom as the creatures of God's mercy. Evangelical freedom is the freedom which God bestows on the creatures who, in seeking freedom apart from God, have ruined themselves and fallen into slavery. Its origins lie in the Father's grace, in the omnipotent goodness of God in which he secures the creaturely freedom which he purposes. Its establishment is in the person and work of the Son of God, who is the embodied act of God's liberating of sinners from bondage to decay and death. Its end is in the Spirit's reconstitution of creaturely life and liberty in company with the triune God. In what follows, we offer, first, a sketch of some of the constitutive features of modern understandings and practices of freedom, and, second, the briefest of Christian dogmatics and ethics of freedom as the freedom for which we have been set free.

II

Modern understandings and practices of freedom are a central feature in one of the most important shifts in Western culture which began before the Renaissance and Reformation in the rise of nominalist philosophy and which continues to shape our socio-economic and political order as well as our reflective images of ourselves. The shift is one in which human selfhood comes to be morally, politically and metaphysically fundamental. As part of this transition to an anthropocentric culture, freedom is radicalized; that is to say, freedom is turned into the very root of human authenticity and dignity. Freedom comes to be constitutive of that which is inalienably human; its inhibition comes to signal the destruction of the humane.

What we might call 'fundamental freedom' – freedom as the basis and distinguishing property of humankind – consists in self-constitution or self-government. Freedom is, first, the distinctively human capacity for self-constitution through action. A human person is human in so far as she is free; and she is free in so far as she can properly be identified as the originator of purposive action. For to be is to act, and to act is intentionally (voluntarily, without overwhelming external constraints) to realize oneself. Truly human action, that is, is a matter of the human agent's self-constitution. In free action, the human agent puts into effect her intentions and so makes herself in a way which is fundamental to her being. The agent's action is not merely to be conceived as the externalizing or 'acting out' of what that agent finds herself to be. Authentically human action is not mere action in accordance with a pre-given human nature (such action is judged to be 'mere' role playing, neither intentional nor free), but rather a making of the agent's nature by free action. Tucked inside this concept of freedom, then, is the notion that the human person is best understood, not as substance but as voluntary subject and agent. Being human is not a matter of having a certain nature or being placed within an ordered reality of which I am not the originator; rather, the distinguishing feature of humankind is, at last resort, the will. The agent is characterized, above all, not as a sort of substance, but as enacted intention. The subject is agent, and in her action is demonstrated her capacity for the self-determination which is freedom: in free action, the human subject is self-positing.

Making self-constitution humanly fundamental is, in the end, radically constructivist. Accordingly, freedom is inseparable from self-government. The freedom which the agent realizes in voluntary acts of self-constitution is to be understood as autonomy. The agent is free in so far as she is autonomous, literally, a law to herself. 'Law' – that is to say, the norms by which we govern action, make discriminations between policies and hold up practices for evaluation – is thus radically internalized. Classically conceived, law is the structure of given reality ('nature'), and the imperative force of that reality. To say that reality is law is to say that it presents itself to us as an order which requires me to be shaped by and to act in accordance with its given character. On a modern (and a postmodern) account of freedom, by contrast, 'law' is not an externally derived norm, but rather a corollary of my most fundamental activity of self-projection or self-constitution. It bears upon me only as the object of my choice (political, economic, religious, sexual). And so only as a self-legislator can I be said to be free.

One centrally significant feature of this constructivist under-standing of freedom as self-constitution and self-government is that freedom is often construed in oppositional terms. Freedom, that is, comes to be portrayed as an opposing of the self to forces which seek to inhibit, contain or envelop the self and rob it of its

authenticity, its self-constituted and self-legislated identity. The
dynamic of freedom is thus one of acting against a countervailing
force, whether that force be nature, custom, law, society or God.
Thus, for example, freedom may be set over against nature. To be
free is precisely to stand apart from the supposedly given. The
experience of freedom (like the self-consciousness to which it is
closely allied) is only conceivable if there is a space between the free
self and that which is given: the space of freedom. Nature –
metaphysical, material, political, legal, moral – is always that to
which freedom is opposed and that which may quickly become an
object of resentment. By its very givenness, nature constitutes an
order of reality which is an obstacle to free self-constitution, a
blockage in the path of self-government which must be overcome or
transcended. The goal of free selfhood is thus not self-fulfilment in
accordance with the order of nature, but self-shaping, a making of
the self by struggling free from nature.

Similarly, freedom is to be set over against situation. Freedom is
antithetical to the particular sets of circumstances in which agents
find themselves, which present themselves as an obligation to
undertake certain tasks or a call to certain kinds of responsive (and
therefore responsible) action. Like nature, situation is oppressive
and must be cleared away by the assertion of liberty. In particular,
freedom is real over against social situatedness – over against the
way in which human existence is determined and limited by
entanglements with others. For if freedom is fundamental to
identity, and if identity is achieved by self-constitution and self-
government, then other persons cannot be intrinsic to my freedom,
but must – like nature – be that which I have to negotiate in order
to be free. Society is heteronomy, and therefore erodes the
autonomy in which my freedom consists.

A sketch like this cannot pretend to be anything other than a
rough-and-ready portrayal of a cultural convention in which nearly
all of us are implicated; a full account of the matter would require a
massively ramified history of the intellectual and civic traditions by
which freedom as autonomy is carried. From a theological point of
view, one of the most indispensable components in an understanding of that history is the way in which modern conceptions
and practices of human freedom both trade upon and reinforce
misperceptions of divine freedom. Indeed, it is at least arguable that
the determinative feature of the moral and spiritual landscape
which had to be conquered and obliterated in the establishment of
freedom as self-determination was the existence and freedom of

God. It is often noted that modern conceptions of human autonomy assume a competitive understanding of divine and human freedom. That is, into the idea of freedom as self-determination is built a presumption that God's freedom is intrinsically a limitation upon human liberty, since our freedom and God's are inversely proportional. In so far as God is free agent, his presence and activity will inevitably annexe the space in which human freedom operates; that space must properly be retrieved for humankind if we are to be freely self-constituting agents. More simply: God's freedom will always interfere.

From the point of view of a theology of evangelical freedom, this misperception is a consequence of the retraction of a specifically Christian understanding of God and God's freedom, and the replacement of that specifically Christian understanding by something much more abstract, as well as much more threatening, namely, an idea of God as impersonal causal force, mere absolute power. The retraction of a Christian understanding of God is partly to be explained by the priority accorded to philosophical theism, in which a generic idea of God as transcendent ground of all things is deployed, first as a preliminary to Christian theology and then as a replacement for positive Christian trinitarian and incarnational teaching about the nature of God and of God's relation to the world. But the retraction is not without its theological roots; more than one strand of the history of theology in modernity has failed to appeal to positive Christian teaching in its response to philosophical criticism, at cost to the internal structure of Christian doctrine, and with the result that trinitarian teaching in particular drifted towards the margins of theology, with little real work to do.

Because of this, a theology of evangelical freedom will respond to conceptions of freedom as self-determination by returning to the inner structure and content of Christian teaching, seeking to show that the spectre of an absolutely free deity who is by definition the enemy of human freedom is just that: a *spectre*, and one which has to be exorcized by careful and loving attention to what the gospel announces concerning the nature and purposes of God. In making the character of God's freedom its first concern, theology will seek to exhibit that the construal of human freedom as self-determination is rooted in a misconception of God, one which issues in a misconception of human freedom. Indeed, theology will suggest that to think of the world as the kind of place where human freedom can only be maintained if we think of that freedom as self-governance is to think of the world untruthfully. Far from protecting human authenticity, freedom as self-governance is the expression of alienation from God, and therefore inhumane.

What is required of the church and its theology, therefore, is a dogmatics and an ethics of freedom. Dogmatics and ethics are the church's attempts to submit its mind to the gospel; they are part of the struggle by which the church's thinking and speaking are sanctified as they are taken into the service of the gospel. In its dogmatics, the church orders its thinking towards the gospel as an *indicative*, as a claim to truth. Part of the gospel's claim to truth is a claim about the nature of God's freedom and the nature of the freedom proper to the creatures of God. A dogmatics of freedom is thus an attempt to spell out the character of the free God in his directedness to his free creatures. In its ethics, the church orders its thinking towards the gospel as an *imperative*, as a call to action. For the gospel is not only the announcement of how we are to think aright about God and humankind. It is also a summons to freedom. And so a theology of evangelical freedom will include an ethics of freedom. Dogmatics and ethics are not speculative; they are part of the church's endeavour to orient its life by the truth about God and the human situation, and to discern the shape of truthful human action. Only on the basis of a Christian specification of the freedom of God in relation to the freedom of the creature can a theology of evangelical freedom proceed; and, moreover, only on such a basis can Christian faith offer any attempt to heal us of the hurtful axioms which have so deeply embedded themselves into modern practices of freedom, both inside and outside the church. If the church has been largely tongue-tied or concessionary in bearing witness over the matter of freedom, it is in part because of a reluctance to engage in the kind of theological clarifications by which the gospel shapes the church. What is required is a gospel-derived account of freedom as that which creatures discover in fellowship with the free, self-bestowing God made known in Christ and in the Spirit. Above all, we must set aside the bad habit of polarizing divine and human freedom, and must attempt to display how the gospel concerns their integration.

The task, then, of a theology of evangelical freedom is that of letting our thinking be guided by the account of the nature of God and of God's creatures which is set before us in the history of God's fellowship with us. In that history are enacted the identities of the free God and of the creatures of his grace whom he reconciles and perfects. The theological thinking of the church must not be led by abstract conceptions of freedom (human or divine) taken over from its cultural settings, but rather by the gospel's answers to the questions: 'Who is God?' and 'Who is the free creature whom God reconciles and perfects for fellowship with himself?'

III

As with all matters concerning God, so in the matter of God's freedom: the primary question is not 'What is God?' but 'Who is God?' The former – abstract – question invites answers which determine God's essence in advance of any specific considerations of the mode or manner of God's existence. By contrast, the latter – concrete – question is answered by beginning from the given reality of God's self-manifesting existence and only on that basis moving on to determine the essence of God. Because a Christian theology of the freedom of God is a thinking in the wake of God's revelation, it addresses itself to this latter question. For revelation is of all things the most concrete and particular. It is the communicative presence of God, vouchsafed to us in God's works of creation, reconciliation and perfection as Father, Son and Holy Spirit. In those works God sets before us his identity as *this one*, the triune creator who has reconciled his fallen creature and is now bringing it to its final fulfilment. His freedom is the freedom of the one who does this work, and in so doing manifests that his freedom is freedom to be God for us and with us. In short: if we are to think truthfully of God's freedom, avoiding the abstract antitheses which have so ruined the modern conception of freedom, we must grasp that God's freedom is the freedom of the triune God.

God's freedom is his freedom as God the Father, creator of heaven and earth. God's freedom is not simply arbitrary power or unfocused will. Rather, because God's freedom is made known in the act of creation, it is a freedom which is actual in his purposive bringing into being of another reality to exist alongside himself. God's freedom is not an infinite reserve of potency which could be actualized in ways other than those which he determines for himself as creator; it is rather the undeflected energy with which God follows the direction in which he determines to be himself. His freedom is thus freedom for fellowship with the creature. As creator, *God is free* – standing under no necessity, having no external claims upon himself, in no need of the creature; as free Lord, God the Father is and creates *ex nihilo*. But because God is free *as creator*, his freedom is not a merely empty or formal idea but a very definite direction and act of relation. And, moreover, as an act of relation, God's freedom is teleological – it involves not simply an initial act of making heaven and earth, but also the preservation and governance of the creaturely realm. As creator, that is, God's freedom is the grace in which he promises himself or commits himself to the creature. The free creator is the free Lord of the covenant, the origin and sustainer of fellowship with himself.

God's freedom is his freedom as God the Son, the reconciler of all things. God's freedom as Father involves the grace with which he pledges to maintain fellowship. That pledge is enacted in God the Son, who restores the covenant between God and his creatures after it has been broken by the creature's wicked and false attempt to be free from God. The creature seeks to be apart from God; only in that way, the creature believes, can real freedom be exercised. This attempt to master its own destiny becomes the creature's ruin and misery, because it strikes at the root of the fellowship with God in which alone the creature has its being. In this situation of the absolute jeopardy of the creature, God's freedom demonstrates itself, not as freedom to withdraw from fellowship, but precisely as an utter determination to maintain fellowship (whatever else it may mean, this is part of what is set before us in the story of Noah). And God's maintenance of fellowship culminates in the person and work of the Son who, as God in the flesh, is reconciliation embodied and effective. He *is* Emmanuel, the fulfilment of the free divine resolve and promise: I will be your God, you will be my people. The fulfilment of this resolve is, of course, entirely gratuitous – God fulfils his freedom in that 'the Word *became* flesh'. But, as in the Father's work of creation, so here in the Son's work of reconciliation: God's freedom is freedom for and with, not freedom apart from or against.

God's freedom is his freedom as God the Holy Spirit, who brings all things to their perfection. In the work of the Holy Spirit, the reconciliation of the creature which has been willed by the Father and accomplished in the person and work of the Son becomes real as the creature's own history. By the power of the free Spirit, God sanctifies the creature, completing his purpose for it and so finally establishing the work begun in creation and maintained in reconciliation. It is the Spirit who thus consummates the purpose of God, not the creature itself. The perfecting of the creature by the Spirit is no less a free work of divine sovereignty than any other of God's works. But the Spirit's freedom is known in the work of making real the relation to God in which the creature has life. The

Spirit is Lord, sovereignly free, majestic and unfettered; but as Lord the Spirit is also the life-giver, bestowing upon the creature the life (and therefore the freedom) forfeited in the creature's betrayal of the covenant. As free Spirit, God directs his ways to the final realization of fellowship with those whom he has created and redeemed for life with himself.

What may we draw from this trinitarian sketch of the freedom of God? Two things. First, God's freedom is his aseity – his being from himself. God is the sovereign originator and accomplisher of all that he is and does. Second, we can only grasp what it is for God to be thus eternally and majestically self-moved when we attend to the direction of the divine movement, which is towards us in his work as Father, Son and Spirit. God's freedom is the glorious spontaneity, reliability and effectiveness in which he is the Holy One in our midst.

IV

What of the freedom of the creature? For Christian theology, that question can only rightly be answered after the question of God's identity as the free creator, reconciler and perfecter has received an answer. To begin by determining the conditions of creaturely freedom in advance of an understanding of God, and then inquiring into the compatibility of human freedom with God's freedom, is simply to remain captive to the destructive convention of human freedom as self-government. A theology of evangelical freedom will work from an understanding of God's freedom towards an anthropology of freedom. God's triune freedom, we have seen, is the sovereign purposiveness with which he establishes fellowship. Human history is the 'space' – arena, setting – in which that fellowship is realized. For the Christian gospel, moreover, the history of God with us is definitive of what it means to be human. It is not a mere modulation or particular form of a more general human history, but is ontologically definitive: to be human is to be the reconciled creature of God pointed by God to perfection. Our freedom, therefore, is the capacity bestowed on us by God to take an active part in the history of fellowship with our creator, reconciler and perfecter.

To understand this, we need to lay aside the assumption around which so much of our economic, political and sexual identity is organized, namely the assumption that freedom is autonomy. Freedom is, rather, the capacity to realize what one is. What we are is reconciled creatures, those set free for true humanness by the work of the triune God. To be free is not to exercise the false freedom to invent myself by my actions, nor to be creator, reconciler and perfecter to myself. Nor is it mere unrestricted will. It is, rather, to be what I have been made to be, to fulfil my vocation as a creature of God, and so (and only so) to exist in authenticity. Two things flow from this.

First, human freedom is *given*. Because it is the freedom of creatures, it cannot be wholly self-originating. But the contingency of human freedom, its dependence upon the agency of another, is not a restriction but a specification, a way of characterizing its particular nature. In the same way that our life is no less life for being the gift of God, so our freedom is no less freedom for its dependence upon the free grace of God. Or, we might say, given freedom only seems a lesser reality if we cling to the decision that only absolute freedom is real freedom, and that nothing but autonomy can guarantee our authenticity.

Second, therefore, human freedom is freedom within situations, and not sheerly transcendent. The modern ideal of freedom idealizes freedom as independence, thereby mirroring the degenerate idea of divine freedom which it was designed to negate. But evangelical freedom is not my removal from the realm of contingency and relation; it is, rather, the character of my relations with that which is other than me. Freedom emerges in my occupancy of the space of the material and social world and, above all, of the reality of God as my origin and end. I am not free in abstraction from these relations, nor simply when those relations are a function of my will and exist solely by my sovereign choice. Rather, I become free when I become myself in the space of relations in which I exist. Those relations are the occasions of my freedom when they quicken me to fulfil my nature as creature of God and fellow-creature with others. Freedom is thus not some property or potency which I have in myself anterior to all relations and to the givenness of nature and situation; nor is it something which is necessarily constricted or compromised by relations and situations. Freedom is that which I come to exercise as I exist in freedom-granting fellowship.

Evangelical freedom cannot therefore be conceived or practised as a single spasm, an act of defiance or protest against the fact that I find myself within an order of reality which is not of my invention. Such accounts of freedom, however deeply ingrained they may be, are too thin to furnish a persuasive account of free human selfhood, above all because they reduce all relations to hostile and oppressive determinations. It is certainly true that not all aspects of our situation do quicken freedom: some relations can be life-denying, robbing us of authenticity. But these diminutions of freedom are overcome, not by abstracting selfhood from the dependencies which are fundamental to what it means to be human, but by the restoration of the human self to the space in which freedom can be received and acted out.

Human freedom is, in short, that which we are given as we live in the space of fellowship which is made by God's free acts of setting us free. In that space we are met by God as the maker, rescuer and preserver of our freedom, and by those others to whom we have been bound as fellow-recipients of grace. What is the form of this freedom for which, according to the gospel, we have been set free?

Evangelical freedom is a form of life which acts out the fact that I have been set free from 'the law of sin and death' (Rom. 8.2). Sin tyrannizes and limits God's creatures as they act out the falsehood that in order to be human they must make themselves. Such self-making is self-destruction, because it breaks the human side of fellowship with God. Since it is only in fellowship with the creator that we can have life, sin and death are inseparable; together they form the despotic principle ('law') which enslaves humankind. For the gospel, however, that tyranny has been overcome by 'the law of the Spirit of life in Christ Jesus' (Rom. 8.2): in what 'God has done' (Rom. 8.3) in Christ and in the effective presence of that achievement in the Holy Spirit, sin and its entailments – death and bondage – have been condemned (Rom. 8.3), and life and freedom have been irreversibly established as the condition by which we are governed.

Evangelical freedom, emerging from our being put to death and made alive in Christ and the Spirit, is thus freedom from the *care of self* which so harasses and afflicts the lost creatures of God. My freedom is in part my freedom from final responsibility for maintaining myself, a freedom which is the fruit of my having been liberated from the anxious toil of having to be my own creator and preserver. Evangelical freedom is rooted in a security given to me – not dreamed, imagined or effected by stringent acts of self-realization. That security is such that in Christ I am inviolable, and so free from concern for my own preservation. Such inviolability is not expressed as self-defensive closure of myself against all transgression from without, but as a profound lack of self-preoccupation, a confidence which has its roots in the sheer objectivity of my condition as one set free by God. The compromise of my liberty which I have made by seeking to be my own liberator has been overcome; because by the Spirit I am in Christ, having my centre not in myself and my own acts but in Jesus Christ who has set me free, then all other bonds are set aside. I no longer need to cultivate my freedom; and so I am free. A particular mode of this freedom is the freedom to pray. Prayer is an act of evangelical freedom because in it is expressed our liberation from anxiety and self-responsibility, and our freedom to live on the basis of fellowship with God and trust in the divine promise. Prayer thus expresses the fact that, as we have been set free by God, so we have had taken from us the evil custody of ourselves which we thought ensured our safety but which in fact fastened us to sin and death. Prayer, indeed, is at the centre of the fellowship with God which is determinative of whatever is authentically humane.

Free for fellowship with God, I am thus free also for human fellowship. If freedom is self-governance, it is the end of love; if, however, freedom is the restoration of my identity in company with my fellows, then I am free to act in support of my neighbour's cause. 'Let no one seek his own good, but the good of his neighbour' (1 Cor. 10.24). Far from being a compromise of freedom, such a rule guides us towards the practice of freedom. To 'seek one's own good' is not to realize one's true nature but to mobilize all one's forces in living out of oneself, making oneself by choices; and so it is to place oneself in the hands of death. To seek that which is one's neighbour's is, by contrast, to be free for life. Looking to the neighbour's cause is not mere self-abandonment; it is rather to exist in the human fellowship by which, precisely by not striving to realize ourselves, we attain to the liberty of the children of God.

Such, then, is a sketch of evangelical freedom, for which we have been set free by the gloriously free God, our maker, redeemer and end. Whether such an account of freedom can commend itself to modern culture is not easy to know. Its persuasiveness depends on many factors: on a willingness to stand apart from dominant conventions; on the existence of forms of Christian common life which exemplify the practice of a freedom which is beyond autonomy or heteronomy; but above all on the coming of the Holy Spirit who is the agent of all persuasion in the matter of the gospel. To understand and practice freedom we need to become different people. It is the office of the Spirit to make us such; the office of the church to bear witness in word and action to the Spirit's convincing work; and the office of the church's theology to assist that witness by trying to speak the gospel well.

INDEX OF BIBLICAL REFERENCES

INDEX OF SUBJECTS

INDEX OF AUTHORS